HOWARD
BOOKS

JANET THOMPSON

Author of *Dear God, They Say It's Cancer*

★ HOWARD BOOKS
A DIVISION OF SIMON & SCHUSTER
New York   London   Toronto   Sydney

PRAYING FOR YOUR
PRODIGAL DAUGHTER

*Hope, Help & Encouragement
for Hurting Parents*

Our purpose at Howard Books is to:
+ *Increase faith* in the hearts of growing Christians
+ *Inspire holiness* in the lives of believers
+ *Instill hope* in the hearts of struggling people everywhere
Because He's coming again!

Published by Howard Books, a division of Simon & Schuster, Inc.
1230 Avenue of the Americas, New York, NY 10020
www.howardpublishing.com

Praying for Your Prodigal Daughter © 2007 Janet Thompson

Library of Congress Cataloging-in-Publication Data

Thompson, Janet.
   Praying for your prodigal daughter : hope, help & encouragement for hurting parents / Janet Thompson.
      p.   cm.
   Summary: "A helpful book for parents of prodigal daughters, offering hope and encouragement from praying Scripture, practical how-tos and tools, journaling, and discussion questions for family and support groups"—Provided by publisher.
   1. Parents—Prayers and devotions.   2. Fathers and daughters—Religious aspects—Christianity.
3. Mothers and daughters—Religious aspects—Christianity.   I. Title.
   BV4845.T46   2007
   248.8'45—dc22   2007023322

ISBN-13: 978-1-4165-5186-7
ISBN-10:   1-4165-5186-7

10   9   8   7   6   5   4   3   2   1

Manufactured in the United States of America

For information regarding special discounts for bulk purchases,
please contact: Simon & Schuster Special Sales at
1-800-456-6798 or business@simonandschuster.com.

Edited by Between the Lines
Cover design by John Lucas
Interior design by Jaime Putorti

Some of the names used in this book have been changed to protect the privacy of those who so graciously gave us permission to share their stories.

❖

To my beautiful daughter, Kim, and my precious granddaughter Katelyn. I pray that the prodigal wanderings will cease for the daughters in our family and in future generations.

CONTENTS

SECTION ONE

PRAYING FOR YOUR PRODIGAL DAUGHTER

SECTION TWO

PRAYING WITH PURPOSE
FOR YOUR PRODIGAL DAUGHTER

SECTION THREE

LIVING LIFE WITH YOUR PRODIGAL DAUGHTER

SECTION FOUR

QUESTIONING YOUR ROLE WITH YOUR PRODIGAL DAUGHTER

SECTION FIVE

WELCOMING HOME YOUR PRODIGAL DAUGHTER

APPENDIX

Far be it from us that we should sin against the Lord by
failing to pray for our prodigal daughter.

PERSONALIZATION OF 1 SAMUEL 12:23

A Parent's Prayer

Is there anyplace my daughter can go to avoid Your Spirit?
To be out of Your sight?
If she climbs to the sky, You're there!
If she goes underground, You're there!
If she flew on morning's wings
    to the far western horizon,
You'd find her in a minute—
You're already there waiting!
Then I said to myself, "Oh, He even sees her in the dark!
At night she's immersed in the light!"
It's a fact: darkness isn't dark to You;
    night and day, darkness and light, they're all the same to You.

Oh yes, You shaped my daughter first inside, then out;
You formed her in her mother's womb.
I thank You, High God—You're breathtaking!
Body and soul, she is marvelously made!
I worship in adoration—what a creation!

You know her inside and out,
You know every bone in her body;
You know exactly how she was made, bit by bit,
  how she was sculpted from nothing into something.
Like an open book, You watched her grow from conception to birth;
  all the stages of her life were spread out before You,
The days of her life all prepared
  before she'd even lived one day.

Your thoughts—how rare, how beautiful!
God, I'll never comprehend them!
I couldn't even begin to count them—
  any more than I could count the sand of the sea.
Oh, let me rise in the morning and live always with You!
And please, God, do away with wickedness for good!

PERSONALIZATION OF PSALM 139:12–19 MSG

Dear Parent,

You have picked up this book because in your heart you feel you have a prodigal daughter. All of our stories differ, and probably our definition of what is "prodigal" differs too. Defining "prodigal" behavior is not the message of this book. We will look at some common characteristics of a prodigal daughter, but each parent's tolerance level and idea of what constitutes acceptable behavior will vary.

I do not present myself as an expert—a "perfect parent" who did everything right—quite the contrary! I am a fellow sojourner who stumbled my way through parenting and made mistakes with detrimental repercussions. What I hope to share with you is what the Lord taught me about how to parent His way and how to work with Him in rescuing a daughter who has gone astray.

We can't go back and change the past or the things we wish we had done differently. But we can impact today and the future. This book is about engaging God through prayer to help us deal with the brokenness in our family and calling on Him to restore our daughter to a right relationship with God and with us.

Maybe you are a parent wanting to prevent your daughter from becoming prodigal or you see signs that she could be headed in that direction. This book is for you too! *Now* is the time to be on your knees daily, calling God to send armies of angels to protect and save her from any misstep. In hindsight, many of us parents of prodigals wish we had started praying much earlier.

If you are a legal guardian, grandparent, relative, "spiritual mother," or mentor to a girl or woman who has lost her way, please know that this book is for you as well.

Praying for Your Prodigal Daughter is designed to be used in families, small groups, Bible studies, and support groups. You'll find helpful discussion questions at the end of each chapter.

My prayer is that through my and my daughter Kim's prodigal daughter stories, as well as through the stories of the many parents and daughters featured in this book, you'll find hope and purpose in the midst of one of the hardest trials a parent will ever face: not giving up on your prodigal daughter. With God's help, you can learn to live with the outcome, whatever that may be.

"May the God of hope fill you with all joy and peace as you trust in him, so that you may overflow with hope by the power of the Holy Spirit" (Romans 15:13).

I'm praying with you,
Janet Thompson

ACKNOWLEDGMENTS

My dearest Kim, you will always be my "baby." To share our story, to bare our souls, is no little thing. I admire and celebrate the beautiful, humble, and courageous Christian woman you have become. When I shared my vision for this book, you were on board and willing to let me expose our lives on these pages, all for the glory of God. That's no small concession, since our life together has had many twists and turns—some we regret and others we celebrate. I thank God for making both our paths straight. We were lost and now we're found. I love you, baby.

Dave, my hubby and helpmate—where do I begin? Our life together has been anything but predictable. You're so willing to sacrifice and do without your "wiffy" when I'm on these crazy book deadlines. "Thank you, dear" isn't adequate for never saying enough is enough but instead always saying, "Sure. Go for it. If it's from God, He'll make your dreams and visions for this book come true." You are becoming quite the chef! You are God's ultimate gift to me. I love you with all my heart and soul.

My dear family—how I love being Mom and Grammie. Grandpa Dave and I will pray for all of you, and any future grandbabies and great-grandbabies, for as long as we have breath.

Michelle and Giulio, Kim and Toby, Shannon and Dan, and Sean and Janel—please follow our lead and be praying parents for your precious children.

All the praying mothers, fathers, and prodigal daughters who shared your stories—you willingly, openly, and vulnerably shared your experiences to help and mentor others. I pray that your family relationships will be restored and that your prodigal daughters will return, because you bravely shared from your heart. You have given the gift of yourselves to parents and daughters you may never meet until that glorious day. None of you asked for anything in return but the joy of being used by God—and He *has* used you mightily.

My North Tustin Critique Group—how did I ever write without you? Your input, encouragement, corrections, critiques, love, and prayers have been invaluable both to the writing of this book and to my life. I pray I am half the blessing to you that you are to me.

My writing compatriot and friend, Pat Evans—in spite of the fullness of your career, family, and writing life, you miraculously and selflessly made time to edit this manuscript. Thank you for the immeasurable gift of your time, talents, and heart.

Pastor Tim Westcott, senior pastor, Idyllwild Bible Church—your Sunday messages inspire my writing and your refreshing humility asks for no recognition. Thank you.

Susan Wilson, associate editor, Howard Books—what a joy to work with you again. You have such a way of making deadlines peaceful! Thank you for all you do behind the scenes to make my books the best that they can be.

Melissa Teutsch, senior publicist, Howard Books—thank you for being my cheerleader and for leaving no stone unturned in spreading the message of this book to hurting parents.

John Lucas, cover designer—you have an amazing gift of capturing the message of my books in a cover that says it all even if I never wrote a word! While we have never met, I feel you know my heart. Thank you for sharing your creativity and designing covers that jump off the shelf.

Philis Boultinghouse, senior editor, Howard Books—my friend, my editor. Thank you for the patience, encouragement, and prayers you so graciously extend to me. I always have so much to say. You understand the heart of this book. Thank you for partnering with me.

Chrys and John Howard—you again welcomed me to the Howard Books team. What an honor.

INTRODUCTION

Who am I, my Master GOD, and what is my family, that you
have brought me to this place in life? But that's nothing compared
to what's coming, for you've also spoken of my family far into the
future, given me a glimpse into tomorrow and looked on me,
Master GOD, as a Somebody. What's left . . . to say to this—to
your honoring your servant, even though you know me, just as I
am? O GOD, out of the goodness of your heart, you've taken your
servant to do this great thing and put your great work on display.
There's none like you, GOD, no God but you, nothing to compare
with what we've heard with our own ears.

1 CHRONICLES 17:16–20 MSG

*Kim is confused about what it means to be a Christian. I feel
responsible for this because she saw me as a carnal Christian.
Please don't let her be lost because of me. Let my testimony reach
out to her, however You would have me tell it. I know she'll be
back in Your arms again. I know You love her and are waiting
for her return.*

EXCERPT FROM MY PRAYER JOURNAL,
NOVEMBER 18, 1993—TWO DAYS AFTER I PURCHASED IT

INTRODUCTION

❖

Pray as if everything depended upon your prayer.[1]
WILLIAM BOOTH

Our Family Story

Sobbing and sinking to my knees in the driveway, I watched the taillights of my beloved only daughter's little blue car disappear down the street. This wasn't how I envisioned sending her off to college. I imagined fun shopping trips buying necessities for her dorm room and helping her settle into her first home away from home. Instead, I could barely bring myself to give my precious daughter, Kim, anything to support the college life she'd chosen—living with her boyfriend.

"Where did I go wrong?" I cried out to God. "What can I do? How did this happen?" Did it start with Granny Hazel . . . or maybe even before that?

At eighteen, young Hazel disappeared. She'd always had a wild streak and enjoyed flirting with boys, but she'd never run away from home before. Frantic, her parents and boyfriend, George, went in search of Hazel and found her in a nearby town with a boy she barely knew. Hazel's goal was to make George jealous, and it worked. He proposed, and they were married.

Granny Hazel and Grandpa George soon had a baby boy, and eighteen months later my mother, Marilyn, was born. Growing up, my mom felt overshadowed and neglected by her outgoing, gregarious working mother, so she turned to her dad for the love and support she craved—until Grandpa George strayed, and her parents eventually divorced. Blaming her dad for the divorce, my mom estranged herself from him.

At age eighteen, my mom eloped. And just as Mom's grandparents had searched for their prodigal daughter, my grandparents went after their prodigal daughter and brought her home, annulling the marriage.

At twenty, my mom met and quickly married my dad, and twelve months later I was born. When I was ten years old, my highway patrolman father was shot and killed in the line of duty. My mom shook her fist at God, saying, "No just God would do this to a young man who was protecting his community." Mom had been a Methodist Sunday-school teacher, but she then estranged herself from her heavenly Father just as she had done with her earthly father.

However, in her time of grief, my grandfather reached out to Mom, and she learned that there were two sides to her parents' divorce story. Mom reconciled with Grandpa George but then had a falling-out with her mother. They later reconciled, but Mom didn't attend Granny Hazel's funeral.

I asked Jesus into my heart at a church youth camp when I was eleven and grew in my faith and love of the Lord. I became the perfect daughter—straight-A student, valedictorian of my high school graduating class, and accepted into a good college.

At eighteen I left for college, and it seemed the family prodigal-daughter pattern had ended. However, not wanting to return home after college, the day after graduation I married the boy I'd been dating. That marriage lasted only six years, but we had a beautiful baby girl named Kimberly. After my divorce, I ventured out into the world as a single working parent, quickly forgetting my Christian values. At age twenty-eight, the "perfect daughter" turned into the prodigal daughter. My mom seemed unable to extend unconditional love and support to me, so just as with previous generations, we became estranged. And my grandfather, who had walked me down the aisle at my wedding, turned his back on me also and consequently never got to know his great grandchild, Kim.

I wandered in an immoral wilderness for seventeen years before rededicating my life to the Lord at a Harvest Crusade. I committed myself to God: "Your prodigal daughter has returned. I will go where You send me."

The first step was to reconcile with my mother. The second step was to rededicate myself to the dating relationship I had ended with a godly man, Dave Thompson. I knew God had brought him into my life, but I had let my previous pattern of relationship estrangement interfere with God's plan for us as a couple. We married eight months before Kim left for college.

My daughter didn't date until she was seventeen years old, but she soon began dating an older boy. She'd been an innocent, shy girl growing up, and I never imagined having any problems with her. But when this young man entered her life, Kim fell prey to his worldly lifestyle. She became part of the party scene, even obtaining birth-control pills without my knowledge. Now, at age nineteen, she was going off to college with him.

Kim had always said she wanted to be just like me. I was sure that just as she had imitated my wayward behavior, she would follow suit when I rededicated my life to the Lord, married a godly man, and enjoyed a Christ-centered marriage and home. But she didn't. Instead, Kim was angry and confused at my new Christian life and wanted no part of it.

Sin has consequences. During my prodigal years, I hadn't modeled the Christian life for Kim. I dated a number of men, and at one point we even lived with one of my boyfriends. Kim and I were both devastated when that relationship ended, and I was sure she would never repeat her mother's mistake. But she seemed determined to do exactly that. Kim was following in the prodigal footsteps of her great-grandmother, her grandmother, and her mother.

No amount of talking, pleading, or cajoling convinced Kim not to live with her boyfriend at college. What else could I do? I pleaded with God. I knew the inevitable heartache that awaited her and that she would regret not having carefree coed years. She wasn't listening to me. I felt helpless, yet I couldn't just stand by and do nothing.

It took me until age forty-five to get my life back on track. I was desperate to prevent my daughter from going down that same path, but I wanted to be cautious not to push her away. I went to the local Christian bookstore in a frantic search for anything that would help me rescue her. I picked up a small devotional guide titled *Praying God's Will for My Daughter* and, glancing inside, saw that all the prayers were in the form of paraphrased scriptures, personalized to use in praying for daughters. I decided to insert Kim's name and pray God's Word back to Him. I could do that.

Two months after Kim left for college, I wrote "November 16, 1993" in the front of my little devotional prayer book and started faithfully praying, every single day, and journaling my frustration and pain. When I finished the book, Kim was still living with her boyfriend. In fact, she was more entrenched in the relationship than ever. But I wasn't discouraged. I went back to the beginning of the book and prayed through it again . . . and again . . . and again . . .

Three years later and several weeks after college graduation, I received the long-prayed-for call. Kim was leaving her boyfriend and asked if she could return home and look for work.

Kim still wasn't ready to live a Christian life, so I continued praying for her salvation and for her to find a godly man and a job in a small, family-owned business that would treat her well in her first career position.

After several interviews she received a job offer at a local, family-owned wholesale nursery . . . where she met Toby. I was thrilled about the job but disappointed and confused about Toby, because he wasn't a Christian. When he later asked for her hand in marriage, I showed him my devotional prayer journal and explained that I'd been praying for a godly man to come into her life, and I wasn't sure he was the one. But because of my prayers, I'd trust that God had a plan—His are so much bigger and better than mine.

As an engagement gift, my husband and I boldly gave them Marriage Builders, a biblically based premarital counseling course. God answered my prayers, as both Kim and Toby made a commitment to live a Christ-centered life. At last, my prodigal daughter was truly home!

On the front page of my devotional, I wrote: "November 16, 1993, started praying daily for Kim."

I joyfully wrote below it: "November 1, 1998, Kim baptized." And: "November 14, 1998, Kim married a godly man, Toby."

What I learned in those five years of daily praying for my daughter is my gift to you in this book. I hope that as you read more of Kim's and my story and the stories of other parents and prodigal daughters, and as you pray God's Word for your own prodigal daughter, you, too, will be encouraged and inspired to entrust your daughter to the Lord.

Hope, Help, and Encouragement

In each chapter you'll hear from the parent of a prodigal daughter and from a prodigal daughter herself. Then we'll spend time focusing on the particular topic of that chapter before moving on to the "Parent to Parent" section, where I've offered helpful, practical tips for implementing the suggestions in the chapter.

Next I've included excerpts "From My Prayer Journal," which was my own journal entries regarding my daughter Kim. I pray that these will inspire and encourage you. My journal is where I expressed my feelings, knowing God would listen and not condemn me if they differed from His plan. Journaling allows us to see God at work in answering our prayers. This section is followed by "Let's Pray Together," where you and I will pray for your prodigal daughter. I've also included a few suggestions for "Family and Support Group Discussion."

At the end of each chapter, you'll find journaling prompts and lines to get you started with your own prayer journal entries. There is also a "Prayer and Praise Journal" at the end of the book, where you can make additional entries, but you may want to purchase a separate journal. I found that journaling allowed me to express and work through my thoughts and feelings as well as keep a record of my journey. It was the place where I could cry, scream, and plead my will; and then pray according to Scripture for Kim, which kept me praying God's will. Here are some tips to help journaling become a blessing:

+ Select a journal that reflects your personality and style.

⊕ Pray before you start.

⊕ Get comfortable.

⊕ Freely write what's on your heart and mind. Don't worry about grammar or about sounding spiritual. Let your pen flow with your thoughts and feelings.

⊕ Think of journaling as simply writing a letter.

⊕ Date your journal entries.

⊕ Just like prayer, journaling is a conversation with God; but don't make it one-sided. Periodically stop and listen for what God is saying, and write it down so you'll remember.

⊕ Reflect on the chapter you just read in this book.

✦ Feel free to use the thought-provoking questions at the end of each chapter, but don't feel confined by them.

⊕ If you want to write confidential things but worry that someone might read your journal, devise abbreviations and symbols only you will understand.

⊕ Don't feel that you must be positive all the time. When you're hurt, write that. If you're sad, "cry" on the page. When you're angry, let it out in writing—God can take it. When you want to express what your will is in a given situation, do it.

✦ Document the good things too, and the days when things seem better.

✦ If you don't feel up to journaling, don't worry—it shouldn't be a burden or make you feel guilty. Take a break and return to it when the time is right.[2]

I'm fully aware that the prodigal pattern and chains of bondage in my family could reappear at any time, so I still pray daily for my daughter, for all our children and grandchildren, and for other families. God willing, I will pray for my great-grandchildren.

Praying for Your Prodigal Daughter

If your daughter has wandered off from God's truth,
don't write her off.
Go after her. Get her back.
PERSONALIZATION OF JAMES 5:19 MSG

chapter 1

PRAYING DAILY

Is your daughter in trouble? You should pray. Is she happy? Sing songs of praise. Is your daughter sick? Then call the elders of the church to pray over her and anoint her with oil in the name of the Lord. And your prayer offered in faith will make her well; the Lord will raise her up. If she has sinned, she will be forgiven if she confesses her sins. Pray for your daughter so that she may be healed. The prayer of a righteous parent is powerful and effective.

PERSONALIZATION OF JAMES 5:13–16

I write out my prayers every day; I have not been able to grow in my prayer life any other way. . . . For the miracle of prayer to begin operating in our lives, we must finally do only one thing: we must pray.[1]

BILL HYBELS

PRAYING DAILY

❖

I'm learning how to pray daily for the very lives of my two
prodigal daughters while they are attacked by the enemy of their
hearts, the world's beliefs, and Satan's lies.
ROBIN

💗 A Praying Mother Shares

Our daughter grew up in a Christ-centered home, filled with small group Bible studies, family devotions, and parents madly in love with Jesus. She went to a Christian university and led Bible studies. She knew the talk and the walk and did them well . . . until five years ago, when the spiritual foundation of her life began gradually eroding as the result of sporadic church attendance, the stress of infertility treatments, the influence of ungodly friends, and isolating herself from a family that dearly loved her, to name a few contributing factors.

Daily my husband and I prayed and prayed. Things only worsened. What would it take to bring this daughter to the end of herself? Where was the fruit of the Spirit? We couldn't see any evidence. Parents feel so helpless, especially a mom, who once had the most intimate of ties with this person. Our daughter hit bottom again and again. We continued praying.

Then God intervened. Through an incredible set of circumstances that continue to unfold, God flooded our daughter with the light of His presence. Suddenly she could see the awfulness of her sin and was unbelievably broken. Our daughter is now an avid follower of Jesus Christ.

She has reconnected with her father and me, and her perspective that I was her adversary has changed. How it melted my heart when she told me recently that I'm her greatest confidante. She sees Jesus guiding her life and responds obediently. The spiritual fruit in her life is plentiful and evident to everyone who knows her. As a mom, I praise our all-knowing and faithful God, who takes better care of the children He has given us than we as parents could ever do or imagine. But one thing I learned is that we aren't helpless as moms. Prayer is powerful.

—*Sherrie*

My Daughter Kim Shares

Mom, I saw the book *Praying God's Will for My Daughter* in your bathroom one time, and I felt resentful that you thought I was "lost" and needed you to pray for me. You turned your life around so completely, and I couldn't relate to the new, "weird" you. All the praying stuff was outside of my comfort zone. When I learned you were praying for me, it upset me. I felt that I could take care of myself and didn't need your prayers.

Praying Daily

A prodigal daughter is sick in spirit, and maybe in body, and the Great Physician's prescription is found in this chapter's opening scripture. In James 5:13–16 God tells us to pray for her healing. She may not appreciate our doing this, but when she's physically ill and a doctor tells us to give her medication daily, we don't hesitate to follow his instructions, even when she doesn't like the medicine. Similarly, we must follow God's instructions diligently if we want our daughters to be well.

Praying is the most powerful thing we can do for our prodigal daughters. Too often we turn to prayer as a last resort, when we've exhausted all other attempts to solve the problem on our own. We reserve calling on God for the big crisis instead of realizing that without including God, everything becomes a big crisis!

Perhaps you've been praying while making frantic phone calls, researching counselors, crying, screaming, pleading, and asking others for help; but I'm suggesting that prayer take precedence over everything else you're doing. How can I say that? Because I've been in your shoes. I know what it's like to watch your best efforts fail to change your daughter. My daughter's life turned around only after I acknowledged that daily prayer was my best effort. Not instantly—God doesn't usually work like that. Your prodigal daughter may not even change in your lifetime. Regardless of the timetable, are you willing to place her well-being in God's capable hands? Can you surrender to His timing and plans?

I know how hard that is and what a test of faith. But God gave our daughters to us, and He asks us to trust Him enough to talk to Him about them. That's all prayer is—just talking to God. In this first section of the book, we'll learn how to pray with a clean heart and right motivation; but for now let me ask you: will you pray for your prodigal daughter daily and as if her life depended on it? It does, you know. So I hope your answer is a resounding yes. But if you aren't sure, spend some time alone with God, asking Him to change your heart and motivate you to be a praying parent.

What prompted me to pray daily was asking myself: How badly do I want my prodigal daughter to change her ways? The answer: with all my heart, I wanted Kim to repent and find her way back to God. I knew that as a praying parent, I would be working with God to accomplish that goal.

A daily quiet time with God is a wonderful way to draw close to and petition Him. I have my quiet time in the morning, so I actually kept my *Praying God's Will for My Daughter* devotional guide in the bathroom, where I knew I would see it every morning. Sometimes I had to lock the door to steal a few moments alone, but I did whatever it took to ensure that I didn't miss a day of praying for Kim.

This daily, peaceful time with God helps us to rest in His presence: Psalm 46:10 tells us: "Be still, and know that I am God." In Matthew 6:6–8 Jesus said, "Here's what I want you to do: Find a quiet, secluded place so you won't be tempted to role-play before God. Just be there as simply and honestly as you can manage. The focus will shift from you to God, and you will begin to sense his grace. The world is full of so-called prayer warriors who are prayer-ignorant. They're full of formulas and programs and advice, peddling techniques for getting what you want from God. Don't fall for that nonsense. This is your Father you are dealing with, and he knows better than you what you need. With a God like this loving you, you can pray very simply" (MSG).

Sometimes even the most mature Christians aren't convinced that our prayers are adequate or necessary. Chris Tiegreen, author of *The One Year Walk with God Devotional: Wisdom from the Bible to Renew Your Mind*, assures us that our prayers are vital:

> We are not commanded to convince a reluctant God to do what He is loath to do; we are commanded to be a catalyst for His intervention. Not only is it acceptable to make our appeals to Him, it is required. God gives us the impression that His activity in the affairs of men is somehow contingent on the prayers of intercessors. If we don't pray, He doesn't act. In His divine arrangement with this planet, our prayers are essential. It is His plan for us to ask; when we don't, we violate His plan....
>
> ...His plan may hinge on your pleadings. Plead however—and whenever—He leads.[2]

I hope the Holy Spirit is prompting you to pray daily for your prodigal daughter and that you realize it's more than a suggestion or an option: it's a necessity. If you aren't yet a believer, know that God does hear your prayers; but His promises are for those who believe in and follow His Son Jesus Christ. Will you consider accepting God's plan for your life? If so, turn to the prayer on page 33 and ask Jesus to come into your heart right now. It's a decision you'll never regret.

I'm just an ordinary mom who understands that God listens and responds to our prayers. He waits for them. I don't understand how He hears all our petitions, but I know that He does. This book will be ineffective unless you also surrender your will to God's will and pray with an undoubting heart. I plead with every parent to search your heart for any shadows of doubt. If you find any, ask God to remove it, and implore others to pray on your behalf until you can say to God, as the psalmist did, "Oh, how I love your instructions! I think about them all day long. ... Your word is my source of hope." (Psalm 119:97, 114 NLT).

As you begin reading and praying from this book, let me offer one caution. Kim saw my prayer devotional in my "secret closet of prayer," the bathroom, and was offended that I was praying for her. I never knew that, or that my praying made her resentful, until she wrote down her thoughts for inclusion in this book. It's tempting to think your daughter will be glad to know you care enough to pray for her, so you "just happen" to leave this book out for her to see. That's probably not a good idea. I hope the day will come, as it did for me and Kim, when you can share with your daughter how fervently you prayed for her. But until then, I suggest keeping this book in a private area of your room or office.

Even if your daughter does see this book, don't let that deter you from reading it and praying. Many things you do probably aren't agreeable with your prodigal daughter right now anyway; but someday she'll thank you, as mine thanked me, for loving her enough to pray for her.

Parent to Parent

When I began praying daily for my prodigal daughter, my life was full, as I'm sure yours is also. I had a career, a new marriage, new stepchildren, and a new ministry. Where would I find the discipline and time to pray for Kim every single day? My motivation came from realizing that nothing I'd done so far was working. I might even have pushed my daughter further away. I knew that God was the only answer, so I vowed to redirect all my frustrated energy into petitioning Him on Kim's behalf. I put my precious prodigal daughter into God's capable hands. I know you can do this too.

Suggestions for Fitting Prayer into Your Daily Schedule

- Set a regular time to spend with God in prayer, as you would set a recurring appointment.
- Choose the time of day when you focus best.
- Think about what you could eliminate from your schedule, if necessary, to make room for this special time.

+ Turn off the TV earlier, or turn it on later, and spend that time in prayer.

+ Pray while you walk, jog, or exercise.

+ Set your alarm a half hour earlier.

+ Go to the office early, or pray while eating lunch.

+ If you can pray daily for three weeks, prayer should then be an established part of your daily routine.

From My Prayer Journal

NOVEMBER 16, 1993

Started praying daily for Kim.

Let's Pray Together

Lord, praying daily and spending quiet time with You is a new act of obedience. Our prayer is that it will become enjoyable and not merely dutiful. Let us feel Your presence when we pray, and let our daughter reap the benefits in her life. Help us to pray daily, but please never let our devotional time fall into the realm of the mundane. We love You, Lord. Amen.

Family and Support Group Discussion

1. Are you willing to pray daily for your prodigal daughter? Why or why not?

2. When can you schedule in a quiet time?

3. Do you believe in the power of prayer? Why or why not? If you're unsure, what will you do to become more confident?

4. Discuss whether you believe God can save your prodigal daughter and the reasons why or why not.

 Your Prayer Journal

Release your anguish and pain. God is waiting with a listening ear and compassionate heart. He wants to hear from you.

_____

_____

_____

_____

_____

_____

_____

_____

_____

_____

_____

_____

_____

_____

_____

_____

_____

_____

_____

PRAYING BIBLICALLY

The Bible is "a manual for living, for learning what's right and just and fair; to teach the inexperienced the ropes and give our young people a grasp on reality. There's something here also for seasoned parents, still a thing or two for the experienced to learn—fresh wisdom to probe and penetrate, the rhymes and reasons of wise men and women. Start with God."

PERSONALIZATION OF PROVERBS 1:3–7 MSG

You can develop a meaningful prayer life! . . . Just know that it will come little by little, growing with your increasing knowledge of God's Word and understanding of God's will. It will come with application, with time, with experience—with the doing of it.[1]

KAY ARTHUR

PRAYING BIBLICALLY

❖

*Biblical prayers must eventually fall in line with
the biblical agenda: displaying the glory of God.
There is no better way to gain victory in crisis than to shift our
focus from our purpose to God's.*[2]
CHRIS TIEGREEN

♡ A Praying Mother Shares

Liz was shy as a teen, and acceptance among her peers was crucial. A high school friend invited her to church and to a youth group. Liz felt comfortable and started reading her Bible and talking about God. I had embraced the world's ways and declined Liz's promptings to attend church, even though I saw that she had a new contentment and zest for life. I knew deep inside that I needed a change as well. Finally I agreed to go with her, and after several worship services, I felt the hardness in my heart soften and asked Jesus into my life as Lord and Savior.

Liz, however, was feeling hurt and betrayed by gossip about her in the youth group and walked away from the group, church, and God.

As my relationship with God grew stronger, I felt progressively disconnected from Liz. I weighed my words, so as not to offend her, and didn't mention God because that usually set her off. My recourse was to talk openly with God in prayer.

I've learned to pray for my daughter by praying back the Scriptures to God. For example, I pray Ezekiel 36:27–29 for Liz's heart to soften and for her to return home: "God, give my daughter Liz a heart of flesh to replace her heart of stone toward spiritual things. Through Your Spirit, move her to follow Your decrees and carefully keep Your laws. Help Liz to return home. Allow her to live in the land You, God, gave to her spiritual forefathers; may she be Your child, may You be her God. Save her from all her uncleanness."

It's been twenty years since Liz rejected God and me. She's still in that "faroff land," like the prodigal son, along with my three other children. I may not see the answers to my prayers for my children's return to the Lord, but I continue to find comfort in praying God's promises, such as Jeremiah 31:17, which says: "'There is hope for your future,' declares the LORD. 'Your children will return to their own land.'"

—*Alice*

A Prodigal Daughter Shares

I was fairly certain my parents were not "praying people." We never prayed together—except for the annual Christmas prayer, a few sentences written on a tablet and muttered aloud while the rest of us giggled at the painful artificiality. In my family, prayer had been associated with anxiety. No one could even say a few sincere words aloud to our Lord, let alone memorize two lines' worth of this manufactured Christmas prayer. We even mistakenly used it once at Thanksgiving.

I contemplated asking Mom if she'd prayed for me during the years I rejected Christ, but I didn't want her to feel bad if she hadn't. Prayer was a private, unspoken concept in my family. My mom always said she "hoped" I'd return, and I knew she meant "spiritually come home," but I couldn't entertain the notion that hoping meant interceding for my salvation. Several people were integral in my ultimate conversion, but I considered my own parents to play somewhat of a background role. Or at least it seemed so in my self-centered, independence-driven, young-adult mind.

Just yesterday Mom told me that she and Dad had joined an empty-nesters Bible-study group that kept prayer lists of everyone's adult children and unsaved family and friends. The door was open. I asked, "Mom, did you ever pray for my salvation when I wasn't walking with the Lord?" Without hesitation she replied, "Oh, yes, I did." I had to ask again just to be sure.

Mom then confided how she had prayed for my return to Christ, as she was deeply concerned about my distorted worldview. My dad even admitted to praying often during the wee hours of the night for the Lord to move me to physically "come home." The catharsis of realizing both my parents had been praying for me was absolutely overwhelming; I felt too weak to even mutter, "Thank you."

The Lord had revealed to me yet another detail in the workings of His divine plan for my life. Today I praise our faithful Lord for integrating my parents into my journey home.

—*Loren*

Praying Biblically

I hope you see from Loren's story that parents don't have to be experts at prayer. Even though Loren's parents weren't proficient in verbalizing prayer, their prayers were effective nonetheless. I'm sure her mother and dad became more at ease in prayer when they joined the Bible-study group. Jesus said in Matthew 18:3 that we must become like little children, and sometimes the immature, innocent days of our faith are when we pray with the most enthusiasm and expectancy. So please don't think you have to be a spiritual giant to pray for your prodigal daughter.

Loren herself came a long way from using cue cards for a Christmas prayer to understanding the concept of intercession, which simply means to stand between, mediate, arbitrate, advocate, plead for, petition for, step in, or intervene. I think of it as empathizing with a person to the point of feeling his or her pain so that I can prayerfully stand in the gap between the person and God, pleading for Him to intervene in his or her situation. It also means taking a stand against our enemy, Satan, to fend off his attempts at hurting the person or blinding him or her to the truth.

Loren's story also exemplifies the importance of both parents praying. We'll talk more about this in chapter 9, but I want to assure you that this is a book for both mothers and fathers. God used two parents to create your daughter, and He wants to hear both of your pleas. So if you're married, be sure to read this book and pray together. If you're a single parent, and if it's possible, consider giving a copy of this book to your daughter's other parent. Your prodigal daughter needs the prayers of both of her parents.

One purpose of this book is to serve as a devotional guide—a study of how God's Word, the Bible, applies to our lives and, specifically, to our prodigal daughters' lives. Only the Bible can give us the direction, peace, and answers we seek. It is our guide for life. Nothing fills the deep need, the hole in our hearts, except for God and His Word. Like Alice in the opening story, we'll be learning how to pray through the Scriptures for our daughters. That simply means we'll personalize passages of Scripture by inserting our daughters' names and adding personal pronouns. Alice said of her experience praying Scripture:

> As parents we pray because we love our children, and as Christian women we believe God's Word. It's all about having confidence that God will align our desires with His purposes. Matthew 21:22 states: "If you believe, you will receive whatever you ask for in prayer." God changes hearts to accept His Spirit and motivates His people to follow His Word and will. When I pray scriptural promises to God, I'm encouraged in knowing He will answer because He wants all His children to come to know Him as Lord.

Why am I suggesting we pray using Scripture? Because as I prayed the Scriptures for my daughter, I became aware that as a parent I thought I knew what was best for her, so I probably had been praying more for my will to be done in Kim's life than for God's will. That was a huge *aha!* moment and a point of surrender for me.

Think of most prayer requests you've heard or offered yourself. We usually say what we want God to do or what we want the outcome to be: "Please, Lord, bring our daughter home." "Please, Lord, help her to stop drinking." "Please, Lord, make her stop dating that boy."

Naturally, our prayer requests often are self-centered. We want our family life to straighten out. We don't want to deal with these problems anymore. Our daughter is an embarrassment: she's a reflection of our parenting skills . . . or lack of them. We're tired of living in fear of what she'll do next, or we're just plain tired of the whole struggle. Our lives would be better if our daughter would just straighten up and fly right.

I wanted my daughter to accept Jesus as her Savior and to live a godly life because I feared for her eternal soul, and that fear haunted me. I also had my own plan for how this should happen. It's easy to assume we know what's best for our daughters—after all, we are their parents!

But I learned that my best weapon in a spiritual battle is the sword of the Spirit—the Scriptures. I decided that I would love my prodigal daughter unconditionally and pray for her daily using God's Word. I was determined to break our family pattern of disowning and estranging, and I knew that God was my only hope.

Evelyn Christenson, in her book *What Happens When God Answers Prayer*, discussed what she calls the "My Will, Not Yours" prayers: "Sometimes, we try to thwart God's will by the prayers we pray. But God then answers, 'You are praying the wrong prayer.' We must never forget that God is sovereign."[3] She also said, "At times we may pray for something good and even scriptural that God has decided is not for us. For other people perhaps—but not for us. And our persistence in this prayer does no good for this can be one of God's 'you prayed the wrong prayer' answers."[4]

Are you wondering how to know if yours is a "wrong prayer"? Here's how Christenson answered that question: "First, we must stay in the Bible to become aware of what is right and what is wrong in God's eyes. This will enable us to identify those prayer requests that are innately evil in themselves. Then, after praying a request, we wait in God's presence, letting Him examine our motives for praying what we did. And God will bring these wrong motives to our minds and guard us from praying 'wrong prayers.'"[5]

I find that praying using God's own words and promises keeps me in line with His will. I also begin my quiet time every morning with a prayer for protection based on the armor of God described in Ephesians 6:10–18. "Lord, I put on the belt of truth. Thank You that You provide us with the truth and that the truth has set me free. Next, I put on the breastplate of righteousness, which I know I have protecting me because Jesus is in my heart. Then I fit my feet with the readiness that comes from the gospel of peace, and I pray that I will walk in peace today and take every opportunity to share the Good News of Jesus Christ with those I meet. I take up the shield of faith to guard my heart against all the flaming arrows of the evil one. I put on the helmet of salvation to protect my mind. Then, fully clothed in my spiritual armor, I take up the sword of the Spirit, which is the Word of God and the only true weapon I have to fight the raging battle that surrounds me."

My husband and I pray this "armor of God prayer" as diligently as we brush our teeth. We wouldn't face our day without being *spiritually* clothed any more than we would go out the door without being *physically* clothed, because 1 Peter 5:8 warns us to be alert: "our enemy the devil prowls around like a roaring lion looking for someone to devour"—someone spiritually unprotected. Your daughter isn't the enemy—Satan is. But your daughter is his prey right now, so you must prepare to fight the spiritual battle to win your daughter back from the forces of evil.

I realize that may sound daunting, but you have God fighting on your side. Before I learned to pray using Scripture, I gave my concerns about my daughter to the Lord in prayer but took them back as soon as I said amen. Then, instead of feeling peace, I was laden with worry and fear.

Psalm 55:22 instructs us: "Cast your cares on the LORD and he will sustain you; he will never let the righteous fall." If we truly learn and understand what it means to cast our cares on Him, we'll know that in spite of our dire circumstances, we're safe in God's hands—it's the difference between fear and faith. This can be a difficult concept to grasp; I know it was for me. Chris Tiegreen talked about it in his book as well:

> When we trust Him [God] with our concerns, we ask Him to manage them. We acknowledge our own futility, and we rely on His power to resolve them. We actively watch, not ignorantly wait. We expectantly believe, not aggressively inter-

vene. We act when He says to act and sit still when He says to sit. We obey His instructions because we know He's in charge—and we're comfortable with that. We can go to sleep at night knowing we can do nothing more effective than acknowledging His wisdom, power, love, and lordship. We can wake up without a single burden, because our burdens are on His shoulders. We refuse to micromanage. We will hope only in Him, because He is where our cares have been cast.[6]

Praying biblically keeps us working with God. He doesn't want us washing our hands of any responsibility—which is what we do when we say things like, "Well, God wants to teach her a lesson, so I'm not going to interfere" or, "I'm just praying for God's will to be done in her life" or, "God's in control, so I'll step back." We're not to take passive roles in our prayer or parental life. God wants us to actively petition Him in prayer. To do that effectively, we must know God's Word and use it. The Bible is called the sword of the Spirit for good reason: it's our only offensive weapon to fend off Satan's attacks on us and on our beloved prodigal daughters.

Parent to Parent

The "Forty Days of Praying Scripture for Your Daughter" located in the appendix of this book will help you get started personalizing scriptures specifically for your daughter. There also is a place to put a picture of her to look at while you pray. Gazing into your daughter's eyes and feasting your own eyes on her beautiful face as you intercede for her, will afford you renewed insight and compassion.

Also, praying and personalizing the Psalms always brings me comfort during a crisis, so I've included a number of Psalms, and you might want to try praying through the entire chapter.

Since we'll be personalizing scriptures, the passages won't match exactly the original text. Let's practice:

Original text: "Listen! The Lord's arm is not too weak to save you, nor is his ear too deaf to hear you call" (Isaiah 59:1 NLT).

Personalize and pray this scripture for your daughter by inserting her name in the blank lines:

I believe, Lord, that Your arm is strong enough to reach down and save my daughter _____. And You are not deaf. You hear me when I call, and You hear my daughter _____ when she calls. I pray that she will call out to You for help, and I call on You, Lord, for my daughter's salvation and return.

Wasn't that easy? It's simple yet so profound.

From My Prayer Journal

DECEMBER 3, 1993

Dear Lord, I learned about hell last night at church, and I fear for Kim's soul. I want my precious baby to be saved from that horrible place. Reach into her heart, Lord—let her speak to You in her quiet moments and know that You are the Savior who can spare us all from that horrendous fate. Love her through me.

Let's Pray Together

Lord, to some of us this is a new way to pray—thinking about putting on Your spiritual armor every day, fending off Satan, and praying through Scripture. Help us to learn, grow, and become comfortable praying Your will and using Your Word. Amen.

Family and Support Group Discussion

1. Have you ever prayed using Scripture before, and if so, how did it feel?

2. For practice, try personalizing and praying these scriptures for your daughter: Zephaniah 3:17, Revelation 21:4, Philippians 4:13. Discuss how you adapted them to use as prayers.

3. How will praying God's Word back to Him help you to focus on God's will for your daughter?

4. Read Ephesians 6:10–18 and practice prayerfully putting on the armor of God with each other. Talk about how you can remember to pray this every morning and pray it for your daughter.

Your Prayer Journal

Write whatever comes to mind today about this concept of praying biblically for your prodigal daughter. Pour out your will if it makes you feel better. Then ask God to help you surrender to His will.

_____

_____

_____

_____

_____

_____

_____

_____

PRAYING EXPECTANTLY

Believing-prayer will heal you, and Jesus will put you on your
feet. And if you've sinned, you'll be forgiven—
healed inside and out.

JAMES 5:15 MSG

*We prayed persistently, expecting God to answer, even when we
didn't know what to pray.*

BETTY

PRAYING EXPECTANTLY

❖

I realize she has a free will and makes her own decisions, but I continue to pray she will listen to the Holy Spirit. I will not give up hope, but I live in peace.
CHRIS ADAMS

♡ A Praying Mother Shares

We raised our children "in the church," prayed with them at bedtime, sent them to Christian schools, and tried to walk the Christian walk. We thought if we did these things, all would be well. Our daughter Sarah was a nearly perfect child, always cheerful, fun, and bringing joy to our family. She graduated from high school with honors and started college, but after she attended a missions conference, things changed. Years later, she said she feared making a total commitment to the Lord.

Sarah moved to Hollywood to pursue goals in singing and music and began using drugs. Her father and I were in denial until we saw needle marks on her arms. A visit from the police revealed to us that she also had become involved in prostitution to support her drug habit. A low point for us was visiting her in jail after her arrest for selling drugs. I took my Bible and read the verse to her: He who began a good work in you is faithful to complete it. Tears rolled down her face.

All this time, her father and I were praying for Sarah. After her release from jail, miraculously Sarah found a Partnership for a Drug-Free America postcard in a phone booth with the words: "Once upon a time there was a girl named Sarah who was very beautiful and had lots of friends. But one day Sarah took heroin and got addicted and now Sarah is dead." On the back of the card was a handwritten phone number of a halfway house that took her in and started her on the road to recovery from drugs and prostitution, and she's been clean and sober for nine years.

But to our dismay, Sarah became a lesbian and broke off contact with her family. I was shocked and repulsed. I didn't want to pray for her anymore. I removed her pictures from my walls and tried removing her from my heart, but I couldn't. I began praying for her to repent of this sin. It's been a roller-coaster ride. I keep praying. Every night I bring her name before the Father. I know He listens. I'm not the patient sort. It's been many years now, and I wanted everything fixed right away. Yet, still I pray.

—*Betty*

My Daughter Kim Shares

Mom, I was really uncomfortable with prayer. I didn't understand it, and I resented that you thought I wasn't good enough just the way I was. You changed your life, and I didn't understand it and was suspicious. You expected me to change too, but I didn't want to. At the time, I liked my lifestyle, and I didn't appreciate your wanting or expecting something different for me. Today I'm glad you had a higher opinion and expectation of me than I had for myself.

Praying Expectantly

I'm sure many of you can identify with me when I say I wish I'd started praying for my daughter earlier. The day she was born wouldn't have been soon enough; the day I found out I was pregnant would've been best. Probably I did pray generic prayers for healthy development of the baby and a safe delivery. Honestly, I didn't think to pray that my baby would not be a prodigal. I doubt many of us do.

As my little girl grew, I prayed in relation to the stages of life she was in at the time, but I didn't let my mind or prayers cross over to the possibility of waywardness. In those early, sweet years, we don't want to think of bad things happening to our precious baby girl, and so we often fail to pray protectively against the evil influence of this world. We're so sure of God's best intentions for our young and innocent bundle of joy that we pray with great expectancy and anticipation for the wonderful things we want for her life—fun, happiness, excelling in school and sports, meeting Mr. Right, succeeding in her dream career, traveling, having a family. That is, of course, if we pray at all.

Today I encourage expectant moms to pray for spiritual protection of their unborn babies. Most pregnant mothers know the gender of their baby, so they can pray specific prayers for their daughter or son. After the birth, feedings—when we're holding and cuddling our babies—are perfect times to pray for their future and commit to raising them in a godly household. Kim was dedicated in the church when she was a baby; but somewhere along the way, I forgot the commitment I'd made during that ceremony to raise her in a godly way.

My husband, Dave, has had the privilege of dedicating both of Kim's babies, and part of the ceremony is a charge of those in attendance to support the new parents and keep them accountable to their vows of raising their children in a Christ-centered home. Dave and I take that role seriously. I wish someone had kept me accountable when I was a young mother.

If you're thinking, *Well, I blew that—I didn't pray over her as a baby*, don't despair. It's never too late to start praying. Would it have helped to pray earlier? Probably. Should you beat yourself up over it now? No! Regretting the past is a normal reaction, but it's unproductive. You can't go back and change history; so acknowledge your feelings of I-wish-I-had, but then move on and make a commitment to start praying *now*.

God doesn't listen less intently to our current prayers if we didn't pray earlier. He's a gracious and forgiving Father who waits patiently for us to realize that He's the central parenting component we've been missing.

Pray with Confidence

It can be difficult to pray for a daughter with the same confidence, expectation, and anticipation of a new parent when we're trying to pray her out of a dark hole; or maybe, as Betty admitted, we don't want to pray for her anymore. It's difficult now to see the great plans for her that God has and that we had. Hopeful and happy prayers give way to desperate and doubtful pleas. We wonder, could this problem be too big for God? Some problems we never even bring to Him because we're sure they're irreversible or that even God couldn't bring good out of the situation. With our finite minds and limited insight, we question the infinite power and unlimited resources of God to change the spiraling course of our daughter's life.

Ah, we of little faith. We forget that God is the God of miracles. He is the same God who parted the Red Sea for the people of Israel; as Jesus He walked on water, raised Lazarus from the dead, then died and rose again three days later! *Nothing* is too hard for our great God.

While the best help you can give your daughter is to believe confidently in what you're asking of God, if you have not fully given your life and heart to Christ, you won't be able to pray with complete confidence. Maybe becoming a believer is a step you've wanted to take, but you haven't yet asked Jesus into your heart. Let me give you that opportunity right now. Here's the most important prayer you will ever pray:

> Dear Lord, I want You to come into my heart. I know I'm a sinner who has not lived a life pleasing to You, but I want to change all that from this day forward. Please, through the death and resurrection of Your Son, Jesus Christ, grant me forgiveness for my sins. I do believe that Jesus suffered death on the cross and rose again so that I might have eternal life with Him. Help me, Lord, to live a life that honors You from this day forward. In Jesus's name I pray, amen.

If you just prayed that prayer, welcome to the family of God! Your sins are forgiven, and the slate is wiped clean. God has granted you a fresh start and eternal life in heaven. Nothing can take that away from you—absolutely nothing. That's good news! Hold on tightly to the promises of God. "Be strong and courageous. Do not be afraid or terri-fied because of them [the enemy], for the LORD your God goes with you; he will never leave you nor forsake you" (Deuteronomy 31:6).

Whether you're new to faith in God or have been a believer for years, you can pray for your prodigal daughter with confidence, knowing that God will answer. Here's a prayer I often prayed with conviction and in-cluded in my journal during Kim's prodigal years:

NOVEMBER 23, 1993

Dear Lord, I pray for Kim's deliverance. Bring her into a right rela-tionship with You, Lord, and don't let her be deceived by cultic or worldly thinking. Please don't condemn her for her sins, but love and protect her until the day she fully knows You, Lord. Help her to over-come Satan and to know that she's saved by Your Son's blood. Watch over her, Lord, and help her to know You and want Your salvation.

Pray with Expectation

Even when we don't *feel* expectant, we must pray like we believe there will be a good outcome. Our positive action of praying expectantly will change our negative feelings of hopelessness. I prayed for Kim and treated her as if she already was the godly woman I wanted her to become. I tried not to label her or treat her as a person "living in sin," and I didn't pray with that attitude. I prayed expectantly for Kim to live a godly life:

DECEMBER 23, 1993

Dear Lord, Kim is lovely and beautiful, and even though Your ways are not her ways yet, she is close. I know someday soon she'll under-stand and follow Your ways and You will use her mightily. Kim's heart is so big, so ripe, so full . . . she only needs to know You better, and she will!

Pray with Anticipation

As you pray with confidence and expectation, you anticipate God's gracious answers to your prayers. This adds an element of excitement and eagerness to replace the discouragement and gloom that can often permeate our minds and prayers as parents of a prodigal daughter.

During the early years of my praying daily for Kim, I didn't see any tangible results. If anything, it seemed she became more firmly entrenched in her chosen lifestyle. She was moving further away from the life I dreamed of and prayed for her. And yet, here's what I wrote when I prayed using verses with a theme of anticipating the time when Kim would serve God:

SEPTEMBER 23, 1994

Dear Father, Kim will be such a good servant for You. She cares more for people than many Christians I know. Surely You will use her gifts for Your glory. I wonder, how? When?

DECEMBER 12, 1994

Dear Father, I know Kim will want to serve You, and I'm anxious to see what form that takes. Put the desire in her life to ask questions, Lord, so that one day we will celebrate her salvation.

One of the things I always remind myself is that faith and doubt cannot coexist in the same heart. If I'm doubting or anxious, my shield of faith, which we talked about in chapter 2, has slipped. The Bible tells us in Hebrews 11:1 that "faith is being sure of what we hope for and certain of what we do not see." God is looking at the big picture, of which we can only see a small part. Having faith doesn't mean we won't have setbacks or discouraging moments, but if we're going to enlist the mighty powers of heaven on our daughter's behalf, we must learn to pray with confidence, expectation, and anticipation that God will grant her, and us, all He promises in the Bible.

Pray with an Open Mind and a Willing Heart

We also must understand that God may answer in a way we're not expecting (or wanting) Him to answer. Are we willing to do His will and follow His instructions even when we don't like them or agree? We have to answer yes, with no reservations, if we want to have the mind of Christ. His instruction cannot be considered simply one of our options or plans of action. God doesn't offer advice that we can take or leave. He provides solutions for us to implement. When we ask Him for help, we "must believe and not doubt, because he who doubts is like a wave of the sea, blown and tossed by the wind" (James 1:6). We must pray not only expecting an answer but also expecting to act according to His answer.

☕ Parent to Parent

Tips for Praying Expectantly

+ Pray with conviction.
  + Search your own heart and clear out any cobwebs of doubt. Is it difficult to put your full trust in God? Are you clinging to control in some areas of your life, just in case God doesn't come through?
+ If you can't answer yes to the following questions, talk with a pastor, elder, or mature leader in your church, or join a church if you're not a member of one already. These people can pray with you and help answer your questions and confirm your faith.
  + *Do I truly believe what I say I believe?*
  + *Do my lifestyle choices match my beliefs?*
  + *Do my actions reflect my values?*
  + *Do I believe in the Trinity—Father, Son, and Holy Spirit?*
  + *Do I believe that Jesus died and rose again?*
  + *Do I believe the words of Jeremiah 29:11? ("'I know the*

plans I have for you,' declares the LORD, 'plans to prosper you and not to harm you, plans to give you hope and a future.'")

+ Do I believe that all things are possible with God?

+ Do I believe that God still performs miracles?

+ Do I believe in the inerrant Word of God—the Bible?

+ Do I believe I have the same audience with God as does any pastor or priest?

+ Do I believe that God gives second chances?

+ Do I believe that God will forgive my daughter and forgive me?

+ Have your daily quiet time and read the Bible, focusing especially on God's promises. Reflecting on God's faithfulness will increase your faith and help you to pray confidently, expecting Him to answer and to work in your and your daughter's lives.

📝 From My Prayer Journal

FEBRUARY 27, 1995

Dear Lord, I see Kim starting to act out of love to serve others. This is such a positive step.

🙏 Let's Pray Together

Lord, we want to pray with confidence, expectation, anticipation, and conviction for the fulfillment of all You are planning for our daughter, but it's hard when she seems to be moving further away from You and from us. Please help us keep a vision in our minds and hearts of the godly woman she can become. Help us not to dwell on who she is now but on who she could be with You in her life. Amen.

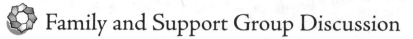 Family and Support Group Discussion

1. What stops you from praying with confidence? expectation? anticipation? conviction?

2. What steps could you take to overcome these barriers?

3. Will you agree as a family or group to find positive things to say, pray, and think about your prodigal daughter?

4. How can you as a family or group keep each other accountable in trusting God's strength more than your own?

Your Prayer Journal

Write down the vision you have of your daughter returning to the Lord and to you. Dream a little about what that would look like, then pray with conviction and expectation that it will become a reality ... and thank God for it even before it happens.

PRAYING PERSISTENTLY

Pray in the Spirit at all times and on every occasion. Stay alert
and be persistent in your prayers.
EPHESIANS 6:18 NLT

*God is the consummate persuader. He is able to convince the
mind of the scientist and to sway the heart of the poet. No corner
of the human psyche is out of His reach. No mental or emotional
wall can withstand His strongest overtures for long. The key to
someone receiving His truth is prayer on behalf of the receiver.
Does someone come to mind? Pray—diligently, persistently,
repeatedly. Pray that God will open eyes and hearts to
His wisdom.*[1]
CHRIS TIEGREEN

PRAYING PERSISTENTLY

❖

*Prayer is being in process before God. It's keep on asking.
Keep on seeking. Keep on knocking. And our transformation is
what glorifies God.*[2]
PATRICIA RAYBON

♡ A Praying Mother Shares

When my daughter, Nicole, was in high school, I gave her a ceramic heart with "A mother's love is forever" painted on it. She threw my gift across her bedroom, shattering it and my heart. But I found another one just like it and gave it to her.

One day, during my prayer time, when she was living on her own and in her wild stage, I looked up and saw a picture of her that had been taken about a month before, when she was home. And I knew deep down that she was into drugs. I never said anything to her—it wouldn't have done any good, she would've denied it anyway—but the next Sunday in church, my husband and I went to the altar. My prayer was "Lord, save her from herself." A month later, Nicole called to tell me she was pregnant out of wedlock.

I believe the pregnancy was God's answer to her parents' prayer. He knew what it would take. God saved my prodigal from herself when the baby in her womb became more important than her drug habit. If it weren't for God's mercy, grace, and intervention, I don't know what would have happened to Nicole. Now she calls home frequently, and "our time" is Tuesday or Thursday mornings, when we have coffee together. One morning we talked for an hour and a half! We're seven hundred miles apart, yet we're closer than we ever were.

—*Michele*

 My Daughter Kim Shares

Mom, I grew up knowing you one way, and then all of a sudden you changed into this weird, praying, Christian person. You had lived with a boyfriend once, so I didn't think that was so bad. I don't know what you could have done differently, but anything you said or did just drove me further away.

Praying Persistently

"Pray Hard," the words on my watch face remind me when I check the time. My husband has a T-shirt with a picture of legs in frayed jeans, holes worn through the knees. In large, bold letters above the picture are the words PRAY HARD with the scripture reference 1 Thessalonians 5:17. While we wait for God to do His part, it's good to be reminded of the work God calls us to do on behalf of our prodigal daughters. After we commit to praying with confidence, expectation, anticipation, and conviction, the next step is to pray as 1 Thessalonians 5:17 says: "Continually."

I prayed and continue to pray at least once a day for my daughter during my quiet time, but I also pray as she comes to mind throughout the day. Praying continually gives us a sense of peace that surpasses all understanding. You'll see changes in your own life even if you don't readily see them in your daughter's. Most prodigals don't suddenly see the error of their ways and make an abrupt turnaround. In fact, things often get worse before they get better. When you don't see the change you're hoping for, you may be tempted to give up or feel you're wasting your time by praying instead of doing something more tangible to rescue your daughter.

But seldom does prayer provide instant results. God isn't like a giant vending machine where we put in our prayer card, and immediately His answer pops out. Neither God nor life works that way. For those of you like me, who want instant gratification and are short on patience, this can be very discouraging.

It helps when we learn to see God's hand at work in ordinary circumstances. That's where He often reveals Himself. Nothing is a coincidence in a believer's life. God is behind those *aha!* moments when we see someone we've been thinking about or when just the person we need to talk to calls. When I faithfully look for God in every situation, I'm reassured by how He's always there. I'm frequently acknowledging His presence with a "Thank You, God" or, "You knew I needed that" or, "God, You're so amazing!"

For example, I always asked for prayers for Kim's salvation. Whenever anyone asked for prayer requests, that was mine. Then one day, after making my usual request during the prayer time at a conference, the woman sitting next to me asked the most unusual question: "Are you sure your daughter isn't saved?" I'd never considered that possibility. I mumbled something about being sure I would know if she were, but God used this woman to plant the seed in my mind that maybe I'd been praying for the wrong thing. So I added to my prayers for her salvation that if Kim already was saved, she would desire a renewed personal relationship with God and want to live a Christian lifestyle. It was simultaneously humbling and comforting to acknowledge that only God knew her spiritual condition, what she needed, and how to get her where she needed to be.

Later, when Kim returned home from college after leaving her boyfriend, I felt compelled to put my mind at ease and pointedly asked if she had ever prayed the "invitation prayer" when our pastor prayed it in church. Without hesitating she answered, "You mean when you go down in front and confess your sins and ask Jesus into your heart?" Since we don't actually "go down in front" at our church, I sat for a moment in speechless amazement and shock. The woman at the conference was right—Kim was saved, and somehow I had missed it! Finding my voice, I said, "Yeah, like that." That's when she openly shared that she had accepted Jesus at a church youth camp but hadn't told me about it. However, she made it clear that she wasn't ready to live a committed life now.

I was disappointed but not discouraged. Like so many of us who made commitments to Christ in our youth but were never nurtured or discipled in how to live a Christian life, she followed what she saw modeled by me—the world's ways. After my rededication to the Lord, I founded the Woman to Woman Mentoring Ministry to help the multitudes of spiritually young women who needed to learn the Christian life from spiritually older women (Titus 2:3–5). My own daughter was one of those young women who didn't have a mentor when she needed it most, but I could be that godly role model for her now.

I persistently prayed with renewed hope and confidence that she would recommit her life to the Lord just as she had seen me do. Knowing that she had Jesus in her heart, even though she had hidden Him from sight at the moment, was actually encouraging, because I now had a place to start in helping her find her way back to the Lord.

I also saw Kim's physical homecoming as an opportunity to pray that when she started dating again, God would bring a godly man into her life. I knew that would be a major influence in her returning to the Lord. Her journey back to God would be a recommitment and eventual lifestyle change that was still a few years away.

The Lord hears every prayer and answers—but not always in the time frame or manner we expect or hope for. Still, He is at work, and He wants to hear that we are too! In the opening story, Nicole's parents trusted God enough to pray, "Lord, save her from herself." Essentially, they were saying, "Whatever it takes, Lord." Then they watched Him bring their daughter back in His own time and in His unique way, knowing that His ways are best. God does not condone sin, but He can bring good out of our circumstances and wrong choices. Nicole's parents understood that. If they had thrown up their hands in defeat and stopped praying, who knows how the story might have ended.

Charles Spurgeon once said, "By perseverance the snail reached the ark!"[3] How many times have we given up while the snail was still on its way? I encourage you to pray persistently, even when it seems God isn't hearing or answering your prayers, for nothing could be further from the truth. Ruth Bell Graham wrote in her book *Prodigals and Those Who Love Them*, "When I am dealing with an all-powerful, all-knowing God, I, as a mere mortal, must offer my petitions not only with persistence but also with patience. Someday I'll know why."[4]

We don't know why God allows certain things to happen, why it takes so long to see positive change, what God is working in the life and heart of someone we love, but someday we will. Most significant changes take time. When we go on a diet, we can't expect to reach our desired weight in a week, even if some advertisements, preying on people's desire for quick results, claim it's possible. As we shed those first few pounds—often with great pain, effort, and deprivation—we're chagrined at how little change we see. No immediate reduction in clothes size or visible figure alteration. No one may even notice the results of our efforts for a long time. It's easy to get discouraged and abandon our new regime, and sometimes we give up just as we stand on the brink of transforming our bodies and our lives. Only we'll never know how close we were, because we gave up before we saw results.

When we start out on a cross-country road trip, we know we're not going to arrive in a day. Every town gets us closer to our destination, but they aren't our final goal. Yet without covering that ground, we'd never complete the trip and reach our journey's end.

Believing a dream is achievable—whether it's wearing a smaller dress size or finally arriving at our destination—encourages us to stay the course. Likewise, we have to believe our daughters' return to the Lord—and to us—is an achievable dream . . . even as we go through the valleys, where it's two steps back for every three steps forward, and we encounter disappointment and frustration at every turn. Many parents describe the journey as a roller coaster of emotions. While that might not be encouraging, it's realistic. Acceptance of the battle ahead and faith in God's ultimate victory on behalf of our daughters will keep us persevering even when we feel like throwing in the towel.

We cannot afford the luxury of giving up praying for our daughters. Their very lives depend on the persistent prayers of their parents. God entrusted our children to us. Our responsibility to them extends beyond feeding, clothing, and providing shelter—we must pray for their spiritual health and protection. This takes persistence and diligence.

After several years of praying daily for Kim, I cried out to the Lord in anguish that it just didn't seem to be working. She was moving deeper into her sinful lifestyle, not away from it. It was at that moment I heard the Lord's comforting words: "I want her back more than you do!" What a relief that was to me—and a turning point. With renewed faith and diligence, I prayed and prayed and prayed.

It's natural to become discouraged when we faithfully and persistently pray yet see little progress. But we must be aware that when it comes to our prodigal daughters, something beyond the natural is at work. The battle for our daughters is spiritual and has eternal significance. Satan fights with everything he's got to keep people from reconciliation with God. Therefore, he works overtime to deceive and lead astray our daughters, but he also diligently seeks to defeat their Christian parents. How? Satan wants us to become discouraged so we won't pray. That's why, in chapter 2, I suggested praying a daily prayer for the protection of the armor of God (Ephesians 6:10–18). Richard A. Burr wrote of his spiritual battle for his prodigal son in his book *Praying Your Prodigal Home:*

> I am convinced that the primary mission of Satan is to undermine God's people with discouragement, doubt and deception, particularly in the area of prayer....
>
> ...Prayer is a battleground. And yet, the secret closet of prayer is also a place of refuge—especially for the parents and loved ones of prodigals. When you are hurting and your children are in rebellion, the tendency is to go horizontally—to other people—and you may possibly receive some temporary encouragement that way. But I learned years ago that the key is *not* going horizontally, but going vertically—to God....
>
> It is God's desire to use His people to draw prodigals to Himself, and prayer is the way he has ordained to accomplish this task. Prayer is the ministry above all other ministries; without it we actually limit God's chosen method of work. And when you couple prayer with the Word, they become the chief means by which our Lord grows His Church.[5]

The battle against Satan is for our daughters' minds and our own. Body and soul follow mind. If our attitude is one of discouragement and giving up, it will show in our physical appearance, our conversation, and our prayer life. However, if we resist the temptation to let anxious thoughts consume us, we'll talk, act, and pray confidently and persistently, knowing our prayers are making a difference.

Today I was reading in my daily devotional a discussion of Isaiah 50:2: "Was my arm too short to ransom you? Do I lack the strength to rescue you?" The comment was, "If you've ever maintained hope when problems are solvable and then given up hope when they are not, you have forgotten the God of the impossible. Your situation does not scare Him. He is not desperately trying to figure it out. He takes great pleasure in bursting into an impossible situation with an answer no one had thought of. . . . He looks for faith so that when He bursts in, He will be recognized. It must be genuine faith, persistent faith, and bold faith. . . . Remember that He stands ready to save."[6]

We must continue praying for our daughters even when it's discouraging, even when we don't see visible changes. How can we do that? By praying in the Spirit as the opening Bible verse instructs. We fight in God's strength. The New Life Version says it this way: "You must pray at all times as the Holy Spirit leads you to pray. Pray for the things that are needed. You must watch and keep on praying" (Ephesians 6:18). Noted missionary Amy Carmichael echoed that concept when she prayed, "Holy Spirit, think through me till your ideas are my ideas."[7]

The Holy Spirit is part of the trinity—God the Father, Jesus the Son, and the Holy Spirit. When we become believers, the Holy Spirit dwells in our heart as our divine counselor. Burr explained it this way:

> Unfortunately, some . . . think that the power of the Holy Spirit is "something" they can pick up and use, *rather than a Person who wants to use them!* Therefore, as we are emptied of self and yielded to the Spirit of Christ, we will discover that we can pray effectively, live victoriously and bear much fruit.

"His divine power has given us *everything* we need for life and godliness" (2 Peter 1:3)....

In other words, there is no true prayer without the enabling power of the Holy Spirit. Do your prayers for your prodigal seem weak and worthless? The Spirit desires to join His strength with our weakness, in order that we may be the recipients of His promise, "The prayer of a righteous man is powerful and effective" (James 5:16).[8]

☕ Parent to Parent

As long as we pray for our daughters, we haven't given up on them—or on God. Corrie ten Boom once said, "When a train goes through a tunnel and it gets dark, you don't throw away your ticket and jump off. You sit still and trust the engineer."[9] The Lord knew that persevering would not be easy for us, so He gave us scriptures to cling to while resting, reorganizing, refocusing, and resisting discouragement.

Let's pray some scriptures together, starting with Psalm 143 (NLT).

Admit to God that you're tired, afraid, and feel like giving up. "I am losing all hope; I am paralyzed with fear" (verse 4).

Remember who God really is. "I remember the days of old. I ponder all your great works and think about what you have done" (verse 5). "Let me hear of your unfailing love each morning, for I am trusting you" (verse 8).

Ask God to show you the next step. "Show me where to walk, for I give myself to you" (verse 8).

Trust God for strength and persistence. "Teach me to do your will, for you are my God. May your gracious Spirit lead me forward on a firm footing" (verse 10).

Expect God to fulfill His promise to reward your persistence. "We must not get tired of doing good, for we will reap at the proper time if we don't give up" (Galatians 6:9 HCSB).

Rejoice when God honors your faithful persistence. "You have heard of Job's perseverance and have seen what the Lord finally brought about" (James 5:11).

Tips for Overcoming Discouragement
When You Feel Like Quitting

+ *Sleep*—Parents of prodigals often grow exhausted from worry, trauma, guilt, stress, and sleepless nights. A nap or weekend getaway can bring new perspective and revive the spirit. Everything looks worse through tired, bleary eyes.

+ *Sing*—Play worship music in your house, at the office, on your iPod, and while driving. Sing along!

+ *Smile*—It's hard to stay down with a grin on your face. When you feel tense, your jaw usually tightens and your eyebrows furrow. Relax your facial muscles, breathe in and out, and smile.

+ *Serve*—Helping brings healing.

+ *Scream*—Shut the door to your room or office or go out to the garage or backyard, and let it all out.

+ *Socialize*—We need human contact . . . especially hugs.

+ *Savor Serenity*—Have daily quiet times with the Lord and rest in His peaceful presence.

From My Prayer Journal

JANUARY 29, 1994

Dear Lord, I'm waiting on You to enter Kim's heart. I know that prayer is my best tool. She doesn't know that You are who she's waiting for, but I'm confident she will soon.

Let's Pray Together

Father, there are times when we just don't feel like praying. Days go by, and it's hard to start up again. Help us to be diligent in the pursuit of Your will for our daughters and to stay faithful to them and to You.

When we don't know what to say and our hearts are heavy, please, Holy Spirit, put our pleas into words. Keep us disciplined and never forgetting why we pray. Amen.

Family and Support Group Discussion

1. What tips can you share with each other to resist discouragement and keep from giving up—especially in prayer?

2. Have you started praying daily for your daughter? If so, has it helped you to have peace? If not, what's stopping you?

3. What helps you to pray even when you don't want to?

4. How can you keep your eyes on the long-range goal of restoration with your daughter?

Your Prayer Journal

Write whatever the Holy Spirit brings to mind. Don't weigh your words; just pour them out as you feel them or as the Spirit prompts.

_____

_____

_____

_____

_____

_____

_____

_____

_____

CHAPTER

5

PRAYING
SACRIFICIALLY

With prayer and fasting the parents committed their prodigal
daughters to the Lord in whom they had believed.
PERSONALIZATION OF ACTS 14:23 ESV

I believe the power of fasting as it relates to prayer
is the spiritual atomic bomb that our Lord has given us
to destroy the strongholds of evil and usher in
a great revival and spiritual harvest around the world.[1]
BILL BRIGHT

PRAYING SACRIFICIALLY

❖

*Setting aside our deepest emotions and speaking words of praise
and trust—especially when we have doubts about what God
allows in our life—are sacrificial.*[2]

MAYO MATHERS

♡ A Praying Mother Shares

In the introduction, "Our Family Story," I shared that Kim met Toby after she returned home from college. Their engagement perplexed my husband and me because we'd been praying that Kim would meet a godly man. As an engagement gift, we gave them Marriage Builders, the same Bible-based premarital course Dave and I took before our marriage. They both accepted Christ during that course. We were thrilled! We knew the next step was baptism as a public confession of their faith, but baptism had been a closed topic with Kim in the past, and Toby, baptized as a baby in the Catholic church, wasn't convinced he needed to do anything more.

We also knew we couldn't persuade them; this had to come from their hearts. During this time, in God's sovereignty, I attended a women's conference where the speaker talked about fasting and praying for her own child. She asked us to write down two things: an urgent prayer request for our children and the one thing we'd find most difficult to give up. Without hesitation I wrote Kim and Toby's baptism as my prayer request and Diet Coke as my hard-to-give-up item. I drank Diet Coke all day—the bigger the container the better.

Then the speaker challenged us to lay down that item before the Lord willingly and sacrificially—give it up completely—and fast and pray for the need we had named. I decided to take that challenge. When I came home and explained this to Dave, he agreed to join me. He gave up tortilla chips, which were a daily "staple" in his diet: we bought indus-trial-size bags just for him. A friend of mine, wanting to support us, sac-rificed sugar and sweets—her addiction. We were three people going through withdrawal cravings for caffeine, junk food, and sugar—so we did a lot of praying as we fasted together.

We started our fast in mid-September. By the end of October, Kim and Toby, of their own accord, started asking questions about baptism. They wanted to know what the Bible taught about baptism and had questions about why Toby should be baptized again, by immersion.

Then came a miraculous breakthrough. On November 1, 1998, I journaled: "Dave and I, along with Pastor Brett, baptized Kim and Toby at church on a glorious Sunday afternoon in front of friends and family, with camcorders rolling and cameras clicking! Just two weeks before their wedding on November 14. God is seldom early, but He's never late!"

—*Janet*

A Prodigal Daughter Shares

When I was in my early twenties, my two brothers and our mother gave their hearts to the Lord. I had two small children and was on my second troubled marriage. I didn't want to hear Mom's "nagging" about turning my life over to Jesus. I was glad they seemed happy with their newfound faith, but I didn't see any reason to get so radical. I believed in God and tried to be a good person—though I failed miserably. Still, shouldn't that be enough? Despite my emotional and relational turmoil, I tena-ciously clung to my right to live life my own way.

On the morning of July 2, 1974, Mom's birthday, she awoke to the Lord's whispering in her heart that He had a special gift for her. She knew it was my salvation. Immediately she called her two prayer part-ners, and the three of them covenanted together to pray and fast "until Kathi [me] came to the Lord!" Setting no time limit on their bombard-ment of heaven, they got down on their knees and went to work.

More than a thousand miles away, I inexplicably felt torn down the middle. I couldn't eat or sleep. On the third day of the women's fast, I called Mom. "I don't know what's wrong with me," I said. "I think I'm going crazy."

"You need Jesus," my mother answered calmly.

Should've known better. I called my mother for practical advice, and all I got was spiritual platitudes. I tried getting off the phone, but Mom wouldn't let me until I promised I would pray. Impatiently, I promised and quickly hung up.

I suddenly felt dirty and took a shower. It didn't help; I felt dirty inside. Remembering my promise to Mom, I fell on my knees asking God to forgive me for being such a selfish, sinful person my entire life. I've walked with the Lord now for over thirty years. Though I now pray for my own prodigals, I've never forgotten the faithful example of my mother and her two friends who agreed to pray and fast until my salvation.

—*Kathi*

Praying Sacrificially

Fasting may be a new concept for you or something you thought only happened in Old Testament times. Actually, the New Testament church fasted and prayed, especially when facing a crucial task like sending Barnabas and Saul on a ministry trip: "As they were ministering to the Lord and fasting, the Holy Spirit said, 'Set apart for Me Barnabas and Saul for the work that I have called them to.' Then, after they had fasted, prayed, and laid hands on them, they sent them off" (Acts 13:2–3 HCSB).

My husband and I had our first fasting experience as newlyweds. Six months after our wedding, my fifteen-year-old stepson, Sean, came to live with us. Six weeks later, my seventeen-year-old stepdaughter, Shannon, joined us. Kim hadn't yet left for college. My older stepdaughter, Michelle, lived nearby but often spent the night with us. Suddenly we were a large family learning to live together and adjusting to each other in cramped quarters.

Dave and I were on our knees constantly, crying out to God for wisdom in parenting our blended family. We wanted to be a happy, united family, but we had many obstacles to overcome.

One day I suggested sacrificially fasting and praying for our new family. Dave agreed. As we researched and considered the particulars of our fast, we determined that it should be a sacrifice. We would give up something that, in so doing, would cause a bit of discomfort. That way, when we felt pangs of hunger or craving, we would seek the Lord for fulfillment instead of the object of our desire. Fasting involves abstaining from something we think we can't do without and, in the process, discovering that God is all we need. He can quench our thirst, satisfy our hunger, and fulfill the craving of our bodies and souls.

So we settled on going without food and drinking only water and juice on Mondays. When we felt hunger pangs, it signaled us to pray for the needs of our family and for protection against anything that might come against us. Our common cause drew Dave and I together. We called each other throughout the day to pray when we were tempted to eat something or needed the other person's encouragement. We made it through those difficult first years of blending our family, and today our children are brothers and sisters lovingly united in our family and in the family of God.

Dave and I learned in our research of the Scriptures that fasting is a private matter between the Lord, ourselves, and perhaps an accountability partner. The Bible says we should not draw attention to ourselves when we fast so we won't become prideful by earning the accolades of others or by feeling overly pious for our sacrifice. When that happens, we get the glory instead of God. Matthew 6:16–19 (MSG) states it beautifully: "When you practice some appetite-denying discipline to better concentrate on God, don't make a production out of it. It might turn you into a small-time celebrity but it won't make you a saint. If you 'go into training' inwardly, act normal outwardly. Shampoo and comb your hair, brush your teeth, wash your face. God doesn't require attention-getting devices. He won't overlook what you are doing; he'll reward you well."

Those "rewards" are often beyond our expectations. As I shared in the opening story, Dave and I fasted and prayed for Kim and Toby to want to be baptized, but I never would have imagined asking God for the privilege of personally getting to baptize them! Even though Dave is on staff at our church and I was a ministry leader who can participate in baptisms, the thought just hadn't crossed my mind. But here we were getting ready to go with our precious children into the baptismal. Before the baptism, Pastor Brett, who performed Kim and Toby's marriage ceremony and oversaw their baptism, interviewed Toby and me. I tearfully said, "You give birth to your daughter, but as a mom I can't tell you the joy of being a part of her rebirth in Christ. It's a double blessing!"

Toby proudly proclaimed, "We're getting married in two weeks, and we want Christ at the center of our marriage." As I heard Toby's words, my mind flashed back to all my prayers for Kim to meet a godly man and how this end was not always apparent. When she told me she'd found "the right one" and it turned out to be Toby, I was disappointed that "Mr. Right" didn't care about his faith. It was hard not to think my prayers had been in vain. Kim went on to tell me that Toby was an uncommitted Catholic (we are Protestant), but she assured me that the differences in their religious background didn't matter, because religion didn't mean that much to either of them anyway!

My heart dropped into my stomach, and I quickly offered a silent prayer for guidance. I knew that getting hysterical or lecturing her would only make her defensive.

She continued happily, "Mom, you're *really* going to like him." I had no doubt I would like him, but could I give my approval if he was taking my daughter further away from the Lord?

Thankfully, I didn't overreact or try to talk her out of marrying Toby. I'd been praying about this, so I went directly to the only One who could change their hearts—God—who had it all under control. He prompted us to give them Marriage Builders, and here they were now getting baptized together.

Do I think our fasting made a difference? Absolutely!

If I haven't convinced you that prayerful fasting pleases God, let me give you one more fasting miracle story.

Kim and Shannon both struggled with infertility, so Dave and I had been faithfully praying for them to become mothers. One Easter the Lord challenged me to pray sacrificially for my girls. Would I fast from sugar and sweets for them? I bargained with the Lord: "How about abstaining during the week but taking a break on the weekend?" Then the Lord asked me this question: "How badly do you want your daughters to become mothers?" He had me there. When I arrived home, I went up to my office, and on the computer screen was an e-mail article with the heading "Cancer Loves Sugar." Since I was recovering from breast cancer, I knew God was trying one more way to get my attention about fasting from sugar.

I told Dave about my new fast, and he said that he would fast desserts. We didn't tell the couples what we were doing. One year later, on Father's Day, Shannon gave birth to our miracle grandson Joshua. We praised God for this little one but knew that our fervent fasting and praying days were not over, because Kim still didn't have a child. It was an especially hard Christmas season that year, since by then all her brothers and sisters had children.

Then two weeks after Christmas, God opened up doors to adoption, and Kim and Toby became the proud parents of newborn baby Brandon. By that time there'd been enough birthday celebrations at which Dave and I hadn't eaten birthday cake that the family knew we were fasting sugar and desserts until all our children were given children of their own. So as Kim was on the way home from picking up Brandon, she called and told us to go get hot fudge sundaes!

As we rejoiced in the answer to our fasting prayers, we had no idea God was planning to reward us even more. Exactly nine months and three days after Brandon's birth, miracle baby Katelyn was born to Kim and Toby.

When I asked Kim how she felt when she learned Dave and I were fasting for her and Toby to become parents, she said, "Mom, I felt you guys were more dedicated and steadfast than we were! It meant so much to us that you would give up something important to you as a sacrificial offering to God. I almost felt a little guilty that you were giving up something while we were going about our lives. I knew you really cared about us and loved us so much that you were willing to fast something for us—just like God sacrificed His only Son for us. I guess I see it as you suffering along with us."

So I have a message of encouragement for parents of prodigal daughters: I know you feel you've made many sacrifices for your blatantly ungrateful daughter, and perhaps you weren't too excited about reading this chapter. I understand. But remember that Jesus made the ultimate sacrifice of giving His life for us while we were still blatantly ungrateful and undeserving sinners so that we could be reconciled to Him forever. It's called grace. God's grace set you and me free from our sinful lives. Now, following His example, we sacrifice, fast, and pray for our undeserving daughters with our hearts full of grace.

Allow me to challenge you with the same kind of questions God put before me. How badly do you want your daughter to change her ways? How badly do you want her to have Jesus in her life? You may even have sacrificially spent thousands of dollars toward that outcome, so why not sacrificially fast instead? Why not try something that costs no money?

Fasting is often a double benefit, since we probably didn't really need the items we gave up in our lives anyway. You don't have to limit your fasting to food. You might consider giving up television, computer games, golf, tennis, manicures, watching sports, surfing the Web . . . anything that means a lot to you and to which you devote quite a bit of time and probably energy and money. Even if you think you could never give up a certain thing—maybe especially if you feel that way—consider it. Even benign or good things can become an addiction. When you have a longing for what you've given up or feel tempted to give up your fast, pray to God on your daughter's behalf, and the craving will pass.

Once you determine what you're willing to sacrifice, give it up—"cold turkey" if you can. It might be tough at first, and you may have a headache if what you're giving up is caffeine, but such side effects should pass within a week or two. If you can't go cold-turkey, try slowly weaning yourself by progressively diluting your caffeine drink or having it every other day, then every third day, and so forth, until you're completely free.

If you have a medical condition, be sure to check with your doctor before starting any food or caffeine fast, but remember: you don't have to choose food as the item you give up.

Also realize that seeing this through to the end could take years. A long delay doesn't mean God isn't listening. Did you accept Christ the first time you had the opportunity, even though you heard He had sacrificed His life for you? Probably not, but He didn't give up on you. As parents we may have to let go, but we won't give up on our prodigal daughters either.

☕ Parent to Parent

If you are married, it's great if you can fast as a couple, but it's not necessary. One of you may start and the other join later. And you don't have to fast the same thing—whatever God lays on your heart is what you personally should give up. If you're single, consider asking a trusted friend or relative if he or she would like to join you in your fast or be your accountability partner.

Tips on Fasting

1. *Establish a goal.* Choose one area of your prodigal daughter's life about which to pray and fast. Even though you'd be happy with any visible change, try narrowing your focus to something observable and measurable, if for no other reason than being encouraged when it happens.

2. *Select the item to fast.* Pray for God to reveal to you what you should give up.

3. *Consult your physician before you fast.* If you take prescription medication or have any ailment, check with your doctor before starting any food fast, including caffeine.

4. *Try fasting for a day.* If you want to fast from food for twenty-

four hours, determine if you'll drink juices or just water. Juices reduce hunger pangs and provide energy. Avoid caffeinated drinks. Start by eliminating one meal until you work up to a whole day. Pick a day when fasting won't interfere with your activities.

5. *Make time to pray.* Remember, fasting is not just about eliminating something; it's about having focused prayer time.

6. *Commit.* Determine to continue fasting and praying for as long as it takes to see your prayers answered—or even if you don't see them answered.

7. *Select an accountability partner.* This person may or may not fast with you, but he or she should pray for you and be available to offer encouragement. Keep your fast as private as possible: it's really just between you and the Lord.

8. *Have faith.* If you have any doubt as to whether fasting is effective, wait until God confirms it in your heart.

9. *Don't give up.* If you go off your fast, don't quit. Satan will try to discourage you, so expect some harassment. Just pray, recommit, and get back on that horse.

10. *Listen for God.* You will experience a keen awareness of God's presence in your life when you fast. Even if you don't see significant changes in your daughter, you'll notice them in your own spiritual life.

For more information on fasting, go to www.billbright.com/7steps.

From My Prayer Journal

OCTOBER 4, 1998

Father, please give us endurance to keep praying and fasting for Kim and Toby to want to be baptized and make a public confession of their faith and decision to follow You.

🐰 Let's Pray Together

Lord, You know the desires of our hearts. Please reveal what You want us to sacrifice as we pray for the return of our precious daughters. Give us willing and obedient hearts. Help us to take this step of faith and to grow in our own spiritual lives as we learn the value of sacrificial love. Amen.

🌼 Family and Support Group Discussion

1. How has the sacrifice that Jesus made changed your life?

2. Are you willing to fast while you pray for your daughter? If so, what will you sacrifice?

3. Read Judges 20 and note how the Israelites were miserably defeated until they fasted and prayed (verse 26), and the Lord led them to victory.

4. Discuss being each other's accountability partners when you're tempted to cave in or give up your fast.

📑 Your Prayer Journal

What are your thoughts on prayerful fasting? Express any concerns as well as anticipation of what God might be asking you to do. If it seems daunting, tell Him how you feel about it.

_____

_____

_____

_____

_____

PRAYING UNCEASINGLY

We keep on praying for our daughter, asking our
God to enable her to live a life worthy of His call. May
He give her the power to accomplish all the good things faith
prompts her to do.
PERSONALIZATION OF 2 THESSALONIANS 1:11 NLT

*I continue to pray specific prayers that speak to where she is. For
example, that she will know the truth and it will set her free from
her world of deception.*
CHRIS ADAMS

PRAYING UNCEASINGLY

What does it mean, then, to pray without ceasing?
It means to stay in communication with God, to talk to your
Father about everything. When we live like this, we show our
dependence on Him and the value we place on His wisdom
and leadership in our lives.[1]
KAY ARTHUR

♡ A Praying Mother Shares

Both my daughter and stepdaughter have walked away from Jesus (as have both my sons). We pray every day during this "season," thanking God for completing a work in their lives and building a great testimony in them for that day when they return to Him. My knees are worn and calloused, but we serve a mighty God who hears the tearful interceding prayers from a mother's heart.

Our daughter, Anna, gave her heart to Jesus when she was six years old. During adolescence, her life reflected a relationship with God. As a teen she ministered and shared the gospel with others and felt a calling to go into missionary work. Shortly after graduating from two Christian universities, she found a great job and went on short mission trips to several countries.

At work Anna met a recently divorced man, an avowed atheist, and began sharing the gospel with him. But within three months she walked away from her Savior, gave up her chastity, declared the Bible evil and harmful, and moved in with this man. For the next three years, she staunchly defended her newfound worldview of "peaceful" and godless beliefs while decrying the "bigotry and hatefulness" of Christians and their alleged world mission to take away the freedoms and rights of people.

They married four years later, but their marriage lasted just over a year. Today, more men and a diagnosis of sexually transmitted disease later, she is husbandless, friendless, jobless, and homeless. She went from a life filled with truth and purposeful dreams to one of eviction and abandonment.

I know God isn't done with her, and I choose to see her the way He does. I'm full of hope and faith that she'll return to the Lord. I know that in some small corner of her shrouded heart, the flames of absolute truth and grace still flicker. I truly believe the Holy Spirit will fan that flame and bring my daughter back. When that time comes she'll have a powerful testimony for others who have been down the same path.

—*Suzanne*

My Daughter Kim Shares

Mom, part of my hesitation to follow you as a Christian was that I thought I wouldn't be able to have a good time anymore. I remember asking you if I would still be able to have a beer with pizza. I worried a lot about what my friends would think—would I even have any friends? Then I decided it would be their loss if they didn't want to be my friend anymore. I saw that you and Dave had zillions of friends, and you always were laughing and having fun. I knew I would have to give up my critical spirit that said sarcastically, "Hey, check out that dude!" when I didn't like how someone looked. I finally began to see that as a good thing. I began to understand more of where you were coming from, and I didn't think you were so weird after all.

Praying Unceasingly

I'm sure many of you related to Suzanne's story about her daughter Anna, who hasn't yet returned to the Lord, and yet Suzanne continues praying for her without ceasing. Someday—maybe here on earth, maybe not until heaven—Suzanne will better understand how God was working in Anna's life, tearing down the obstacles she'd erected, confronting the questions and issues in her life, drawing her slowly, unrelentingly back to Himself.

You may have questioned why I chose the opening verse, which ends with "May He give her the power to accomplish all the good things faith prompts her to do." I trust that my Kim's eventual return answers that question for you. As she shared in the story above, a prodigal daughter's returning is a process. It takes time. We may never suspect the extent to which God is working in our daughters' lives or the progress they're making at this stage of the process. That's why it's so important to pray unceasingly for them, no matter how little effect our prayers seem to be having.

So far we've talked about praying daily, biblically, expectantly, persistently, and sacrificially, and now we're focusing on praying unceasingly. Unceasingly means *never* giving up . . . during the crisis, when it gets worse, when it gets better, when it seems over . . . a praying parent's job is never finished.

I hope this is more encouraging than daunting. Praying is such an incredible privilege. The God of the universe lets us talk with Him! Who better to converse with about our daughters than God? We talked earlier about praying expectantly, with high hopes for the future, and praying persistently, even when things seemed to be getting worse. Now we come to the reality that if we really want God's best for our daughters, we must pray for them as long as we have breath.

When I thanked the pastor who led Marriage Builders, where Kim and Toby made a decision for Christ, he said, "The prayers of the parents paved the way. I was just the fortunate guy who happened to be there at the right time."

Once Kim returned to Jesus, she still had a long journey ahead of her as she learned to live out her faith. Life was not suddenly perfect. As for every Christian, there would be challenges and hurdles. So continuing unceasingly in prayer for her was and is crucial.

I know unceasing prayer can sound burdensome, especially when the daily challenges that come from having a prodigal daughter—dealing with grief, pain, sorrow, and anger—weigh heavily on our shoulders. Sometimes it feels difficult just to stand up straight—which is why on our knees is such a good way to pray. Some of you have found yourselves prostrate on the floor, too weary even to sit, too broken to bring yourselves face to face with the Lord. You feel like you can't get any lower. Without a doubt, every parent sharing the story of their prodigal daughters in this book felt the same way at one time. But I hope it encourages you that when they came to the end of their strength and their own resources, they readily admitted the situation was beyond their capabilities to change, but not beyond God's. You may recognize Psalm 23:4 as a verse you learned as a child or have heard at funerals: "Even though I walk through the valley of the shadow of death, I will fear no evil, for you are with me; your rod and your staff, they comfort me." I think we would all agree that having a prodigal daughter in the family is like walking through a dark valley. Some of us feel we're walking in the shadow of death every moment, not knowing whether our daughters are dead or alive.

But notice that the verse speaks of walking *through* the valley. In other words, we must not become paralyzed, thinking, *I just can't do this anymore.* If you've ever been on a hike and found yourself in the middle of a valley, you know that the only way out is to keep walking, putting one foot in front of the other.

Every valley has a beginning and an end. We can count on that. But when the end is not in sight, the mountains on either side can seem foreboding, as if they are closing in on us. Yet the psalmist tells us we don't have to be afraid. Believers need fear no evil, no matter how dark the valley. How is this possible? Because the Lord, our Savior, will never leave us or forsake us. His rod will beat back any enemy attack. His staff is ready to draw us close to Him as He comforts and assures us that we can make it through this valley.

Parent to Parent

Tips for Praying Unceasingly When a Prodigal Daughter
Has You Walking in a Dark Valley

1. *Relax*—don't run. "Even though I *walk* . . ."

2. *Refuse* to quit. "Even though I walk *through* the valley of the shadow of death . . ."

3. *Remember* God's presence. "Even though I walk through the

valley of the shadow of death, I will fear no evil, for *you are with me . . .*"

4. *Rely* on God completely. "Even though I walk through the valley of the shadow of death, I will fear no evil, for you are with me; *your rod and your staff, they comfort me.*"

1 Thessalonians 5:16–18 (MSG) encourages us: "Be cheerful no matter what; pray all the time; thank God no matter what happens. This is the way God wants you who belong to Christ Jesus to live." Notice that this verse tells us (1) to be cheerful, (2) to pray, and (3) to thank God "no matter what happens." We aren't thanking Him for bringing this difficulty into our lives—although I know people who do pray that because going through the valley has transformed them—but we are to thank Him, as some translations say, "in everything." That's a tough order and not something that comes easily, but God instructed us to pray this way for our own sanity and peace of mind, as we rest in His sovereignty.

From My Prayer Journal

APRIL 22, 1996

Lord, help me continue praying until Kim comes to know You. Let me trust Your timing.

Let's Pray Together

Lord, it's so hard to keep praying when we see no results. It's torture watching our daughters continue down this destructive path. We're weary and beaten down and sometimes don't even feel like praying. Give us the desire and the words, and when we can't come up with anything to say, please fill in the blanks for us. Please renew our faith and our will to never give up. We want to work with You, Lord. Help us keep up the fight. Walk with us through this dark valley. Amen.

Family and Support Group Discussion

1. Discuss how God's Word encourages you to pray unceasingly for your prodigal daughter. What are the verses you hold on to?

2. What value do you see in continuing to pray for your prodigal daughter even after she returns home to God and to you?

3. What keeps you praying when you want to quit?

4. How did you feel when you read that praying for your daughter is a lifelong calling?

Your Prayer Journal

Can you see yourself praying for your daughter as long as you have breath? Are you okay with that, or does it feel overwhelming? Talk to God about it.

_____

_____

_____

_____

_____

_____

_____

_____

_____

_____

_____

_____

_____

_____

_____

_____

_____

_____

PRAYING THANKFULLY

Don't fret or worry. Instead of worrying, pray. Let petitions
and praises shape your worries into prayers, letting God know
your concerns. Before you know it, a sense of God's
wholeness, everything coming together for good, will come
and settle you down. It's wonderful what happens when
Christ displaces worry at the center of your life.
PHILIPPIANS 4:6–7 MSG

*I'm so grateful God removed my old heart of stone and gave me
such a wonderful NEW one! Oh, I praise Him!*
ROBIN

PRAYING THANKFULLY

❖

The reason God wants me to praise him is because he knows the
pattern this forms in me. If I'm praising, I'm not doubting . . .
if I'm not doubting, I'm trusting . . . when I'm trusting, I'm
praising . . . when I'm praising, I'm not doubting—and so on.
A continual attitude of praise protects me against
debilitating doubt.[1]

MAYO MATHERS

♡ A Praying Mother Shares

Following are excerpts from my Prayer and Praise journal spanning a
thirteen-year period that began shortly after Kim left for college with
her boyfriend. I prayed with thanksgiving and praise, awaiting Kim's
return to the Lord, then celebrated the fulfillment of God's faithfulness
to a mother's unceasing prayers.

DECEMBER 14, 1993

Lord, thank You for Kim. She's everything a mother dreams of in a
daughter. Please help her to know You through our life together. Let
her see Your light in me.

JANUARY 14, 1994

Dear Lord, let Kim know You are ruler of the universe and worthy of
our praise for Your magnificent glory. Open her heart to You. I love
You. Thank You for all You do.

SEPTEMBER 13, 1994

I thank You for Kim. She's such a joy to me, and I'm so grateful that
You gave her life physically through me—please use me to help her find
spiritual life in You.

FEBRUARY 16, 1995

I praise You, Lord. You are sovereign. You know exactly when Kim will come to You. I just have to be faithful in prayer.

AUGUST 24, 1996

I think Kim is starting to understand praise.

MAY 23, 1997

I praise You, Lord, for Kim.

JULY 10, 1998

Lord, please help Kim see that she should thank You for all You do for her.

NOVEMBER 1, 1998

Praise You, Lord! Thank You for the amazing gift of Kim giving her life to You, and my being able to baptize her! I never could have imagined such joy. You're awesome! She took a public stand. You are so powerful, Lord. We give You all the glory and praise this day.

JANUARY 14, 1999

I pray, Lord, that Kim will learn to publicly and boldly praise You and be glad when she does. Give her a heart of praise.

SEPTEMBER 8, 2000

Lord, help Kim to praise You in spite of her circumstances. Show her Your hand at work in her life.

MAY 4, 2002

Dear God, it might be hard for Kim to think of praising You in her sorrow of infertility. Please help her to give You thanks for her salvation and for ALL You've done in her life.

SEPTEMBER 20, 2005

Please keep praises on Kim's lips for the blessing of her two babies! Let her never forget that they came from You!

DECEMBER 3, 2006

Today Kim stood with her husband on the stage of their church and publicly gave You all the praise and glory for the miracle of their children. Thank You, Lord, that I was there to see Your faithfulness and fulfillment of this mother's prayers. Praise You, Lord. You are amazing. Words cannot express my gratitude.

My Daughter Kim Shares

Mom, thank you for always loving and believing in me and not giving up, even when I acted like I wanted you to. I didn't always appreciate your prayers; in fact, they did nothing but embarrass me. I didn't understand prayer because I didn't understand God. Now I thank God and you that I'm saved and have a wonderful life and family. Things could have turned out so differently. Thank you for not losing hope.

Praying Thankfully

Quin Sherrer and Ruthanne Garlock, who are praying mothers of prodigal children, acknowledge: "Our human tendency is to wait until we see our prayers answered, and then offer praise. But that requires no faith. When we offer praise to God, focusing on His mercy, love and power, it reinforces our faith and sends confusion to the enemy. By praising and thanking Him before seeing the answer, we are declaring God's victory over the evil one."[2]

As you see from my journal entries, over the years I praised God for what I hoped and prayed He would do. I was praising and giving thanks expectantly, even when I saw no visible change in Kim.

Writing these out for you, I became even more aware of all God's answers to my prayers. I was reminded that I had asked to be part of Kim's spiritual birth, and God answered by allowing me to participate in her baptism. I continuously prayed that she would want to praise God publicly, which she did just this year, without hesitation, in front of the entire congregation of her church—at two services! This is why journaling our prayers and praise is helpful and encouraging.

I have to admit, when I first started writing this book, I hadn't included this chapter. I was so intent on helping others learn how to pray for the deliverance of their prodigal daughters that I overlooked one of the most important aspects of prayer—thanksgiving. Whenever I construct a prayer journal, I always title it "Prayer and Praise Journal." I put a column on the right side with the heading "Praise." Periodically I review my prayer requests and note how God answered. Often He answers differently from what I expected, but I always give thanks that He did answer. I've included a Prayer and Praise Journal for you, too, in the appendix.

Ruth Bell Graham recalled one night when she was awakened and was praying for her prodigal: "Suddenly the Lord said to me, 'Quit studying the problems and start studying the promises.'"[3] She continued:

> I realized the missing ingredient in my prayers had been "with thanksgiving." So I put down my Bible and spent time worshiping Him for who and what He is. This covers more territory than any one mortal can comprehend. Even contemplating what little we do know dissolves doubts, reinforces faith, and restores joy.
>
> I began to thank God for giving me this one I loved so dearly in the first place. I even thanked Him for the difficult spots that taught me so much.
>
> And you know what happened? It was as if someone turned on the lights in my mind and heart, and the little fears and worries that had been nibbling away in the darkness like mice and cockroaches hurriedly scuttled for cover.
>
> That was when I learned that worship and worry couldn't live in the same heart: they are mutually exclusive.[4]

Lloyd Ogilvie, in *Conversation with God*, made an important distinction between praise and thanksgiving: "When we *give thanks*, we glorify God for what He has done; when we *praise* Him we glorify Him for what He is in Himself. Praise concentrates on God for Himself rather than His gifts and provisions. . . . The depth of our praise measures the quality of our relationship with Him"[5] (emphasis added). Then he wrote (and I love this statement), "What's more, when we praise we have a foretaste of true joy, the ecstasy of heaven."[6]

Ogilvie explained further:

> The old saying, "Prayer changes things," is only half-true. What it also changes is our attitudes as we relinquish our worries and anxieties to the Lord. Often, then, when we leave the results to Him, He intervenes and does what we could not do. Also, prayer changes our perception of what is possible and recruits us to be part of the solution, not part of the problem.
>
> And it's during the step of praise in our prayers that we experience relinquishment. You cannot really *praise the Lord of all* and *keep control of all* at the same time. With praise in times of difficulty, dark moods are lifted; our troubled spirits are transformed; and our unwilling hearts are made receptive. Plus I find that bright times of success and smooth sailing are elevated with praise into joy. But whatever the circumstances of life, praise brings us to the heart of God.[7] (emphasis added)

How much less stressful our lives would be if we followed the Scriptures literally. Look back at Philippians 4:6–7, which opens this chapter. It tells us not to worry about anything but instead to pray when we feel anxious—and not just pray for our current traumatic situation, but prayerfully reflect and thank God for the many past blessings and the ones we know He still has in store for us. It may seem strange to you to think about being thankful. After all, perhaps you haven't yet seen anything to be thankful for in the situation with your prodigal daughter. Ah, friends, thanking and praising God is acknowledging our gratitude that He is in this with us. It's letting Him know that we understand we can't go it alone.

Imagine if our children only came to us with requests of what they wanted and how they wanted it, and every time we granted their request, they just asked for something else without ever saying *thank you*. Or if they were only grateful we were their parents when we gave them things. How long would it take us to decide this wasn't healthy for them or for us? But aren't we often that way with God, our heavenly Father? We come begging and pleading—maybe demanding—that He do something, without ever acknowledging all He already has done or giving Him credit for what He could do in the future.

Thanking God probably is something we do more readily, but praising God may be a new concept. One way to praise God is simply to acknowledge His attributes. Every time I get an e-mail from Robin, who shared the opening quote, it's peppered with praises for God. She writes His name in uppercase letters and uses exclamation points. I almost can hear her shouting passionately and excitedly how great our God truly is!

Some people like to praise God by using His various names when they pray—such as Jehovah-Jireh, which means "the Lord is my Provider"; Jehovah-Rapha, "the Lord is my Healer"; Jehovah-Nissi, "the Lord is my Banner" (in times of war); El-Shaddai, "God Almighty"; Yahweh Sabaoth, "the Lord of hosts"; El Olam, "Eternal God"; and Jehovah Shalom, "the Lord is my peace."

One way I like to praise God, especially in a group setting, is going through the alphabet and naming the qualities of God that start with each letter: A—God, You are awesome; B—benevolent; C—Creator; D—delightful; and so on.

☕ Parent to Parent

Kim has a phenomenal gift for finding Mother's Day and birthday cards praising me as a mother and expressing how thankful she is that I'm also her friend. I keep every card and marvel at the messages that come from her heart, telling me how she values and loves me. She isn't asking me for anything . . . she's just grateful. And in that act of grace, I am tearfully humbled. Let me give you an example of one such card that exemplifies the difference between praise and thanksgiving as well as how they go together. The front of the card has words of praise for me as a mother:

> Mother
> Ally
> Coach
> Mentor
> Confidante
> Advocate
> Teacher
> Inspiration
> Friend

Inside the card comes thanksgiving:

> For who you are,
> And everything
> You mean to me,
> I thank you from
> The bottom of my heart
> With love on Mother's Day[8]

Then, in her own handwriting, Kim wrote: "This card says it all! You truly mean the world to me, and I thank God for our relationship. Happy Mother's Day! I love you."

The card and Kim's own words weren't thanking me for all the things I'd given her or I've done for her. While there is a place for that kind of thanksgiving, the words of praise that touch our hearts the most are the ones saying, "I'm glad you're my parent and that you're in my life." That kind of praise and thanksgiving warms God's heart too, just as it does ours.

Our circumstances might not change while we offer praise and thanksgiving to God, but our attitude toward them will. We'll discover a peace and joy that surpasses all understanding and allows us to approach our prodigal-daughter situation with a calm and hopeful heart. We'll find ourselves letting go of areas we have no control over as we praise God for His omnipotence and thank Him for watching over our daughters when we no longer can.

From My Prayer Journal

APRIL 26, 1996

Lord, I give You thanks for all You do in our lives, and I praise Your sovereignty. I know You have great and wondrous plans for Kim. Thank You for letting me partner with You by praying for that outcome.

Let's Pray Together

Lord, we do praise You for who You are and not just for what You do for us. We realize that it's a gift to be Your follower. We thank You in advance for the mighty work You're going to do in our daughters' and our lives. We thank You that we can come to You with our requests and pleas, and You never turn a deaf ear. You are a great and glorious God, and we praise You. Amen.

Family and Support Group Discussion

1. How have you been able to praise God even when you don't see any changes in your prodigal daughter?

2. Practice the alphabet method of praise by taking turns going through the alphabet and using each letter to start a word that describes God.

3. For what can you be thankful that God has done or shown you during this prodigal journey?

4. In the praise column in your Prayer and Praise Journal in the appendix, use a different-color ink pen to thank and praise God each time you see Him answering a prayer request.

Your Prayer Journal

Today, write words of praise and thanksgiving to God. It will lighten your heart and your load.

Praying with Purpose for Your Prodigal Daughter

The word of God is living and active. Sharper than any double-edged sword, it penetrates even to dividing soul and spirit, joints and marrow; it judges the thoughts and attitudes of the heart. . . . Let us then approach the throne of grace with confidence, so that we may receive mercy and find grace to help us in our time of need.
HEBREWS 4:12, 16

It is God who works in you to will and to act according to his good purpose.
PHILIPPIANS 2:13

CHAPTER

8

PRAYING TO BREAK GENERATIONAL SIN

God, slow to get angry and huge in loyal love, forgiving
iniquity and rebellion and sin; still, never just whitewashing
sin. But extending the fallout of parents' sins to children into
the third, even the fourth generation.

NUMBERS 14:18 MSG

Was I handing the same set of problems to the next generation? . . .
We often parent the way we were taught simply because we don't
know better. In my case, pinpointing these generational patterns
gave me the opportunity to not only break the cycle, but explore new
methods of relating to, disciplining, and encouraging my children. It
helped me to view history through the eyes of an adult.[1]

T. SUZANNE ELLER

PRAYING TO BREAK
GENERATIONAL SIN

❖

*There is nothing new under the sun. The problems your family
experiences frequently have their roots in patterns of dysfunction
that are handed down from generation to generation.*[2]
DR. DAVID STOOP AND DR. JAMES MASTELLER

♡ A Praying Mother Shares

My oldest daughter, Heather, accepted Christ during her teen years and
passionately sought truth; however, she became disillusioned watching
me being religious and legalistic instead of merciful and loving. I remarried two days before Heather left home at the age of fifteen to go to
boarding school. The years of damage from my two previous husbands,
not to mention the fact that I didn't marry Heather's father, were
enough, even without the generational bondage added to her short life,
to push her away from me and the God I professed to know.

My youngest daughter, Jessica, accepted Christ in her early years, but
as a teenager she hung out with the intimidating kids who were influenced by the "dark side" and wore black. Much to my displeasure, she
moved out when she was seventeen to live with my stepson from a previous marriage. Lately she has allowed me back into her life, and restoration is taking place. However, both she and Heather choose not to
converse with me on the subject of God.

I grew up under the authority of the Jehovah's Witnesses. My mother
was hostile and drowned her pain in alcohol. My parents stayed together while I grew up, but with critical verbal accusations and physical
violence present, and living under that threat, you can imagine that there
was never peace or a feeling of safety in our home. I later realized my

father was emotionally absent and couldn't express his feelings lovingly to my sister, my mother, or me.

I desperately wanted more for my daughters, and I tried not to pass on the generational brokenness. In my lack of understanding the way God renews our minds and lives through a personal relationship with Christ through prayer, meditation, and memorizing His Words, I was unaware that I couldn't truly help others in living something I didn't have myself—most definitely not my own children.

Now I choose to be active in my church, surrounding myself with godly women who hold me accountable to live a holy life in Christ. The Holy Spirit is teaching me daily to be a faithful prayer warrior as I stand in the void for my daughters. I'm learning how to fight for their very lives while they succumb to the world's beliefs and Satan's lies.

—Robin

My Daughter Kim Shares

Mom, I didn't realize until you started writing this book that the cycle of the prodigal daughter has plagued our family for generations. I now feel a new sense of responsibility to stop the pattern from repeating in my daughter. I look at Katelyn, so precious, perfect, and innocent, and I don't want to mess her up. The world is a tough place to live, and children are so easily influenced. I just hope I can provide her with a strong foundation that will help her stay faithful to God.

Praying to Break Generational Sin

Have you heard these sayings? "Like mother, like daughter!" "To see what your wife will look like in twenty years, look at her mother."

There's some truth in them. I enjoy observing how frequently mothers and daughters resemble each other—Kim and myself included. When Kim lived nearby, she would often show up at the door to pick me up for some outing, and we would both be wearing the same color and style clothes. When that happened she always said, "Oh, Mom, you have to go change." Or we would meet at church, and sitting side by side, we often giggled as we saw a reflection of ourselves in the others' outfit. Last Christmas Eve we dressed alike right down to our black leather boots!

When I changed to an organic, raw diet, Kim was quick to follow.

My husband and I lead or participate in Bible study small groups, and Kim and her husband have done the same.

I faithfully worked out at the gym throughout Kim's life, and now she's a gym instructor.

My daughter has watched me run a sales business, and today she has her own successful Pampered Chef business. Growing up, Kim was shy, though I'd never had a fear of speaking in public. Now, as a Pampered Chef consultant, Kim frequently gives public demonstrations, and people often comment that she is "just like her mom."

Every five years we have a blended-family portrait taken, and people can usually tell that I'm Kim's mom by our smiles.

Recently, at a reunion of my dad's family, a cousin surprised me by exclaiming how much I resemble my mom!

Even though daughters strive to differentiate themselves from their mothers, subconsciously they often follow many of their mothers' patterns and traits. My friend Jane noted that when she shortened her hair, several weeks later her teenage daughter did the same. This is natural. From birth, Mom has been the closest role model and mentor—for good or bad—of what it's like to be a woman.

The older we get, the more similarities seem to appear. But appearance and mannerisms aren't the only ways in which daughters resemble their mothers—our daughters often imitate the behaviors they've seen in us over the years. They're watching us all the time. And even as they emulate our choices of clothes and hairstyle, our daughters often repeat the sins of their parents. Countless times I've heard of women whose past became their daughter's future: maybe they were unmarried teen mothers, or had abortions, or hurriedly married because they were pregnant, and find their daughters, years later, are in the same situations.

Perhaps Mom battled an eating disorder in her youth, and now her daughter overeats or is obsessed with being thin. Or Mom's alcohol abuse is resurrected in her daughter's drug abuse or self-injuring behavior. Robin (from the opening story) and I were prodigal moms who unintentionally raised prodigal daughters. And fathers are not exempt either from passing down bad habits and addictions to their daughters.

At age fourteen Kim announced her life goals: she wanted to go to college, marry a potentially wealthy man, pursue a business career, have children, get a divorce, get a master's degree, and travel the world—in that order. I stood in silent shock as she elaborated that while she was in the "married phase," she wanted to live in a big, beautiful home in Newport Beach, California, and she and her husband had to have prestigious jobs and make lots of money.

I was forced to take a hard look at where these goals were coming from, and I didn't have to look far. Except for the part about marrying a wealthy man and living in Newport Beach, I had done everything she'd described—I went to college, married the day after graduation, became a dietitian, bought a house, gave birth to Kim, divorced, earned my MBA, became a business professional, and traveled extensively for both work and pleasure. Now Kim wanted to be "just like Mom."

During my days of not walking closely with God, I was worldly and materialistic. We had "things," and lots of them. I thought they were important. My mother had always told me we didn't have "things" growing up because both my parents didn't work, so I decided I would always be a working mom. That way my family could have whatever we wanted whenever we wanted it. Unintentionally, I'd transferred those values to my daughter.

When Kim was twelve, I took a job that required extensive travel. Swedish nannies lived with us and cared for Kim while I was gone. These eighteen-year-old girls were great "big sisters," but they couldn't replace her mother. I remember Kim crying one night before I left on a trip. She told me how much she missed me when I was gone. I explained that I could stop traveling if she really wanted me to, but I wouldn't make as much money, and we wouldn't be able to have the same lifestyle.

She decided to keep the lifestyle. But I had set her up for that decision. I had modeled that money and work were more important than our time together. Much later I was saddened to learn that she poured out in her diary how much she hated my job and how lonely she was.

As you read at the beginning of this book, in "Our Family Story," the thread of divorce, estrangement, and disowning family members was woven through the generations of my family: My maternal grandfather disowned his only son and me. My mother estranged herself from her father, her mother, and me and disowned my sister and me in her will. My daughter and her dad became estranged.

Divorce also was an accepted pattern in our family, starting with my maternal grandparents, who each married and divorced three times. Both my parents had failed marriages before they married each other, numerous aunts and uncles divorced, and so did I.

My maternal grandmother lived with her boyfriend, I lived with my boyfriend, and Kim lived with her boyfriend. Our family is a perfect example of how the sins of the parents often are repeated in the lives of the children. But it doesn't have to be that way. Someone can take a stand and say, "This can stop in my generation, and I will take every step possible to make sure that happens." Of course, this requires first admitting that we have a problem.

When I was in seminary, I took a Family Therapy and Pastoral Counseling class taught by Dr. David Stoop. One of our assignments was to make a genogram—a diagram charting aspects of our family's behavior patterns over several generations. We were to plot our family tree and then look for relational, emotional, and physical themes down through the generations. Dr. Stoop commented that every family has a black sheep in each generation, and skeletons in the closet or elephants in the room—secrets or issues no one talks about.

One classmate's genogram showed no dysfunctional relationships. He said there weren't any, but Dr. Stoop remarked that my classmate's family was in denial. Ever since Adam and Eve sinned in the Garden of Eden, families have been dysfunctional—starting with their oldest son, Cain, who killed his brother Abel out of jealousy.

Then consider the family of Abraham. Abraham and Sarah were infertile, so Sarah arranged for Abraham to have a child with her maidservant, Hagar. Ishmael was born, and Sarah claimed him as her own son. Later Sarah became pregnant and gave birth to Isaac. Sarah then rejected Ishmael and Hagar and insisted that Abraham disown them emotionally and physically.

When he grew up, Isaac married Rebekah, who gave birth to twin sons, Esau and Jacob. Isaac favored Esau while Rebekah favored Jacob. Rebekah schemed with Jacob to trick Isaac into giving Esau's rightful family blessing, which traditionally went to the oldest son, to Jacob. Esau, who had been born first, was enraged. Jacob was forced to run for his life and spend the next twenty years estranged from his family.

Jacob met and fell in love with Rachel, whose father, Laban, tricked him into marrying Rachel's sister, Leah, first. Jacob had already worked seven years for Laban, and now he had to work another seven years to earn the right to marry Rachel. He had children with both sisters and with their two maidservants. Leah's son Reuben was the firstborn, yet Jacob favored Joseph, the first son of Rachel. Joseph's half brothers became jealous of him, sold him into slavery, and lied to their father that he was dead. Jacob's sons deceived him just as he had deceived his father, Isaac.

Fearing for his life, twice Abraham told his wife, Sarah, to pose as his sister, and his son Isaac followed suit in a similar situation by asking his wife, Rebekah, to pose as his sister.

Each generation of Abraham's family was marked by a division of loyalties between parents, favoritism toward certain children, brothers becoming enemies, and estrangement. Lies, deception, murder, attempted murder, jealousy, envy, hatred . . . each generation's problems had roots in the sins of the previous generation, and things got even worse throughout the generations recorded in the Old Testament. Years later, this lament was recorded in the book of Judges: "After that generation died, another generation grew up who did not acknowledge the LORD or remember the mighty things he had done" (2:10 NLT).

In the twenty-first century we still live in a fallen world where relationships, actions, and family dynamics—the good, the bad, and the ugly—are passed on to successive generations. The Bible tells us that "all have sinned and fall short of the glory of God" (Romans 3:23). By not acknowledging or accepting this reality, we live in denial and severely hinder our effectiveness in praying for our prodigal daughters. It's true that we cannot change the past, but we can keep it from defining the future and sentencing our prodigal daughters to walk the same ominous path—or worse. We must make a determined choice to alter negative family patterns.

Unchecked, sin becomes magnified in each succeeding generation. Someone once said: What the parents do in moderation, the children do in excess. It grows darker ... more sinister ... more dangerous. Children's easy access to money, transportation, and the Internet has had a horrific impact on the types and magnitude of sins luring our daughters. News stories tell daily of runaway girls caught up in pornography, sex slavery, prostitution, drug abuse; having abortions; falling victim to Internet predators; living on the streets; often dying by their vices. And many stories go untold. Sadly, it's only getting worse.

HOW THE TIMES HAVE CHANGED[3]
Public school teachers rate the top disciplinary problems.

1940	1990
Talking out of turn	Drug abuse
Chewing gum	Alcohol abuse
Making noise	Pregnancy
Running in the halls	Suicide
Cutting in line	Rape
Dress-code violations	Robbery
Littering	Assault

I want to speak a moment to adoptive parents who might be wondering how all this applies to your family. You may not know or want to uncover the history and genealogy of your adopted daughter's birth parents. But there was undoubtedly some reason the birth family wasn't a healthy environment, or you wouldn't have your daughter. However, it's not inevitable, or even probable, that an adoptive daughter will become a prodigal. Chris Adams's prodigal daughter is an adopted twin, but the sibling twin daughter did not present the difficult challenges her struggling sister did.

Your adopted daughter is now part of your nuclear family, and so you'll benefit from the following steps for breaking generational sin, even if you don't know the specifics of the birth family.

☕ Parent to Parent

Below are some practical steps you can take to help break the chains of generational sin in your family and stop it from being passed down to future generations. They also might help identify the root cause of your prodigal daughter's problems. Gather your family and extended family members together, and ask them to work through these steps with you. They may be hesitant, but explain that you're asking them to help you with your daughter and to possibly prevent similar problems in their own families. Don't worry if everyone doesn't participate . . . just start with those who do.

Steps to Help Break the Chains of Generational Sin

1. Pray, asking God to bring unity and healing to your family and to help everyone be open and honest in addressing these sensitive issues.

2. Admit that sin and dysfunction exist in your family. God already knows, but He wants to hear you confess it to Him.

3. Identify the sin if you can. It's important at this step not to justify, rationalize, minimize, or marginalize the problem. It is what it is, and it won't help to make excuses. If you know the specific sin or sins passed down through the generations, name them: _____.

4. Ask God to forgive you for any part you played in contributing to the pattern of generational sin. Ask God to bless any lives adversely affected by your sin—including your prodigal daughter.

5. Receive God's forgiveness for your own sin. You can't receive it for others or for past generations, but you can have peace in your own heart knowing that God has forgiven you.

6. Repent and sin no more. Take steps to change your own ways and help your family break the dysfunctional patterns of sin. Discuss what everyone is willing to do to accomplish this.

7. Petition God to break the generational chains of sin in your family from this day forward. Pray together that God will accomplish this, starting with the current generations.

8. Pray daily that God will bless your family.

9. Embrace freedom. No more worrying about keeping the family secrets. They're out in the open for prayer and healing. They no longer hold their old power over your family.

10. Praise God for what He has done and will continue doing to restore your family, and thank Him for the bonding that has taken place through this gathering.

Our families will sin again—maybe in the next hour. But as long as we're aware of our family weaknesses, we can keep each other accountable and not let Satan get—or keep—a foothold among us ever again. Just as the bondage and effects of sin are multigenerational, so can be the blessings of restoration.

From My Prayer Journal

JULY 24, 1994

I pray today that You will deliver Kim and break any generational chains that bind her and keep her from You.

Let's Pray Together

Father, it's difficult admitting and discussing the failings in our family—things we would rather forget and not deal with. But our earnest prayer is that You will help us to break those sinful chains. Lord, let the restoration start with us and extend to our children and their children. Keep us ever aware of the dangers of sin lurking in our own lives and those of our family members, and help us to be diligent in taking steps to prevent these generational sins from resurfacing. We want to be victorious, and we know that with Your help, we can. Amen.

Family and Support Group Discussion

1. Sharing family "secret sins" releases the hold they have on us. Try talking to each other about some of those "skeletons in the closet" in your family tree.

2. What insight have you gained through this chapter into what might be going on in your prodigal daughter's life?

3. Discuss why knowledge and acknowledgment are powerful tools in preventing the perpetuation of dysfunctional and sinful patterns in our lives and those of future generations.

4. Pray for each other that the strongholds of sin would be broken in each of your lives and in the lives of your family members.

Your Prayer Journal

Ask God to uncover generational sins and for wisdom to stop them from recurring in the next generation. Ask Him to heal both you and your daughter and protect you both from the repercussions and consequences of those sins. Pray that God will break the sin chain in your family for good.

PRAYING AS A COUPLE

If Christian parents, who are called by My name, will humble
themselves and pray and seek My face and turn from their
wicked ways, then will I hear from heaven and will forgive
their sin and will heal their family.
PERSONALIZATION OF 2 CHRONICLES 7:14

*Teens want to know that their parents are praying for them on a
daily basis. They believe that a parent's prayers protect and help
them, even when they are struggling.*
T. SUZANNE ELLER

PRAYING AS A COUPLE

❖

*They [my parents] prayed, not knowing what to pray but
allowing the Spirit to groan for them before the Father.*[1]
CAROL SPROCK

♡ A Praying Couple Shares

My husband, Chuck, and I babysat our two young grandchildren when
our daughter and her husband took a weekend trip to Colorado to inves-
tigate the housing market. Our kids had never lived outside of California,
so this adventure was appealing to them. They returned exuberantly ex-
tolling the "promised land" they had found, with its wide-open spaces, tall
trees, plentiful sunshine, huge yet affordable homes, and the promise of a
new beginning. Throughout dinner they gave us a room-by-room description of the home on which they'd placed a down payment. We were in
shock, but we tried to listen through our haze of disbelief. Our fear had
become reality: they were moving. Tears were not far behind.

We had been an integral part of their young lives. We knew the difficulties they would be facing with no family close by to help with the
kids and having to adjust to a different climate and culture. Rationally,
we knew they should do what they felt best for their family. Emotionally, we were heartbroken. We asked questions to help them think
through their decision, but they had decided. With the wind gone from
our sails, we resigned ourselves to the inevitable. We had no choice but
to let go and leave it in God's hands.

Control freak that I am, and deeply hurt, I knew I needed damage control so my reaction wouldn't make them never want to visit. Chuck and I
knew God had given us an opportunity to practice what we often say to
each other, "Err on the side of grace." So we helped them sell their house
in California and decorate their new house in Colorado. We opened our

home to them during the transition and prayed, as did many of our praying friends. We cried a lot too; but together we took our tears and fears for our children and grandchildren to the Lord in prayer. With His help, we showed our daughter grace, even when our hearts were breaking.

Chuck and I had learned the value of praying together for our children when our son was a teenager trying to find his way. He was a normal teen, working through his own challenges, frustrations, and family issues. We knew that, as imperfect parents, the way we handled his struggles would impact him spiritually for life. As youth leaders in the high school ministry, we were keenly aware that teenagers scrutinize their parents' faith with a heightened sense of right and wrong.

We went for long walks around our neighborhood, praying and crying out to the Lord for wisdom to help our son. We especially prayed that we would not hinder his walk with the Lord through our words and actions. To overcome our own insecurities and fears, we asked God to rein in our feelings and let us see our son and his struggles through His eyes. Only God's grace could give us the extra measure of love and patience we needed in dealing with our son. Today he is a godly Christian man with a rock-solid faith and witness.

We asked God for that same grace in dealing with our daughter's decision to move. It wasn't easy, but we let them go as graciously as possible. And six weeks after our daughter's family moved away, she called to say they were moving back home to California. We're so glad we agreed, as a couple, to take these hurts and heartaches to the Lord in prayer together for both our children and to let God work in their hearts—and ours.

—*Linda*

A Prodigal Daughter Shares

(*Continued from chapter 2*)

Even though we were not the model of a mature Christian family while I was growing up, my dad prayed for my physical return while my mom prayed for my spiritual return. When I finally surrendered myself to

Christ, my "all or nothing" tendency drew me closer and closer to Him through His Word. The Lord has allowed me to grow alongside my parents as we experience new life in Christ. The Lord has opened the opportunity for me to minister to my parents with the zeal of a new believer. Prayer brought their prodigal daughter home, and now we're all growing closer to the Lord together—and to one another. I'm certain that if I stood before God today, I would be with my family, together in His home.

—*Loren*

Praying as a Couple

I feel Linda and Chuck's pain in the opening story. Dave and I were in a restaurant with Kim and Toby the first time they talked about moving from where we all lived in Orange County, California, to Idaho, and I burst into tears. Several years later, when they actually did move four hours away, it was difficult, but we found comfort in knowing they were still living in California. Dave and I prayed and knew we had to accept their decision. Now we look back and realize that if they hadn't moved, they probably wouldn't have adopted Brandon, who was born in a city near their new home. We all can see God's plan and His hand in their moving away, even though it was sad not having them near us. As Linda and Chuck learned, through prayer we can rest in the assurance that the Lord has a greater plan and purpose for our lives and the lives of our children and grandchildren than any we could imagine.

As I sit writing this, I have to rely on the truth of that last sentence. A new chapter is unfolding in my daughter's life. Earlier this week Kim told us they are moving to Idaho with our two beautiful grandbabies—for many of the same reasons Linda's daughter and husband moved to Colorado. My heart is breaking just as Linda's did, and I cannot imagine how we will bear being even longer-distance parents and grandparents . . . and yet we must.

Linda and I are walking buddies. As we walked and talked about this new development, she asked if she could pray for me, just as I had prayed for her when her heart was breaking. As she put her hand on my shoulder and began praying, I felt an incredible peace. My tears are still fresh and wetting the keyboard this very moment, but I know that with God's help and many prayers, Dave and I will get through this season.

If you're a single parent, you may have felt tempted to skip over this chapter. I understand, because as a single parent I often thought messages directed at couples couldn't possibly have anything to offer me. However, the principle of finding a caring, supportive person—a friend, your sister, an aunt—to pray with you for your prodigal is an important message for everyone.

If you're divorced, perhaps you can pray in agreement with your ex-husband or ex-wife for your prodigal daughter. I know that's a long stretch if you aren't agreeing on many things now; but if you both have your daughter's best interest at heart, agreeing to pray for her could help you reach a common ground. Separated, divorced, or never married—in any case, God used you together to create or adopt your daughter, and the power of both parents' praying just might help her turn her life around. I hope this is a possibility for you.

Having a blended family, Dave and I learned early in our marriage the importance of praying together as a couple. It dismays and alarms us the number of Christian couples who admit to not praying together— even couples in ministry! Surveys show that couples cite a myriad of reasons and excuses, none of which would likely impress God, who joined each couple together in marriage to become one. Notice in the following verses that God says the only reason husbands and wives should abstain from physical intimacy is to engage in spiritual intimacy through prayer: "The wife's body does not belong to her alone but also to her husband. In the same way, the husband's body does not belong to him alone but also to his wife. Do not deprive each other except by mutual consent and for a time, so that you may devote yourselves to prayer" (1 Corinthians 7:4–5).

Most couples who pray together, including Dave and me, say it's the most intimate experience of their married relationship—even more personal than physical intimacy. Yet some couples are more comfortable naked than speaking to God in front of each other. Don't deny yourself this wonderfully intimate time of prayer together. Once you start, you'll wonder how you ever got along without it.

Praying together also helps ensure that we're in one accord when it comes to best handling the situation with our prodigal daughters. Otherwise we might find ourselves praying for opposite things in our private prayers.

Ideally, couples would learn to pray together before they have children. Then, when the babies arrive, praying for the children would become a new dimension of their married prayer life. However, the reality is that it often takes a crisis, such as a family problem or a prodigal daughter's rebellion, to bring couples to their knees—together.

I'm not just talking about praying before we eat a meal. I mean serious time spent in prayer together as a couple. Linda and I meet to walk at seven A.M., and it's not unusual for her to apologize for being a few minutes late because she and her husband had been having their morning prayer time together. Or when we finish walking, she'll often say, "I have to hurry back so Chuck and I can pray together before he leaves for work." By the time they faced their first big challenges with their children, they already knew what to do. They had established a pattern of praying together daily.

My husband and I also enjoy the blessings of daily prayer times. We pray together every morning before either of us leaves the house—even if it means waking up the other person. Our favorite prayer position is hugging, but often we sit next to each other and hold hands. We usually each pray that the other's day will be blessed, but we also pray for family and personal issues. We pray together again at night before we go to sleep.

Even when I'm out of town, Dave calls in the morning and again in the evening for our prayer times. If I'm in a different time zone, already on a plane, or engaged in speaking, when it's 7:50 A.M. at home in California, Dave is leaving my daily prayer message on my cell phone. Before leaving me at the airport, he hugs me and prays as I stand in the baggage-check line. As with Linda and Chuck, this spiritual habit has seen Dave and me through many tough times and possibly warded off numerous perils we never even knew we escaped.

As newlyweds, we made prayer a priority in our marriage. We read books on prayer, studied the Bible, listened to sermons, took classes, and practiced until it was a natural part of our daily life together. If praying as a couple is a new experience for you, your initial prayers will likely be for the current situation with your prodigal daughter. But as you become more comfortable in this wonderful time with God and with each other, you'll soon begin sharing all your praises and pleas. Praying as a couple is the best way to heal a hurting marriage, strengthen a marriage going through a trial, or grow closer in good times or bad. Together you can cry, discuss problems, disagree, arrive at mutually agreeable solutions, and most importantly, seek God's guidance and wisdom.

Parent to Parent

Tips for Praying as a Couple

If you haven't experienced praying as a couple, these suggestions might help.

+ Make praying together a priority in your day.
+ Find a place where you can pray without interruption.
+ Determine a time that fits both your schedules, and put it on your calendars.
+ If you choose morning, make it a pleasant time over a cup of coffee or tea.
+ If you choose evening, pray before you get into bed, because both of you probably will be exhausted at the end of the day, and it'll be hard to stay awake.
+ Begin each prayer session by going to the "Forty Days of Praying Scripture for Your Daughter" in the appendix and praying aloud a scripture prayer. Then continue with your personal prayers.

+ Take turns praying. If one of you is more comfortable than the other praying aloud, have that person start and the other spouse join in or say his or her own prayer. Or do conversational prayer, in which you alternate praying, just like talking to each other.

+ Start with short prayers until you get used to praying together.

+ Write down things you want to remember to pray about. It's okay to pray with your eyes open so you can look at your notes.

+ Hold hands or embrace while you pray.

+ Remember that prayer is simply talking to God. You don't have to use big theological terms or sound "spiritual." Just pour out your heart to the only One who can really help.

From My Prayer Journal

FEBRUARY 15, 1994

Dear Father, Dave and I are so grateful for the peace You have given us. Praying together lifts a big cloud that has hovered over our home.

Let's Pray Together

Dear Father, perhaps praying should come naturally as a couple, but sometimes it doesn't. Help us to be open and vulnerable with each other and to develop spiritual intimacy. Don't let us become discouraged; motivate us to make learning to pray together a priority in our lives. Guide us to pray in agreement for the return of our prodigal daughter. Amen.

Family and Support Group Discussion

1. Do you pray together as a couple? If not, why not? Will you commit to do so daily?

2. If you do pray together as a couple, how has this united you in dealing with your prodigal daughter?

3. Read the story of Samson's parents in Judges 13:2–24 and discuss how they asked for instruction in how to raise their son (verse 8).

4. Close your group time by praying as couples. If this is a family group, let your children hear you pray together. Praying parents are great role models for the next generation.

🖺 Your Prayer Journal

How do you feel when you pray with your spouse? Do you enjoy it, or is it intimidating? Ask God to give you confidence and a renewed sense of commitment.

_____

_____

_____

_____

_____

_____

_____

_____

_____

_____

_____

PRAYING AS A FAMILY

I'll let you in on the sweet old truths, stories we heard from
our fathers, counsel we learned at our mother's knee.
We're not keeping this to ourselves,
we're passing it along to the next generation—
God's fame and fortune, the marvelous things he has done.
PSALM 78:2–4 MSG

What better small group can you imagine than your own family?
It is among this small group of people that God desires to work,
allowing each family member to see faith put into action.
It is here, as we teach our children the things of God,
that the idea of approaching the Creator of our universe
becomes real and possible.[1]
TRICIA GOYER

PRAYING AS A FAMILY

❖

*Teens do want parents to pray for them, but they aren't talking
about quickie prayers over tacos or lectures disguised as prayers,
like, "Dear God, help my daughter to figure out how to stop
back-talking." Quickie prayers have little or no impact.
Sermon prayers push your teen one step away from faith.*
T. SUZANNE ELLER

♡ A Praying Mother Shares

We have not seen our prodigal daughter in eight years or heard from her in over four years.

We pray for her daily, knowing God is huge and can do anything. I pray for her to find peace with God, restore relationships with others, find help mentally and emotionally, and find true joy.[2]

Our other daughter was angry at times because of the tense situation in our home. Sometimes she felt neglected. She also worried about her sister and was also angry at her much of the time. We prayed with her and prayed together for her sister. She saw the pain we experienced. She also saw how much we had to invest in her sister during this time, sometimes having little energy left to deal with anything else. As an adult with children of her own, she cannot understand how we have been able to continue in the situation, yet have peace, hope, and joy in our lives. I pray she never has to know.[3]

—Chris Adams

♡ My Daughter Kim Shares

Mom, while I was still living at home, I remember one Easter when you wanted the whole family, including Dave's parents, to go to the Crystal Cathedral for their Glory of Easter performance. I agreed to go because it was Easter and it was your birthday request. Michelle and I met after work for shopping and dinner at Carl's Jr. in the mall before joining the rest of the family.

To my surprise and alarm, when we sat down to eat, Michelle asked, "Do you want to pray, or should I?" I was thinking, *Hey, this is weird. We're only at a fast-food restaurant in the mall! You don't pray over fast food in public. And one of us is going to pray? I'm only comfortable with our parents praying at family Christmas or Easter dinners in the privacy of our home. I don't even like it when they pray over other meals, but I go along with it as long as we're at home.*

Resigned, I mumbled, "Okay, you pray." I kept looking around hoping no one saw us. I was so embarrassed.

🌣 Praying as a Family

A prodigal daughter affects the entire family, especially other siblings, who probably feel neglected and angry and yet grieve the loss of closeness with their sister. They may have mixed loyalties between the sister they love but seem to have lost and the parents who struggle to help her. Sometimes we think it best to protect the rest of the family by shielding them from the crisis surrounding the prodigal. But it can become a case of ignoring "the elephant in the room." And as everyone focuses on avoiding the elephant, they begin avoiding each other.

Talk about the elephant. Be honest with your children about what's happening with their sister. Their fearful imaginings about what's going on could be worse than the real thing. Admitting your concerns and including brothers and sisters in the solutions—and the prayer—is empowering for the entire family.

Dr. David Stoop and Dr. James Masteller have pointed out that a problem child usually is acting out in response to an underlying family issue. It's never just about the child: "A family is more than a group of individuals who happen to share the same address and the same last name. Many of the riddles of 'why you are the way you are' can be unlocked by looking at the family as a system of relationships and interpersonal dynamics."[4]

My husband asked if I really thought families would read this book together and discuss the "Family and Support Group Discussion" questions at the end of each chapter. I said, "If they want the family to stay intact and the prodigal daughter back, I would hope so!" When one member goes astray, it's a problem for the entire family. Families that pray and work at the problem together will experience healing.

When our family was newly blended and first dealing with all the issues that entails, I read every book I could find on the subject and tried implementing many of their suggestions. But the book that helped the most was a book of devotions for blended families. Unfortunately, by the time I found the book, Kim had already left for college with her boyfriend.

We all had full lives. Sean and Shannon were young adults with jobs, and both Dave and I were working. The only time we could fit family prayer and devotions into our schedules was to roust the family out of bed at six A.M. on Sunday morning. Reluctantly, the kids came staggering out in their pajamas, often wrapped in the blankets from their beds. I always had something in the oven while we shared our devotional time so that when we finished we could eat breakfast together. It was a precious time with each other and with God before heading to the morning church service. Afterward, we all went our separate ways.

That might sound radical or like too much trouble, but my husband and I believed in the importance and power of centering our new family on God and His Word. We put up with the kids' complaints and struggles to get out of bed. It was a huge sacrifice for us too, but one I wouldn't hesitate to repeat, because we achieved our goal—putting God first in the new Thompson family.

Did our kids appreciate these spiritual times together? Probably not at the time. But I hope that as they look back now, being adults, they have a sense of how much God and their parents love them.

Dave's oldest child, Michelle, didn't live with us, but she established "family nights" at our house. She came over for dinner, we all played games or watched a movie, and she often spent the night. Michelle actually purchased games and made sure everyone marked the date on his or her calendar. Though she was out on her own, she still longed for the family experience.

Even though Kim was not at home to participate in these family activities and opted out of the family devotional time when she was visiting, she benefited from the way our diverse family learned to come together as a unit. Today our family is no longer merely blended but united by the blood of Jesus Christ, which is much stronger than the ties of human blood.

Spending time as a family, with or without the prodigal, is invaluable for everyone's mental and spiritual well-being. Otherwise, siblings may develop resentment and feel cheated of love, attention, and resources as they watch their parents' dwindling energy and note the money, time, and emotion spent on behalf of a prodigal child. Many siblings act up or withdraw from the family just to turn their parents' attention back to them. Some parents become so worried that the other children will follow the example of the prodigal sibling that they become stricter and more suspicious. Hanging out together can head off many of these potential family problems.

It might be naive to say, "The family that prays and plays together stays together," but I have to believe it's true. It worked for us, and I know it can work for you too. Praying parents are the best role models and mentors for helping children learn how to handle—with God's help—the inevitable challenges and crises of life.

As I read the story Kim shared in the opening of this chapter, my mind flashed back to the countless times our family has prayed together before meals. We always hold hands, and when Kim was in her prodigal days, she would reluctantly put out her hand, but it was limp—not warmly clasping ours as it is today. Still we included her in prayers.

Sitting around the table might be the perfect place to have your family devotions. Our grandchildren love to hold our hands as Grandpa Dave prays and we all joyfully sing out, "Amen." When we go out to dinner with Shannon's family, two-year-old Joshua puts out his hands for us to hold while he prays aloud with his daddy. Kim's twenty-month-old son, Brandon, puts his head down and says, "Amen" every time she puts him in his high chair. She commented that it's a reminder for her to pray with him before every meal, not just when they sit down to dinner as a family. By the way, her family prays before meals now—even in public and at fast-food restaurants!

Our daughter-in-law wrote an article about a time when her family was eating at a restaurant with her toddler son, our now eight-year-old grandson, Caleb. Caleb kept saying, "More amen," insisting they pray again and again. *I'm hungry,* Janel thought in protest. *The food smells so good. We already prayed once.* Then the Lord gently changed her perspective: what a blessing that her toddler wanted to pray!

God was showing these parents, through their precious babies, that it's never too early to nurture their children's desire to pray. When they're small, we think, *Oh, isn't that cute?* But we should be thinking, *How can I foster their desire to pray so they will always have a hunger for "More amen"?*

As children grow into their teens, praying as a family can be a bit trickier. T. Suzanne Eller, author of *The Mom I Want to Be,* offered this insight when I asked her to share her thoughts on families praying together: "Most teens say they want their faith to be a private experience. They want to know their parents are praying. They want to see prayer in action. But at this age they are taking their faith to the next level and making it their own. I know many say that family devotions and praying together is the key—and for some, I'm sure this is true—but after working with teens for over eighteen years, I hear more teens say: 'Be my model and encourage me in prayer, but don't make my prayer a public or family event. Let prayer be private.'"

So don't be surprised if, for a time, your teens resist praying with you or the family; but it's crucial that you still involve them as much as possible and that you continue to teach them how to pray. Tricia Goyer wrote in her book, *Generation NeXt Parenting,* "While I enjoy it when my family gathers to pray or read the Bible together, I find the most joy when my children seek God on their own."[5]

Does this mean if the siblings are praying or participating in family devotions that they won't become prodigals also? There are, of course, no guarantees. Even as our prodigal daughter, Kim, was coming to the Lord, Shannon—the evangelistic sibling who had prayed for her step-sister—went through her own time of angrily questioning God and us as parents during a painful time in her life when she was struggling with infertility. For a period, she disassociated herself from both God and Dave and me. It was a sad and strained time for us all. Dave and I had to admit our part in the problems she was having with us, ask for forgiveness, and keep praying and loving her. I'm grateful that God brought her back to Him and to us. Today our beautiful Shannon is a loving daughter, godly wife—and mother.

Praying as a family and for our family sometimes requires parents to do uncomfortable things, but Dave and I have learned to follow God's lead—no matter how unusual it seems. For example, when Kim and her boyfriend graduated from college, both families came together to celebrate. By now it had become second nature for us to view every time with family, every celebration, as a time and occasion for prayer. But Kim's boyfriend's family was "not religious," so that meant Dave and I had to take the initiative to gather everyone together before the meal. Dave prayed, and Kim didn't protest—she probably expected it.

After the family festivities, the kids were anxious to go party with their friends. Before they left, Dave and I took Kim and her boyfriend aside and told them we wanted to pray for them. The looks on their faces said, "Oh, brother! That's the last thing we want to do." But we didn't give them a chance to react or protest. We placed our hands on them and asked God to bless each of their lives. When we said the final amen, they couldn't get out of there fast enough.

Recently I asked Kim how she felt that day. She told me: "Mom, I was so uncomfortable with prayer back then. Prayer embarrassed me. I remember thinking, *Oh, here she goes again with that prayer stuff—trying to save our souls.* I just wanted to get out of that room."

It was a bold move for Dave and me, but God had a bolder move planned, and He wanted us to collaborate with Him by doing our part. I believe God used that prayer—along with all the prayers we prayed while they were together—to help our prodigal daughter make her final decision several weeks after graduation to come home physically and, several years later, spiritually.

Anytime you mix a prodigal in with a praying family, there's bound to be an uncomfortable or embarrassing moment for someone. Often that person is the prodigal herself, but let's face it, sometimes it's us—or our extended family. It can be tempting to keep grandparents, aunts, uncles, and cousins at a safe distance from our prodigal or from the truth of her situation. We might feel too embarrassed to face them or not want to hear their comments about our prodigal. Admittedly, many give well-meaning but unhelpful advice. But the prodigal daughter is part of their family too, and they love her and are concerned. They want to help even if they don't know the right thing to do or say. So why not give them an assignment? Tell them lovingly that you would appreciate their prayers, and tell them specifically what you need them to pray for. Provide them with a copy of this book, or suggest they purchase one so they can learn how to pray effectively for the family prodigal. We often ask people to pray for us, but many don't know how or what to pray.

When a daughter is far from the Lord, we need an army of prayer warriors battling on her behalf. Who better than family? "And now this word to all of you: You should be like one big happy family, full of sympathy toward each other, loving one another with tender hearts and humble minds" (1 Peter 3:8 TLB).

My paternal grandmother, Granny Reed, prayed for her grandchildren—all twelve of them. My fondest memory of her is when she sat down in her favorite chair, her nylons rolled down, her glasses resting on the bridge of her nose, and her big, black Bible open on her lap. That was the cue for the grandkids to gather around her on the floor in a circle as she read Bible stories and prayed with and for us. I know she prayed for her seven children too, and it broke her heart when my father was murdered and she didn't know if he was a Christian. My dad was a church prodigal, saying he had seen too much hypocrisy, and yet I find comfort in the verse that gave Granny Reed hope: "Train a child in the way he should go, and when he is old he will not turn from it" (Proverbs 22:6).

Several of my cousins were prodigals, and I certainly had my times. I'm one of those prodigals who, when she was old, returned to the way she should go. I truly believe I'm in ministry today because of the prayers of Granny Reed. She never stopped praying for any of her kids and grandkids, even after a stroke took her eyesight and she could no longer read her beloved Bible. I thank God that I had a grandma who loved me enough to pray both for and with me.

Except for Shannon's family, who lives near us, our other kids and grandkids live scattered throughout the United States, Italy, and wherever the Navy stations Sean and his family, so we can't be involved in the day-to-day activities of their lives. But with the birth of our first grandchild, we knew what God was calling us to do: to pray for our children and our grandchildren. What better legacy to leave than that we prayed for our family and raised a praying family.

Some of you reading this book might be grandparents. Perhaps you're currently raising or are even the legal guardian of a prodigal granddaughter. Please know that everything we discuss applies to you too. Some might feel it's a burden raising a child, especially a prodigal, in this season of your life. But because you're reading this book, you understand that God has a purpose for your being in your granddaughter's life. You love her so much that you're willing to do whatever it takes. There are extra jewels awaiting you in your heavenly crown.

Parent to Parent

Having family devotional times may seem daunting at first if you've never had them before. That's okay. Don't be afraid, just start small. The most important thing is to start.

Tips for a Family Devotional Time

+ Ask what the children want to study or do.
+ Include everyone in the decision of the time, day, and frequency of your devotional time together.

+ Involve all family members in leading or participating.

+ Read this book together. Answer the family discussion questions at the end of each chapter.

+ Help your children learn how to pray by using the prayers in the "Forty Days of Praying Scripture for Your Daughter" located in the appendix of this book.

+ Pray for your children, asking them to share requests, and share your prayer requests with them.

+ Let everyone know how important and powerful their prayers are in helping their sister, your prodigal daughter—and how important their prayers are for every member of your family.

+ Share with your children any good news and answers to prayer you receive, and encourage them to report answers to their prayers.

From My Prayer Journal

FEBRUARY 8, 1994

Please soften Kim's heart toward You and toward our family's Christian ways.

Let's Pray Together

Father, for those of us who haven't been praying as a family, starting may involve a process. Give us fortitude and wisdom to know how to incorporate a devotional time into our family life. Help us reach out to extended family and friends who could join us in praying for our prodigal daughter. We want to be godly role models for all our children. We love You, Lord. Amen.

Family and Support Group Discussion

1. What can you do to better include the entire family in praying for your prodigal daughter?

2. If you've been reading and answering these questions together as a family, how has it helped your family? If you haven't, how could you incorporate this into your family schedule?

3. Brainstorm a list of prayer requests you can give to well-meaning relatives, and keep them informed of the answers and of further needs.

4. Encourage your children to participate in this group, and ask how they are coping with having a prodigal in the family (and with all that entails).

Your Prayer Journal

Record some of the highs and lows your family experiences while establishing a devotional time together.

_____

_____

_____

_____

_____

_____

_____

_____

_____

Living Life with Your Prodigal Daughter

Jesus replied, "If anyone loves me, she will obey my teaching.
My Father will love her,
and we will come to her and make our home with her.
She who does not love me will not obey my teaching. These words
you hear are not my own; they belong to the Father who sent me.
"All this I have spoken while still with you. But the Counselor, the
Holy Spirit, whom the Father will send in my name, will teach
you all things and will remind you of everything I have said to
you. Peace I leave with you; my peace I give you.
I do not give to you as the world gives.
Do not let your hearts be troubled and do not be afraid."
PERSONALIZATION OF JOHN 14:23–27

CHAPTER 11

DEFINING A PRODIGAL DAUGHTER

Our daughter will be made right with God by placing her faith in Jesus Christ to take away her sins. And this is true no matter who she is or what she has done.

For our prodigal daughter has sinned; she has fallen short of God's glorious standard. Yet God, with undeserved kindness, declares that she is righteous. He did this through Christ Jesus when he freed her from the penalty for her sins.

PERSONALIZATION OF ROMANS 3:22–23 NLT

There has never been, and cannot be,
a good life without self-control.[1]
JOHN MILTON

DEFINING A
PRODIGAL DAUGHTER

❖

Believe me, after all the dope and stuff I've done,
smoking's not the worst thing I could do.[2]
ASHLEY SMITH

♡ A Praying Mother Shares

As a single parent I worried about putting my four children through college. But for Jeanne, my oldest, everything fell into place. I said, "Jeanne, do you realize that except for the cost of your books, your whole first year of college is costing us nothing?"

"I know, Mom. And if I get a part-time job, I can start saving for next year so I can transfer to a really great art school somewhere out of state."

I couldn't think about her moving far away again. She'd just returned from a year studying art in Yugoslavia as a foreign exchange student. I was delighted she was going to college twenty minutes away. She even came home on the bus the first weekend.

Two weeks after school began, my daughter Julia called me at work. "Mom, Jeanne's gone! She left a note for the people she was living with saying she was sorry, but she had a chance to move to California with her friend Greg."

I felt like I'd just fallen out of an airplane with no parachute. How could she be so selfish after I worked so hard getting her that scholarship, the grant, and free room and board? How could she throw a free year of college down the drain? How could she up and leave without saying good-bye? Gone with Jeanne were my dreams of sharing a wonderful year with my oldest daughter. Four days later a letter arrived.

"Dear Mom, I know I've hurt you, and although it may take time, I hope you'll eventually understand my reasons and forgive me. I'm not going to California to get married, become pregnant, do drugs, act lazy, join a cult, or escape from my family. I'm going west to improve my life, learn, explore, and seek new opportunities. I know my way will be hard, and that's what I prefer. I'm not leaving you behind—because I love you very much. The only thing I regret about leaving is not having said good-bye. When I decided to do this, I realized I wouldn't be able to discuss this with you in a rational way. Love, Jeanne."

She was right about that last part, and the three-page letter I sent stating what I thought of her sense of adventure made that plain. When Jeanne left abruptly, I got on my knees in prayer. I saw that when she returned from Yugoslavia, I had pulled her back close to me with the lure of a scholarship, a grant, and a comfortable place to live near our convenient, safe, hometown university. But Jeanne had a different education plan, which included sleeping near seals on the beach, working for artists, and filling out her own scholarship, grant, and loan applications. This mother learned the hard way that letting go means letting go her way, not mine.

—*Patricia Lorenz*

A Prodigal Daughter Shares
(Continued from chapter 9)

When I was growing up, my family believed in Jesus Christ as our Savior; it just took us a while to understand what it meant to call Him Lord. Nevertheless, when I was seven, our Christian neighbors, Bill and Joan, baptized my family in our backyard spa. I understood the symbolism of "accepting Jesus Christ" but didn't fully grasp that I was choosing one way of life over another. As far as I knew, Christianity was the only belief system.

I learned what a Christian family looked like by spending time with Bill and Joan, and their daughter Angela "kept me in check." I had a loving, dedicated, concerned family, but we were stuck in spiritual infancy. I thank the Lord my parents pointed me in the right direction, trusting Sunday-school teachers and Christian neighbors to fill in the gaps.

However, as I entered junior high, my relationship with Bill and Joan's family waned. Angela and I attended different schools, and I had to make new friends. I tried carrying what I had learned into those new friendships, but soon I started swearing like everyone else, gossiping, defying my parents—essentially compromising my values. The compromises increased as I learned that God doesn't strike you down every time you sin. It seemed I was getting away with it. I allowed Satan to creep into my life.

High school brought added pressures, added sins, and compulsive lying to my parents. I wasn't good at lying, though, since my conscience knew a fear of the Lord. I kept God in my life but at a safe distance. I recall nights out with friends when I felt scared enough to pray for safety but not scared enough to stay away from the darkness. Many reckless nights I committed every sin imaginable, followed by silent petitions to Jesus, *Please forgive me* . . . a mere mantra. And the cycle would repeat the following weekend.

I stopped going to church, except for occasional holidays, and then I couldn't participate in communion because my heart wasn't in the right place. I was ashamed to stand before God and confront my sins—and reluctant because I would have to change the lifestyle I was growing accustomed to. I was having too much "fun." *Someday* I would return to the Lord, I told myself.

—*Loren*

Defining a Prodigal Daughter

We probably all have different ideas of what defines a prodigal. Some of us might feel our daughter is prodigal if she doesn't do what we think is best for her: if she decides to live life by her plan—go to a different college, not go to college at all, put on a backpack and travel Europe instead of getting a job, live in a car, move across the country, go to Hollywood to be a star, get pregnant, live an alternative lifestyle. Some are like Loren, lured from the light into the dark. Loren openly described her journey to God, away from God, and—we will see later—back to God. Loren's story is a classic example of a prodigal daughter's thought process and response to outside influences.

Maybe your daughter has become one of the "mean girls" who are ruthless in their verbal, and sometimes physical, attacks on other girls. Or perhaps your daughter is acting out because she is the victim of this type of relational or physical aggression by her peers.

Then there are those daughters who are killing themselves with their destructive choices, have run away from home, or remain missing. I could never describe every scenario each of you, as a parent of a prodigal daughter, has experienced. But one definition of a prodigal we all can agree on is that a prodigal is a daughter who is breaking the hearts of her parents—and of God.

A recent phenomenon that's rightfully upsetting parents is "Girls Gone Wild." It started several years ago as a series of videos in which roving camera crews convinced partying (and often drunk) college girls to lift their shirts and flash their breasts. It has recently been adopted as a description of the alarming moral decay that increasingly seems to be modeled by influential women to the current generation. The phrase has been splashed across magazine covers and been the topic of numerous articles and commentaries. *Newsweek*'s February 12, 2007, issue featured the subject. On the cover was a picture of Paris Hilton with an arm around Britney Spears, whose sultry gaze connects with readers' eyes defiantly: "Out-of-Control Celebs and Online Sleaze Fuel a New Debate Over Kids and Values," the cover reads, with the following line: "The Girls Gone Wild Effect." Inside, the article looked at how this trend affects the values of young girls: "Paris, Britney, Lindsay & Nicole: They seem to be everywhere and they may not be wearing underwear. Tweens adore them and teens envy them. But are we raising a generation of 'prosti-tots'?"[3]

Ladies' Home Journal addressed the issue in their article "Girls Gone Wild?" It posed a question that's on the minds of a lot of parents: "Teen girls today have adopted a steamy, super-sexed style. What's going on—and can moms put a stop to it?"[4]

The answer is yes. That's what *Praying for Your Prodigal Daughter* is all about. If your prodigal daughter is a "girl gone wild" or is being influenced by that trend, keep reading—but most important, keep praying.

This new phenomenon is no surprise to God. In chapter 8 we looked at how sin can escalate in each subsequent generation. Paul told the Philippians back in A.D. 61 that they were living in a "crooked and depraved generation," but he said that they could still be "blameless and pure, children of God without fault." Doing so would cause them to "shine like stars in the universe" as they held out the word of life to others (Philippians 2:15–16). Interestingly, the *Newsweek* article echoed that passage of Scripture:

> We're certainly not the first generation of parents to worry about such things, nor will we be the last. . . . One thing is not in doubt: a lot of parents are wondering about the effect our racy popular culture may have on their kids and the women they would like their girls to become. The answers are likely to lie in yet another question: where do our children learn values? Here's a radical idea—at home, where they always have. Experts say attentive parents, strong teachers, and nice friends are an excellent counterbalance to our increasingly sleazy culture.[5]

The *American College Dictionary* defines *prodigal* as "recklessly extravagant; characterized by wasteful expenditure; one who spends or gives lavishly and foolishly."[6] A prodigal often foolishly and recklessly follows the crowd or her own desires and does whatever it takes to fit in, even when it means giving up everything she has—including her own body. She often spends all her money on her friends and new chosen lifestyle and may even steal or prostitute herself to support this habit. She squanders her spiritual, familial, and emotional inheritance and is heedless of the long-term consequences to herself, not to mention her family. In her recklessness, she seems to have no sense of fear of impending danger. She may not have left home physically, but she's checked out on being a team player in her family and in the family of God.

As you can see from the prodigal daughter stories in this book and your own personal experience, prodigals don't always fit a particular profile. Their family situations are as varied as they are. Until we have our own prodigal, it's easy to miss that concept. Perhaps a bit self-righteously, many of us parents believed prodigals came from homes with physical or religious abuse, parental conflict, difficult divorces, struggling single parents, turbulent blended families, insufficient resources, or cultural deficiencies. Then, when it becomes personal—it's our daughter who has "gone wild"—we're forced to rethink what defines and what causes a beloved child to become a prodigal, all the while lamenting, "I can't believe this is happening to us."

Hope, an eighteen-year-old recovering from methamphetamine addiction, admitted: "My parents raised me with good morals. Meth made me give up all my morals. Meth was my life."[7]

Often a prodigal daughter has been raised in a moral environment, maybe even in a Christian home. She actually may have accepted Jesus, but at some point she fails to resist the world's strong pull.

I understand that phenomenon. To outsiders, my first marriage must have seemed like the start of a "perfect life." Our wedding, the day after college graduation, was quickly followed by new jobs, a new car, a new house, and a new baby, in that order. With each step, I thought the next "new" would fill the void in my soul. I had accepted Jesus as my Savior at eleven, but for me it was just a religion, not a relationship. Because I went to church faithfully and did all the "right things," like so many of the prodigal daughter stories, I didn't even realize that a relationship with Jesus was the missing piece. I thought I was okay spiritually, but I wasn't growing in the Word or in my maturity as a Christian. Marrying an unbeliever led me to compromise my relationship with God. In my search for happiness, I gradually spiraled down into the abyss of divorce.

I thought I'd missed out on having "fun" because I'd been such a good girl all my life. I had been a virgin when I married, but the first man I dated after my divorce taught me what it meant to be "single" according to worldly standards. At first I resisted his influence—a lifestyle that normalized sex outside of marriage and leaving my daughter with baby-sitters while I went out on dates—because it went against everything I believed. But it wasn't long before he made it seem acceptable. I know just how Loren felt dutifully sitting in church, hearing God's Word yet knowing I was going to walk out the door and willfully disobey it. Somehow, I thought that if I kept going to church, it would all balance out. Like Loren, I tried to negotiate with God, telling Him, "I'll be back. I just want to have a little more 'fun.'" Both Loren and I put "fun" in quotes because today we look back and wonder, what were we thinking? That wasn't fun. It was blatant, self-destructive sin!

What was missing in my life was a mentor. Loren described how her neighbors mentored her in her early years as a Christian, but when that relationship waned, no one stepped in to continue the discipling pro-cess. But the world was ready to grab both Loren and me and pull us into its clutches. Without a firm foundation of faith and mature Chris-tian role models at home, we were vulnerable prey to the lures of the world.

That's why I have a passion for mentoring. I challenge spiritually mature women to reach out to the spiritually younger women in their spheres of influence. I wish someone had done that for me.

I was careless, reckless, and—for a person who likes to be in con-trol—I displayed little self-control. I was living the "good life" and pro-viding well for my daughter, but by the Lord's standards, I was a sinful daughter who had gone astray. It was the era of "If it feels good, do it," and we were all looking out for "#1" instead of looking at the One. I even had a license plate on our car that touted ME N KIM. I thought I could handle our life all on my own.

Daughters can become prodigals at any age. We often think of them as young girls and attribute their folly to immaturity and peer influence, but I was twenty-eight when I turned from the ways of the Lord to my overtly sinful life. I didn't return to the fold until I was forty-five.

Loren and I can tell you from experience, Jesus kept knocking at the door of our tightly shut hearts. Every prodigal daughter who accepted Jesus at one time is experiencing that same spiritual tug-of-war for her soul. Satan has temporarily lured her astray, but Jesus still resides in her heart.

Don't give up and let Satan win the battle for your prodigal daughter's heart and soul. Though it may seem contradictory, the more rebellious, defiant, stubborn, and argumentative your daughter becomes, the more you should cling to this hope and encouragement: God is working in her heart, and she's resisting. But that means she hasn't surrendered completely to Satan and is experiencing tormenting guilt. God hasn't given up on her yet, and neither should you. There's still hope. Instead, worry when she becomes passive and doesn't care anymore or seems to have no energy left to fight the spiritual battle. When this happens, watch carefully for signs of depression and suicidal tendencies.

Often prodigals move away from home in an attempt to squelch the torment of their own consciences. Nothing brings on feelings of guilt more than being around those who taught you the morality you're abandoning. Such prodigals think that if they can escape their past, their history, and the person they used to be, then the demons will go away, and they can be happily free from guilt. Of course, that's merely Satan's ploy to get them away from everything that might be a positive influence.

After reading many stories—including my own—of girls accepting Jesus as their Savior in their youth but renouncing their faith and values in their teens or early adulthood, I'm convinced Satan is after the products of the wombs of our Christian daughters. He knows if the girls remain followers of Christ, they will likely marry a believing man and reproduce more little believers. So Satan focuses on young women going through puberty and in their reproductive years. If he can keep them blinded with lies, strung out on drugs and alcohol, and hanging out with the wrong crowd, even if they do get pregnant, there's little chance they'll raise the child in a healthy, Christian environment—if they even choose to have the child.

Our daughters may have no idea this battle is raging around them, so they need our prayers to protect them from the attraction and pull of Satan—or to release them from the tight hold he already has on them. While God fights for them, He offers us this encouragement: "This is what the LORD says to you: 'Do not be afraid or discouraged because of this vast army. For the battle is not yours, but God's'" (2 Chronicles 20:15).

As parents we work with God by praying for our prodigal daughters, our innocent daughters, our yet-to-be-born daughters, our granddaughters, and our friends' and neighbors' daughters. Chris Adams told me, "I remember times when I dug my heels in and said I refuse to allow the enemy to win. It was sheer determination to trust and follow God no matter what, and tenacity NOT to allow the devil a victory."

Part of the battle plan is being informed and aware parents. Chris Adams, the Women's Enrichment and Ministers' Wives Specialist for LifeWay Christian Resources, and Vickie Arruda, a biblical counselor, wrote a chapter together titled "Prodigal Children" in the online resource *Women Reaching Women in Crisis*. They compiled a list of characteristics of a prodigal child. As responsible parents, we cannot ignore any of these:

Prodigal Checklist

The following checklist isn't exhaustive but gives characteristics of a prodigal child.

- ✦ Hard, rebellious heart toward God and authority
- ✦ Disrespectful toward others
- ✦ Unteachable: can't tell them anything, knows all, or doesn't care to know
- ✦ Attitude of self-sufficiency: doesn't need anyone
- ✦ Uses those around them for their own means
- ✦ Blames others for their circumstances. Cannot or will not grasp a cause-and-effect principle
- ✦ Manipulative

- Shows no genuine brokenness when confronted with behaviors
- Ignores boundaries and not good at setting boundaries for their own life
- Wants immediate gratification
- Runaway behavior, comes and goes as pleases or has left and not returned
- No regard for how their behaviors affect or interfere with others
- Shows no emotions
- Says whatever they think the parent wants to hear[8]

During puberty, teen years, and even throughout early adulthood, children are trying to establish their own identities, separate from that of their parents. They want to be alone more and keep secrets, but it isn't the time to back off—even though everything they do and say tells us to do just that. We are the parents, and maybe we can prevent our daughter from becoming a prodigal if we keep our antennas up for warning signs. By the time I tuned in to my daughter, she had made irreversible choices and decisions that caught me completely off guard.

Questions to Ask about Your Daughter's Behavior

- Is she doing any one activity to the exclusion of all other activities?
- Does she borrow money and become excessively upset if you ask her why she needs it?
- Does she get defensive when you ask where she's been?
- Does she make late-night or early-morning phone calls? (If she has a cell phone, check the phone records.)
- Are her or the family's possessions or money missing?
- Do you catch her in lies?

+ Is she hanging out with a new group of friends?

+ Has her personality or attitude abruptly changed (more than would be expected from hormonal causes)?

+ Have her grades dropped?

+ Does she no longer want to go to church with you?

+ Is she ignoring phone calls from youth leaders or old friends?

+ Does she become agitated if you enter the room while she's on the computer or phone?

+ Is she "spending the night" frequently at friends' houses?

+ Does she have a new boyfriend you haven't met?

+ Is she criticizing herself and complaining excessively about her looks and weight?

+ Does she spend inappropriately long hours locked in her room or the bathroom?

+ Do you smell alcohol on her breath or cigarette smoke on her clothes?

+ Is she suddenly wearing long-sleeved tops and pants to cover her arms and legs?

+ Does she exhibit signs of depression—trouble sleeping, fatigue, irritability, mood swings, gloominess, expressing feelings of failure, sadness, unhappiness?

+ Is she suddenly painting her fingernails pink or purple?

Did that last one get your attention? Television programs often alert parents to the subculture that's influencing their children. I don't watch much TV, but in doing research for this book, I've been tuning in to programs about children, and I would encourage you to do the same. It's a revelation! I watched an episode of the TV series *Without a Trace* about a lonely teenage girl who put videos she made in her bedroom on the Web, announcing that she wanted to give up her virginity. She "hooked up" with an older man and disappeared. In searching for her, detectives questioned her friends and learned that pink fingernail polish was used to indicate that a girl would give oral sex; purple meant she would "go all the way." I was stunned.

We have to talk to our girls in order to know what's going on in their world. And never, never, never let them have a computer or a video camera in their bedroom. Many girls are sending their own soft or hard porn via computer for the world to see, as well as giving personal information, and they're doing this right from their own rooms. A great resource to help parents monitor and navigate through today's overwhelming digital world is Vicki Courtney's *Logged On and Tuned Out: A Nontechie's Guide to Parenting a Tech-savvy Generation*.

Then there's the drug scene. In his article "How Could We Not Have Known?" Dotson Rader discussed what he called "the methamphetamine epidemic": "Young people are particularly vulnerable. So it is disturbing how seldom the signs of meth addiction are recognized. No parent I spoke with recognized the symptoms in a child until the addiction was out-of-control."[9] Does Rader's comment about unsuspecting parents, echoed in every article and book I've read about wayward kids, shock you as it does me? Don't be an uninformed parent. Note the following list of red-flag warnings of drug abuse:

- *Changes in sleeping patterns.* Staying up very late and displaying energy that's not typical.
- *Unreliability.* Skipping school or work. Breaking promises.
- *Abrupt changes in relationships.* Old friends often are replaced with a new group who are into drugs.
- *Motormouth.* Rapid obsessive speech. Agitation and fidgeting.
- *Irritability.*
- *Weight loss.*[10]

These lists are by no means complete, and your daughter might have other reasons for some of the behaviors mentioned. But they're a starting place for identifying warning signs that your daughter is entering troubled waters. It's much easier to save her when she's only in ankle deep rather than in over her head.

☕ Parent to Parent

Here are a few points to consider about our own behavior as parents. Being aware of these with all our children could possibly help us prevent another prodigal situation.

Checklist for Parents

- Don't always assume our daughter is guilty. Have conversations instead of interrogations.

- Don't nag. It's like a dripping faucet.

- Don't go overboard with rules. Determine what's most important, and offer grace.

- Don't tear our daughter down. Build up her self-respect by finding things to approve, and praise her successes.

- Don't compare our daughter to her siblings or to our friends' daughters. God created her in a unique way that's perfect just for her—and for our family.

- Don't be rude or yell. Talk to our daughter with respect, the same way we want her to talk to us.

- Don't get out of her life when she says, "Get out of my life." She doesn't really mean it, she's just testing to see if we're a parent she can count on—solid as a rock.

- Don't leave children home alone. Kids often get into trouble after school or when left alone for the weekend. Working parents: please hire someone to be home in the afternoons, or find a supervised after-school activity for your children. You might want to check out the Afterschool Alliance, supported by the U.S. Department of Education (www.afterschoolalliance.org).

It's worth the extra cost. When you're going away for the weekend, have an older, trusted person stay in your home. Otherwise, it's a party waiting to happen. Trust me, I know!

+ Don't stop talking to our daughter. The silent treatment is not effective. Take a deep breath, and keep the dialogue going without letting it escalate to an argument.

+ Don't take our daughter's behavior personally, especially if she's in her teens or hormonal. Teens are naturally belligerent as they test their independence, and hormonal changes can cause volatile, erratic mood swings—especially before or during her period. I can tell if Kim is PMS just by the way she answers the phone. I know I need to be extra compassionate and empathetic and not take personally anything irritable she says.

From My Prayer Journal

OCTOBER 12, 1994

Please deliver Kim from the world's ways that she has chosen and help her understand and want Your ways.

Let's Pray Together

Lord, it's difficult admitting that our daughter is a prodigal. How did we miss the signs? Why couldn't we do something to change the direction she was taking? Help us to face the reality and severity of our situation. Remove the guilt and anger that hinders us from giving our daughter the help she needs. We need You, Lord. Amen.

Family and Support Group Discussion

1. What is your definition of a prodigal?

2. What traits from the checklists has your daughter displayed?

3. How could your daughter's alienating behavior toward you be a sign her conscience is troubled?

4. How can knowing this encourage you to pray for her even more?

 Your Prayer Journal

What are the feelings you're experiencing as the parent of a prodigal daughter? Don't hold back. Let it all out.

_____

_____

_____

_____

_____

_____

_____

_____

_____

_____

_____

_____

_____

_____

SETTING BOUNDARIES

❖

*We chose to rescue her many times over the years, but there came
a point we had to decide if rescuing was enabling her to continue
the path she was on, or helping her. . . . One of the things we
learned was to set some sensible boundaries of what we would be
willing to do and on whose terms.*[2]
CHRIS ADAMS

♡ A Praying Mother Shares

I was sure Jennifer would do great things for the Lord. But her last two
years of high school, she pulled away from the church youth group and
became involved with friends whose moral values concerned me. Someone reported Jennifer being "stoned" at school. She vehemently denied it,
but we established ground rules and random drug testing until she
turned eighteen. We also found her a Christian counselor.

With a sense of relief, we sent her off to college. However, Jennifer was
unhappy in the small college town and moved back home. But she didn't
want to follow our rules, have a curfew, or go to church. Arguments esca-
lated until we all agreed she should have her own place. Jennifer was responsible for rent and living expenses, and we continued paying for college.

We suspected she was partying heavily and using drugs. She lost weight,
avoided our company, and discouraged us from coming to see her. It was a
strained relationship. After her sophomore year, Jennifer moved in with a
boyfriend we had never met and who had served time in jail. Her father
and I stopped helping with college expenses. I was angry and hurt. I told
her that sex outside of marriage wasn't part of God's plan, and I couldn't
condone her decisions—but God and I still loved her, and He was waiting
with open arms for her return. We would all eagerly await that day.

—*Leslie*

SETTING BOUNDARIES

The day is Yours, LORD, also the night; You established the moon and the sun. You set all the boundaries of the earth; You made summer and winter. The enemy has mocked You, LORD, and my foolish prodigal daughter has insulted Your name. Do not give the life of Your precious daughter—and ours—to beasts; do not forget the lives of her poor parents who love You and her.

PERSONALIZATION OF PSALM 74:16–19 HCSB

My parents trusted me when I wasn't trustworthy. . . . I think they thought that because I was a Christian, the temptations would not be there. But I was not exempt from any of the world's temptations that pulled me away from God. I was not prepared to handle the choices that faced me. There were so few boundaries in my life. I had always been a good girl and had done the right things. My parents thought that I always would be that perfect girl who knew right from wrong.[1]

A YOUNG WOMAN

💕 My Daughter Kim Shares

Mom, if you set limits I felt were unrealistic, I just lied to you about what I was doing. I told you what you wanted to hear. I didn't get in trouble very often, but when I did, the punishment was pretty harsh. I thought my friends' parents were much more lenient, but now I'd probably say you were okay or could've been even stricter. Your follow-through was lacking.

I got into trouble as a teenager because I had too much freedom and independence. You left me alone a lot but expected me not to get into trouble. You told me I couldn't have anyone over to the house while you were gone; but I didn't want to be alone all the time, so I had people over. When you didn't change the circumstances, I repeated the offense. Kids are going to try to get away with as much as they can.

☀️ Setting Boundaries

On an Oprah Winfrey show featuring uncontrollable three- and four-year-old little girls, psychologist Dr. Robin Smith asked the mothers to consider: "What boundaries have we missed on our watch as parents that might be contributing to our children's problems?"

On my watch, I made a mistake common to many busy parents—I gave my daughter too much freedom and responsibility for her age because it fit my schedule as a single, working mom. Then, when she abused it, I overreacted. But as she said, I didn't change the original circumstances that allowed her to stray. I expected her, the child, to change; but I, the parent, remained the same, and so the pattern continued. I've learned a lot since then.

Christian author, speaker, and single, divorced parent of four, Angela Thomas calls herself a "boundary mom." "Her kids don't have Internet access, e-mail accounts, or MySpace pages. There are movies they don't see and music they don't listen to. 'I feel really strongly that is a part of what I am going to answer to the Lord about—whether I protected them and gave them boundaries that helped them stay pure during their growing up years,' Angela says. 'They have enough years of their life to navigate evil. Satan may attack any one of my kids at any time, but it won't be because he came in through the front door—not on my watch.'"[3]

Admittedly, boundaries put restrictions on both the child and the parents who must enforce the limits and rules. With a prodigal, maintaining boundaries is a difficult, full-time job, and we may feel more like jail wardens than parents. Prodigal daughters are going to bend the rules and step over the line, but we can't set up the boundaries as we go along—boundaries must be set before we can go on.

Discipline isn't being mean; it's actually the most loving thing we can do. Psychologist and Focus on the Family founder James Dobson agrees: "Discipline and love are not antithetical; one is a function of the other."[4] Boundaries provide freedom to roam within established parameters. We're preparing our children for life in the real world, where staying within the law maintains freedom. Break the law and freedom is lost, as many prodigals have already discovered.

Raising children without discipline and respect for boundaries does them a huge disservice. It's almost certain they won't know how to set their own boundaries but will instead make poor choices. And overindulgence without boundaries is a formula for self-absorbed narcissists or insecure crowd-followers. Punishment deals with past transgressions; discipline and boundaries must be set with an eye toward the present and the future.

Few children welcome boundaries. When they balk and disagree with the boundaries we've set, it's important to hear them out, letting them know we still love them, even when they disagree with us. They may not admit it, but they do want boundaries. They need the assurance that we'll act in their best interest and not cave in to their pleas to let them do something potentially harmful. That doesn't mean they won't test us to see if we really mean what we say. They will. The Bible counsels us, "Just say 'yes' and 'no.' When you manipulate words to get your own way, you go wrong" (Matthew 5:37 MSG). So say no in love, accompanied by yes to a better choice. Discuss your reasons for saying no, and offer acceptable alternatives. Some kids take no as a personal challenge, so take the time to connect with them without lecturing.

We need to set boundaries that we're willing to enforce in spite of our children's pleading and pressure. We can take our inspiration from God's example. Why doesn't God bend the rules for us? Because "the wages of sin is death, but the gift of God is eternal life in Christ Jesus our Lord" (Romans 6:23). God doesn't want us dying a permanent death. He's a loving Father who always has our best interest in mind. So He gave us the Bible as the guidebook of boundaries, consequences, and promises to guide our lives as well as our parenting.

As our children grow older, we may become lax at enforcing consistent boundaries. Maybe it's because our lives are busier or we think they already know the rules. We often back off right when they most need us to give our complete attention to regulating their actions and activities. David Walsh, PhD, author of *No: Why Kids—of All Ages—Need to Hear It and Ways Parents Can Say It*, warned that teens "need limits and consequences just like their younger brothers and sisters do. . . . Letting go of rules and consequences too soon. . . . [is] like sending him [or her] out onto a treacherous road with bad brakes and only a learner's permit. Do not let No become a phrase of the past."[5]

Cloud and Townsend, authors of *Boundaries: When to Say Yes, When to Say No to Take Control of Your Life*, offer advice for children at different ages and stages:

During crucial adolescent years from eleven to eighteen: "Instead of controlling your child, you influence her. You increase her freedom, as well as responsibility. You renegotiate restrictions, limits, and consequences with more flexibility."[6]

For a teen who hasn't had boundary training: "You need to begin at whatever point your teens are. When their ability to say and hear no is deficient, clarifying house rules and consequences can often help in the last few years before the youth leaves home."[7]

For older children: "Boundary development will be met with more resistance. In their minds, they do not have a lot to gain by learning boundaries. You'll need to spend more time working on it, getting more support from friends—and praying harder!"[8]

For prodigal children: "The too-strict parent runs the risk of alienating the almost-adult from the home connection. The too-lenient parent wants to be the child's best friend at a time the teen needs someone to respect. At this point, parents should consider consulting a therapist who understands teen issues. The stakes are simply too high to ignore professional help."[9]

A manipulative prodigal excels at pitting one parent against the other. Parents who disagree about discipline, boundaries, or consequences should discuss their differences away from the children. That goes for divorced parents too! In an episode of *Supernanny*, Jo Frost firmly told separated parents who were having problems with their youngest child that they must agree on the same rules and discipline for each home. If a child misbehaved in one parent's home, the other parent had to enforce the consequences in his or her home as well. She warned them to agree to support each other in disciplining their children, or the problems would escalate.

If yours is a two-parent family, go before the Lord together, asking God to bring unity and to help the two of you agree on an effective parenting style so your prodigal can't divide and conquer. As Mark 3:25 reminds us, "If a house is divided against itself, that house cannot stand." It's imperative also, as parents, to assess our own boundary issues. Whether our prodigal daughter is living at home, outside the house, or, especially, if she has returned home, boundaries are not an option for her or for us!

Setting Boundaries When a Prodigal Daughter Is Still Living at Home

Sometimes parents are so fearful their daughter will run away that they cave in on discipline or enforcing the family rules, and something worse happens than if she had run away for a few days. Pick your battles. Inevitably, a prodigal will test the limits, and you must determine what your position will be. When possible, stay one step ahead of her. For example, decide before the issue comes up in your home: is a pierced nose, eyebrow, or tongue okay, but no tattoos? Or are tattoos in areas normally covered by clothing okay, but no piercings? Do you need to approve the type of tattoo? Or is it, no piercing and no tattoos, period? Daughters need to know.

Often parents are shocked when their daughter comes home with some new body art or piercing, yet the parents had never discussed with her their opinion regarding such issues. Kathy's daughter thought her parents would be happy because she had "Believer" tattooed across her lower back. Kathy and her husband had never dreamed she would do that without consulting them. When later their daughter announced plans to move in with her boyfriend, they told her they wouldn't pay for any future wedding. She didn't make the move—and even stopped dating the boy.

One time I sensed that Kim might be considering a tattoo; so rather than waiting for her to show up with one, I decided to bring up the topic and let her know my thoughts. She admitted she was contemplating it. This was around the time of Princess Diana's death, so I asked Kim what she would have thought if she learned that Princess Diana had had a tattoo. "Diana is royalty," she replied. "It wouldn't be right." I told Kim she was *my* royally beautiful princess, and I didn't think it would be tasteful on her body either. Today Kim's glad she never got that tattoo. Maybe you're fine with tattoos. Whatever your feelings, let your daughter know your position. It doesn't mean she won't go ahead and do it, but at least you have been clear that she is going against your wishes.

What about drinking? If we as parents drink, it will be difficult to raise kids who don't. Some parents say they would rather have their children drink or do drugs at home because they're going to do it anyway. That's Satan's lie. Just ask the parents arrested for serving alcohol in their basement to underaged friends of their children after two of the kids died in a car accident on the way home.

Instead of having implied or expected boundaries or trying to outguess what the next issue was going to be, I wish I had written down specific guidelines and discussed them with Kim in advance. I now see that it's important to let our children know what the boundaries are for specific areas: Curfews? Dating? What constitutes a date? Sex? Birth control or "Morning After" pills? Abortion? Friends? Grades? Smoking? Refusing to attend church? Dyeing hair, getting a Mohawk, or shaving her head? Style and color of clothes? Makeup? Parties? Drugs? Drinking? Marijuana? Quitting school? Cutting classes? Driving? Owning a car? Giving out personal information on the Web? Personal Web pages? Sending computer videos? MySpace? Add your own concerns to the list.

You might think, as I did, that if you don't discuss these subjects, she won't think of them herself. But that's naive and dangerous. She lives daily with these issues, and peer pressure is pushing her to partake and experiment. It's much easier for her—and for you—to have a game plan rather than making snap decisions under pressure that you both might regret later. Try creating a "Family Survival Plan" of boundaries and consequences that everyone discusses, agrees to, and signs. Post it in a place where everyone will see it frequently, like on the refrigerator. If your prodigal won't commit to obeying and signing it, don't let that keep you from being committed to enforcing the consequences.

If we don't know how to set boundaries, we won't raise children who abide by them. Believe me, I know. When Kim turned sixteen, I got a wake-up call. I started assessing what I was modeling to her and quit my lucrative job that required extensive travel. I learned a new career that allowed me to work close to home so we no longer needed a nanny. It was a start, but we still had a long way to go because that left Kim home alone when I did go away. I tried to ignore the telltale signs she was having people over when I was gone. She lied . . . I wanted to believe.

I just assumed my sweet, innocent Kim would always stay that way, regardless of my lifestyle. But I was in for a rude awakening. I went away for a weekend, leaving Kim and a teenage houseguest staying at a friend's house . . . or so I thought. I came home early to find them in our backyard smoking marijuana. I grounded Kim for a month. Certain it must be the other girl's fault, I sent her home.

I also wasn't expecting a midnight call from police telling me that my teenage daughter was at a party with drinking, loud music, and no parents. If I didn't want her trotted off to jail, I should come pick her up. I thought she was hanging out with her girlfriends. She was: they were at the party too. My response was, "No parties ever again!" This only perpetuated Kim's lying to me.

Because I hadn't set boundaries in advance, I wasn't ready with appropriate consequences. So we talked it out and found a balance: Kim agreed to leave a party if the parents weren't present and the kids were drinking or doing drugs. I never got another phone call in the middle of the night again, but I made a few when she didn't come home one night. Again, I had gone away for the weekend and returned early to find a note telling me she was "spending the night at a girlfriend's house." Several phone calls later, I discovered she actually had gone to Tijuana with her boyfriend and a group of friends. I had just read about that being the party spot for Orange County high school kids because it was right over the border, and underage teens could drink and party in the streets all night.

I was shocked and horrified that my "baby" had become part of that wild scene. To her surprise, I was waiting for her when she returned with her boyfriend. She wasn't expecting me home yet and had planned on slipping in ahead of me, thinking I would never know about her escapade. Because she had been with her boyfriend overnight, I confronted her about how far their relationship had gone. To my surprise, she admitted that "to be responsible," she had obtained free birth control pills at a clinic that didn't require parental consent. I was completely unaware—I didn't even know such places existed. I felt heartsick. I had just assumed Kim would wait until marriage to have sex, but I'm not sure I ever verbalized that expectation to her.

Later, when Kim didn't want to attend church with me anymore, I didn't push it. Today I know the best boundary is to say, "As long as you're in our home, we all pray together and go to church"—period. No discussion, no negotiation. If it's been an established part of your family's routine, don't change to accommodate the prodigal. If it hasn't been part of your family life, it's time to start. We all need prayer and spiritual support.

Setting Boundaries When a Prodigal Leaves Home

Once a prodigal daughter has left home, setting boundaries involves the parents more than it does the prodigal. If we're financially supporting her at school, we can articulate our expectations and the consequences for not meeting them, but we really can't control what she does outside our home.

However, we can—and should—determine our parental boundaries: How far will we go to meet her needs or bail her out of difficulty? If she has run away from home, will we go after her? Praying as a couple helps us come to an agreement with each other and with God. We can ask Him for wisdom and guidance and to give us peace about our decisions and to protect our daughter while she's shadowed in the darkness of her chosen lifestyle. Chris Adams and her husband had to make tough choices with their prodigal: "A counselor friend said when and if our daughter makes contact, just to listen and not ask a lot of questions. If she is wanting help, even if we did not know whether she was dealing with reality or fiction, we should decide ahead of time what we would be willing to do."[10]

When Kim came home from college for visits, Dave and I set boundaries. She stayed at our house, and her boyfriend stayed at his parents' house. That always caused tension between Kim and her boyfriend, but because she wanted to be with us, she complied. We never gave them presents as a couple, such as things for their house, or did anything to condone their living arrangement. It was awkward and painful, but we drew the line. We stood by what we believed, but we stood by Kim too. We were kind to her boyfriend and prayed for his salvation as we prayed for Kim's.

Setting Boundaries When a Prodigal Returns Home

When and if a prodigal daughter returns home, it becomes important to define a new set of age-appropriate boundaries. It takes time to be able to tell whether she's truly remorseful and repentant or just coming home for a shower, warm bed, and food so she can leave again. Many times it's a revolving door that we may at some point have to close. It's important to pray about setting wise limits.

Some returning prodigals are adult children. Cloud and Townsend warn:

> Many adult children perpetually get into financial messes because of irresponsibility, drug or alcohol use, out-of-control spending, or the modern "I haven't found my niche" syn-

drome. Their parents continue to finance this road of failure and irresponsibility, thinking that "this time they'll do better." In reality, they are crippling their children for life, preventing them from achieving independence.

An adult who does not stand on his [or her] own financially is still a child. To be an adult, you must live within your means and pay for your own failures.[11]

Parents are often so happy at the return home of a prodigal daughter that they're inclined to throw rules and boundaries out the window. But that's groundwork for more problems. When Kim returned home after graduating from college and leaving her boyfriend, we told her she could stay as long as she needed. She set the boundary of three months to find a job and a place to live. That was agreeable to us. It gave me a chance to talk to her about a relationship with Christ and encourage her to go to church with us. It was a time of transition, and I prayed every day that God would maximize our time together.

☕ Parent to Parent

Tips for Setting Boundaries

Some of the following boundaries might seem minor compared to the problems you're having with your daughter, but they could change the future for your other children. Consider including these in your "Family Survival Plan."

1. *Acceptable language.* Establish a curse-free home for everyone. Discuss what language is and is not acceptable.

2. *House rules.* Don't cave in to the manipulative ploy, "Everyone else's parents let them do it," designed to make you feel you're too tough. Let your daughter know calmly, "That's nice, but this is not allowed in our family, and here's why . . ." Remember, you're the "other parents" in someone else's home.

3. *Appropriate dress.* In her article "Kids Behaving Badly," Mary

Mohler told how Roni Chohen-Sandler, PhD, author of *Stressed-Out Girls*, suggested going shopping together. "Let her pick out what she likes, with the understanding that you will then choose among them." Mary concluded, "You'll have veto power, while she'll still end up with clothes she thinks are cool."[12]

4. *Acceptable computer use.* Block violent and pornographic sites, and keep computers in the open—never in the bedroom. There are ways to monitor keystrokes, find out passwords, even observe from another room. Discuss appropriate sites and usage time.

5. *Use of cell phone.* Cell phones can be used to propagate trouble. Monitor cell phone records and check out numbers you don't recognize. This works especially well with shared minutes. Don't wait until you're trying to find your daughter's drug dealer or where she spent the night.

6. *Use of car.* For prodigals, cars are a vehicle for trouble. I know one dad who put a tracking device on his daughter's car, and it only took her getting caught in a couple of lies for her to know her parents were serious about checking up on her. We shouldn't sit home wondering what our child is doing in the car we are paying for or provided for her. Prodigals need to know clearly: "You abuse the car: no gas, no keys. But we'll put air in your bicycle tires."

7. *Keeping tabs.* Know where your child is. Consider requiring all family members to sign out and back in every time they leave the house and return home again. When our kids were living with us, Dave and I had a large message board next to the door, and everyone in the family, including us, wrote down where we were going for the day. But don't stop there. Spot-check. Get caller ID on your phone, and have your child call from a land-line when she arrives at her destination.

8. *Hanging out.* Invite your daughter's friends over. You need to know whom she's hanging out with, even if it appalls you. Set the rules for behavior at your house, but make it fun and wel-

coming so your daughter's friends want to come. Perhaps you can change some of the unsavory influences or weed them out.

9. *Just in case.* Even with boundaries, most prodigals will slip up from time to time. When that happens and she finds herself in a dangerous or difficult situation, let her know that it's safe to call you for help. Offer to come and pick her up—no questions asked. That will be hard, but wait until she's ready to talk. In the meantime, be there for her.

10. *Drugs, cigarettes, and alcohol.* Establish a drug-, cigarette-, and alcohol-free home—for everyone in the family. Studies show that most children have their first experience with these substances at home.

Some of the suggested boundaries might seem a bit intrusive, but in an interview on the *Today* show, family therapist Argie Allen advised parents to weigh breaching your child's trust versus their safety. Privacy versus parenting? Even if your child gets angry with you for invading her privacy, at least she's alive! Allen said that often, when something horrible happens to a child, clues are found on her computer or cell phone, but the parents never knew. Don't let that be you.

Allen also advised being up front with children, telling them, "We're going to monitor you," rather than secretively spying. And if they're into MySpace, be sure to keep their accounts set to "private" and to let them know you'll check their Web page and postings weekly. Don't wait until it's too late. Be proactive rather than reactive.

From My Prayer Journal

JUNE 7, 1994

Dear Father, Kim knows how to be obedient. I just pray she'll understand that Your ways need to be her ways now that she's on her own. As You know, I had my wayward times, and I modeled that for her; but I came back to You. Lord, I pray Kim will also.

✌ Let's Pray Together

Lord, it takes work and consistency to set healthy boundaries. Help us find a good balance—not too strict but not too lenient. You do a perfect job of that as our Father, and we want to parent Your way. Setting and enforcing boundaries is one of the hardest parenting jobs, and we can't do it without You. Please give us wisdom and courage. Help our daughters to respond positively. We need Your help. Amen.

❀ Family and Support Group Discussion

1. What boundaries or guidelines have you established for your children and yourself as parents?

2. How well are they working?

3. What are some additional boundaries or guidelines you should establish now?

4. Discuss how God's "parenting style" with us as His children models how we should parent our children.

✍ Your Prayer Journal

What has God been telling you about any areas in your life or your parenting where you need to take a firmer stand? Maybe you've been avoiding boundary issues. Ask for God's guidance in establishing and enforcing healthy boundaries for yourself and your children.

_____

_____

_____

_____

CHAPTER

13

SURVIVING
IN MARRIAGE

Because of the present crisis, I think that it is good for you to
remain as you are. Are you married? Do not seek a divorce.
1 CORINTHIANS 7:26–27

*Today our marriage is better than it's ever been, but that was
made possible by first seeking God in prayer.*[1]
PATRICIA RAYBON

SURVIVING
IN MARRIAGE

❖

*A part of me wanted to blame all of my daughter's problems
on my husband; his lack of relationship with her did play a role
in her struggles, and blaming someone else
is the easy way to deal with painful issues.*
SHARRON

♡ A Praying Mother Shares
(Continued from chapter 10)

During the hardest time of struggle, there was very little physical or emotional strength left to invest in each other. We had a strong marriage, for which I am very grateful. I am not sure weak marriages can survive this kind of crisis. We did try to get away occasionally, just the two of us, but our thoughts would continue to go back to what our daughter was or was not doing. During a period of time when she lived outside our home in high school, we felt a release of some of the 24-hour-a-day stress of wondering what she was doing. Sometimes we even experienced guilt from feeling some relief. But it gave us some time to focus on our other daughter and each other. We prayed together and trusted God to continue to work in and through our situation. When one of us was really struggling, the other was strong. We didn't often fall apart at the same time. That was God's grace! We didn't always agree on how to handle each circumstance, but we desperately needed each other's strength. Our love and commitment held us together when our life was falling apart.[2]

—*Chris Adams*

🫶 My Daughter Kim Shares

Mom, it really bothered me when you first got remarried that you were going to submit to your new husband, Dave. That didn't sit well with me because I knew you to be a powerful businesswoman who, up to that point, had done it all on your own. In fact, I wanted to be just like you when I grew up. You raised me by yourself, owned your own home, and had a career as a regional sales manager, but now you were going to quit your job, go into ministry, and be submissive to Dave? I didn't trust this religion.

I finally became a bit more open-minded when Toby and I got engaged and you gave us the Marriage Builders course. I was prepared to go along with whatever Toby wanted, and surprisingly, he thought the course sounded like a good idea, since we both came from broken families. With a new goal of wanting a marriage that wouldn't end in divorce, I was more open to something—anything—that might help us.

Pastor Pete's words during the classes spoke to us. I finally understood what it meant to submit and trust in my husband as the spiritual leader in our home. I was beginning to understand more where you were coming from.

One thing Pastor Pete cleared up for me were the spiritual roles of a husband and wife. I thought you had lost it when you said you were going to submit to Dave, but finally it made sense. You weren't going to become a "Yes, dear" doormat. I finally saw how a dominant wife could beat down her husband rather than lift him up. The husband was to become the spiritual head of the house, not an abusive slave driver. We were to submit mutually to Christ, who would love us as His bride.

Also, Pastor Pete told us that if we put all of our faith in our spouse, he or she would let us down, because each of us is only human. Learning about the marriage triangle helped us visualize that if we put Christ at the center of our marriage, it would bring us closer together. I had never really considered how to have a successful marriage. I guess I just thought we'd wing it, and our love for each other would get us through the tough times. Winging it could've been detrimental.

It wasn't any one thing Pastor Pete said that got us thinking about committing our marriage and our lives to the Lord. It was week after week of listening to him tell us that we can't do marriage on our own. We didn't want to end up divorced, like our parents, and we knew the odds were against us. We also started feeling convicted about our lifestyle. It wasn't how we wanted to enter into marriage.

Pastor Pete made it clear we couldn't get to heaven on our parents' faith—something I had been counting on—it had to be our own personal decision and relationship with Christ. That really got us thinking. I know that because we committed our lives to Christ, God has blessed our marriage.

Surviving in Marriage

If you're married, I know I don't have to tell you how having a prodigal daughter can strain even the best of marriages. It will take its toll if we let it. What a gift from the Lord that Chris and her husband never hit bottom at the same time! As long as one of the marriage partners is still thinking clearly and not feeling overwhelmed, your prodigal and her siblings have at least one functioning parent.

When we're losing it but our spouse is not, it's important to see this as a gift rather than working to bring our spouse down with us. We might lash out at our mate because we want the other person to feel as badly as we do. Or, not understanding why he or she isn't in the dumps too, we might think he or she doesn't care as much as we do. Those presumptions are counterproductive. Instead, we should thank God that one of us has some semblance of emotional control while the other indulges in the luxury of falling apart for the moment.

Many people marry someone who is almost their exact opposite. In a crisis that can be a real benefit, since diverse personalities usually react to situations differently. When one panics, the other stays calm. However, these differences can also lead to major conflict and discontent over how to discipline or deal with a prodigal daughter.

Biblical counselor Vickie Arruda wrote: "Because both parents are eager to reach this child, they often take on different approaches as a response to the other parent. For example, if a mother feels a father disciplines too harshly, she will not discipline enough to compensate. This behavior inevitably builds tension between the parents. Often it's unidentified and unspoken. On the other hand, some parents will do everything by the book and collectively take on the role of failure, which eventually affects their marriage."[3]

It's important to avoid the temptation to blame each other if we don't want our marriage to become another casualty of the war for our prodigal daughter. When we yearn to get to the root of our child's problems, it's easy to shift blame and accuse our spouse: you should have been stricter, been home more at night, played less golf, stayed home with the kids instead of working. But this isn't going to help our daughter now. It's bad enough to have a child causing us pain without inflicting additional pain on each other.

Some couples separate, or one spouse walks out to escape the pain, but it only escalates the hurt and anguish. The last thing families under stress with a prodigal daughter need is for the parents to begin fighting between themselves. Matthew 12:25 warns us: "A family that's in a constant squabble disintegrates" (MSG).

Our houses surely will disintegrate if we can't come together as helpmates to deal with our family crisis. We look at each other, thinking, *This isn't what I signed up for. I wanted to get married, have kids, and live happily ever after.* But the truth is, life is hard. That's why God's Word says, "Two people are better off than one, for they can help each other succeed. If one person falls, the other can reach out and help. But someone who falls alone is in real trouble. Likewise, two people lying close together can keep each other warm. But how can one be warm alone? A person standing alone can be attacked and defeated, but two can stand back-to-back and conquer. Three are even better, for a triple-braided cord is not easily broken" (Ecclesiastes 4:9–12 NLT). Dave and I put that last sentence on our wedding invitation with a triple-braided cord in the background. With Christ at the center, our marriage would be indestructible.

We can let a prodigal daughter be a bitter dividing force, or she can actually draw us closer together when we realize that the same love that brought this child into our world—whether by birth or adoption—will see us through. It's our choice. We need the Lord and each other more than ever. Abandoning the marriage physically or emotionally still leaves the prodigal "out there" and the rest of the family members suffering from a situation they didn't create. It's a scenario in which everyone loses. We married "for better or worse," and right now, this is the "worse" part; but I hope you agree that what God joined together, we should let no man—or prodigal daughter—put asunder.

A prodigal doesn't always negatively affect a couple. Any crisis my husband and I have gone through together has only strengthened our marriage and commitment to each other. When we were first married, we agreed divorce would never be an option. We each had been down that road. We wanted to set the example for our family and others that Christian marriages are forever, and with God's help, we could endure anything we faced—together.

If you're a single parent, my heart goes out to you. I was in your shoes and didn't wear them well. But remember God is "a father to the fatherless, a defender of widows, is God in his holy dwelling" (Psalm 68:5). Even though the principles I discuss next are about marriage, focus on the discussion of your personal relationship with the Lord and what might take your focus off God.

At the beginning of each Marriage Builders class, Pastor Pete, who taught the course, would write "God" at the top of a white board. Then, forming a triangle, he drew a stick-figure husband in one corner and a stick-figure wife in the other. Next he drew the lines connecting the triangle, with God at the pinnacle. Then he explained that when the woman and man were pointing a finger and looking only at each other, they were at the farthest points of the triangle. But the closer they moved toward God, the closer they came together until each of their lines merged in God.

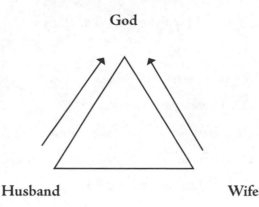

God

Husband   **Wife**

Pastor Pete's point was that every marriage has to have God as the head of the home, and as each spouse works on his or her individual relationship with Him, they draw closer together in their marriage relationship. However, if one of them takes his or her focus off God, they move back toward their respective corner and farther apart.

Marriage Builders was not only a premarital counseling course. Any couple could take it who wanted to strengthen their marriage. Dave and I were excited about this course, and we recommended it to almost every couple we knew. Each came out with a stronger, more committed marriage. Try to find a similar course or weekend marriage retreat offered by your church or a church in your area. Your focus has probably been almost totally on your prodigal, so now it's time to take a break in dealing with the crisis and enjoy your Mr. or Mrs.

Parent to Parent

Marriage can survive a prodigal daughter, but the degree of health of that marriage will depend on each person's willingness to work on his or her individual relationship with God. Pray that both of you will grow closer to God; but if your spouse pulls away, resolve to stay strong in your relationship with the Lord and pray that your spouse will follow your lead. God will see you through this time.

Marriage Survival Plan

+ Have daily quiet times.

+ Read God's love letter—the Bible.

+ Pray alone and with your spouse.

+ Ask others to pray for you and your family.

+ Stay involved in your Bible study group—or join one.

+ Expect God to bless you and your family.

+ Find creative ways to stay focused on the Lord and not your circumstances.

You might find it helpful to see a biblical marriage counselor together to help guide you as a couple through these uncharted waters. Be sure to choose a Christian professional who specifically provides *biblical* counseling, because God's Word is the *only* answer that can bring you the hope and peace you seek in spite of your circumstances. Any other kind of counseling—even from a Christian—is simply someone's educated opinion. The Bible is the only true and helpful counsel. When you learn how to glean wisdom and answers from your own Bible, you may not even need professional counseling (although you may still find talking things out with a counselor very helpful).

Another important key to surviving in marriage is to not abandon doing the things you enjoy together as a couple. If, before the crisis with your prodigal daughter, you played tennis or golf, went to Sunday breakfast before or after church, worked around the house or garden, walked, biked, cooked, shopped, or went to plays together, don't stop. Plan a weekend getaway, and agree for that time to only respond to emergency phone calls, and define "emergency" before you leave.

Continue physical intimacy—in fact, consider increasing it, even when you don't feel like it. You and your spouse need to be unified, and sexual relations is one way God provided for married couples to experience that unity. It can also help relieve tension and bring you both some pleasure. Don't feel guilty about allowing yourself to feel good at this difficult time. "Do not deprive each other of sexual relations, unless you both agree to refrain from sexual intimacy for a limited time so you can give yourselves more completely to prayer" (1 Corinthians 7:5 NLT). So spend time praying together, and then enjoy each other. The Lord says so!

From My Prayer Journal

JANUARY 15, 1994

Thank You for giving me such a loving, giving, servant husband who helps pray for Kim and our family.

Let's Pray Together

Father, thank You for my spouse and for the ways we complement each other. Help us to keep our marriage strong even when outside forces are trying to drive us apart. We need each other now more than ever. Let our love shine brighter during this time than it ever has. Help us keep our eyes focused on You and not on each other or our problems. Give us sweet times of intimacy together. We give You all the glory for our marriage. Thank You for creating our precious daughter. We love You above all others. Amen.

Family and Support Group Discussion

1. Share how your prodigal daughter has affected your marriage negatively and/or positively.

2. What can you do to turn the negative effects into positives?

3. How can you ensure that no matter what happens, you will not abandon each other?

4. What can you do to strengthen your marriage during this stressful time? Hint: discuss the marriage triangle.

Your Prayer Journal

What has God shown you about your marriage and your spouse through this crisis?

_____

_____

_____

_____

_____

_____

_____

_____

_____

_____

_____

_____

_____

_____

_____

_____

_____

_____

MAINTAINING
A "NORMAL"
FAMILY

When you sin against your brothers and sisters in this way
and wound their weak conscience, you sin against Christ.
PERSONALIZATION OF 1 CORINTHIANS 8:12

*We must determine over and over how we're going to live with the
consequences of choices our children or others make. We must try
to look up when circumstances are weighing us down and live
someplace between the hurt and the hope.*[1]
JUDI BRADDY

MAINTAINING A "NORMAL" FAMILY

❖

I also realized we could not allow
the behavior of this one child to consume us.
At times we had to purposefully put
our prodigal out of our minds.
It simply wasn't fair to focus all our attention
and emotional energy on him
at the expense of the other members of the family.[2]
GIGI GRAHAM TCHIVIDJIAN

♡ A Praying Mother Shares

Bobbi's days had been full of usual teenage activities: school, homework, family, and friends—until the Christmas shortly before her seventeenth birthday. It had been a wonderful day, but no one saw Bobbi leave the house. As sunset came and night began to fall, we noticed she was gone. Phone calls to her friends offered no insight as to where she might be. Before she met her boyfriend, Bobbi had exhibited a good deal of common sense, but she ignored our concerns about him. We reasoned that forbidding her to see him might cause her to sneak out, so we gave her an early curfew and limited the amount of time she could spend with him.

No one in our family wanted to believe what we were all beginning to suspect. Finally, one by one, we began: "I wonder if he's talked her into having sex . . . and now she's pregnant . . . and they've run away together." My head was spinning. *She can't be pregnant. That can't be it . . . that must be it. Why else would she leave? Where did we go wrong? What else could we have done to prevent this? Is she safe? What should we do? Oh, Bobbi, where are you? God, help.*

We notified the police, and prayed—hard. Prayer was the one tangible thing we could do, so we prayed continually, believing that God would keep Bobbi safe and someday return her to us.

Months passed without any word. To those who didn't know what had happened, our lives must have seemed "normal," for we came and went as usual. Those closest to us, however, knew of our sleepless nights and anxious moments when the phone rang or there was a knock on the door. One particularly disturbing phone call was from the police requesting a copy of Bobbi's dental records for identification purposes, in case they found her . . . dead.

—Mary

My Daughter Kim Shares

Mom, nothing was "normal" about our family after you married Dave and Sean and Shannon came to live with us. After being an only child all my life, I was excited to have brothers and sisters, but it was definitely an adjustment. You weren't just my mom anymore. Now you had a husband to take care of and more kids calling you Mom. That was strange!

And all of you were Christians—reading your Bibles, going to church, and getting together in small groups—and I wasn't doing any of those things. Because I thought all of you were weird, with your religion that I didn't trust, I did feel out of place a lot of the time. It was awkward when I came home from college and my boyfriend and I had to stay at our parents' homes separately instead of together, like we lived at school. It always was tense and stressful, but I agreed to please you.

Maintaining a "Normal" Family

I know after reading this chapter title, you're probably thinking, *Hey, what's normal? Normal isn't normal at our house anymore!* That's true. You'll never go back to the days before you had a prodigal. This experience now has become a part of your family history and legacy. It's similar to when we have our first baby: we quickly realize that normal—as we knew it "BC" (before children)—is gone forever.

Family life is a series of changing scenarios, each requiring a readjustment of the "routine and normal." Some changes we welcome, like the birth of children or bringing home a new puppy. Other changes, like illness, tragedy, or a prodigal daughter, are difficult and unpleasant, and it takes time to reestablish a "normal" family pattern.

Eventually we adapt to our new life—whether the changes were planned or unplanned. If we don't, the results can be disastrous. We'd live in a perpetual state of unhappiness, chaos, depression, unrest, resentment, fear, and anger. If you're living in one of these destructive and debilitating states right now, I hope this book will help you and your family to move forward.

So how do we return to some state of normalcy even while our world seems to have been turned upside-down? We talked in chapter 10 about the importance of praying as a family, and to do that, we need to include our children and extended family in the inner circle of our lives as we deal with our prodigal. We also looked at the importance of making sure we don't brush siblings aside as everyone focuses on the one child who has gone astray.

What a paradox this can be for parents. We're afraid that if we don't focus our energies on the prodigal, we might lose her forever. At the same time, we worry that if we don't give adequate attention to our other children, they'll get into trouble or feel neglected. What's a parent to do? What's the right thing? How do we determine exactly where to devote our time, energy, and resources?

The parable of the lost sheep in the Gospel of Matthew reminds us that a shepherd doesn't want to lose a single lamb from his flock. He'll go after the one that got away and bring it back. Jesus does the same thing for each prodigal daughter who wanders away from the truth and the safety of His love: "See that you do not look down on one of these little ones. For I tell you that their angels in heaven always see the face of my Father in heaven. What do you think? If a man owns a hundred sheep, and one of them wanders away, will he not leave the ninety-nine on the hills and go to look for the one that wandered off? And if he finds it, I tell you the truth, he is happier about that one sheep than about the ninety-nine that did not wander off. In the same way your

Father in heaven is not willing that any of these little ones should be lost" (Matthew 18:10–14).

That one sheep, by not following the rules and staying with the others, by wandering off perilously to do its own thing, put all the other sheep in danger: the shepherd, leaving the other sheep in the open country, searched for the one who was lost. I've read that story many times, but today I pondered, didn't he care about the other sheep? What if they wandered off too while he was gone?

I prayerfully arrived at the conclusion that the shepherd knew that the remaining sheep were not wayward sheep. When he said, "Stay until I get back," they followed the rules, chomped on grass, and stayed put until the shepherd searched and returned with the lost sheep on his shoulders.

So what does this mean for us as parents trying to tend our entire little flock of sheep and faithfully fulfill our responsibility to each of them—the weak *and* the strong? First, we need to assess our flock. What are their ages? If the siblings are young, they need our full attention . . . or at least the full attention of one parent. Maybe we can divide our duties as parents so that one stays close to home to maintain normalcy for the family— going to school and church functions, soccer games, cheerleading or football practice; eating dinner together; hanging out together watching TV; going to the movies; getting them to ballet or swimming or Bible studies and youth group meetings. Life goes on while the other parent actively pursues the lost child. On weekends, you reverse roles so the children at home have contact and relationship with both parents. If you're a single parent, enlist the help of grandparents, other family members, or friends.

If the siblings are older, determine the stage each of them has reached in life. Do they follow the house rules and walk closely with the Lord? Can they be part of the battle plan for rescuing the lost sibling? Sit and talk with them, asking for their help, ideas, support, and prayers. Reassure them of your love. Explain that if they were the one in danger, you'd go to the same great lengths for them. If they're willing, enlist them in the fight.

Being the sibling of a prodigal isn't easy. If the other children aren't willing to go to battle, it could be a sign they need extra attention. Don't ignore their needs and frustrations. As parents we must be careful not to overextend ourselves mentally, emotionally, financially, and physically in pursuing our prodigal—or we'll destroy our family in the process. However, just because a sibling doesn't want to join the fight right now doesn't necessarily mean he or she will be our next prodigal. Siblings may be hurt, confused, angry, jealous, and just need their parents. That's normal!

It's important not to overreact or overcompensate. Becoming stricter because we fear losing our other children too might only push them away and make them even more resentful. Becoming too lenient diminishes their sense of security. We need to evaluate our parenting and disciplinary tactics. If we honestly think they had nothing to do with our prodigal's waywardness, then we shouldn't change anything in our parenting of the other kids. If, however, we do see areas where we need to tighten or loosen the rules and guidelines in the family, then we must admit it and explain to our children why things are changing. They need to know why the familiar is now different. Don't assume they'll put it all together. Remember, they're children who still need parenting.

I've watched parents assume that their other children understood the urgency of the situation and why they had to focus on the prodigal, only to have one of them act out negatively just to say, "Hey, I'm one of your children too, and I need you. I'm not like my sister. Look at me as the individual I am."

Don't forget fun activities for the family too. Just as parents need a getaway from the trauma, so do the kids. Involving everyone in planning a weekend camping or ski trip, enjoying a theme park, or just going out for ice cream once a week helps everyone take a break from the urgency and tension. If you normally take an annual family vacation, by all means, still go. And if you don't, maybe it's time to start!

☕ Parent to Parent

Prodigals often are manipulative and thrive on being the center of attention or focus in the family. In some cases they only care about what they want and when they want it and may not care who gets hurt in the process. I know this is hard to hear, but the time may come when we have to say to our prodigal (and tell ourselves), "We love you, but we will not let you destroy the family. We'll never give up hope, but we're letting go."

If and when we do this, we must then pray for God to do as He promises in Ezekiel 34:11–16: "God, the Master, says: From now on, I myself am the shepherd. I'm going looking for them. As shepherds go after their flocks when they get scattered, I'm going after my sheep. I'll rescue them from all the places they've been scattered to in the storms. I'll bring them back from foreign peoples, gather them from foreign countries, and bring them back to their home country. . . . I myself will make sure they get plenty of rest. I'll go after the lost, I'll collect the strays, I'll doctor the injured, I'll build up the weak ones and oversee the strong ones so they're not exploited" (MSG).

Letting go doesn't mean giving up. It simply means that we are completely and prayerfully trusting the Good Shepherd, and we're letting Him go after our lost sheep—our prodigal daughter—while we tend to the rest of the flock.

From My Prayer Journal

APRIL 3, 1994

Michelle cooked Easter dinner for the family at our house today and invited two of her friends from school. It was a new way for us to spend the holiday. Instead of being chained to the kitchen, I was able to spend enjoyable time with Kim, who came home from college for the weekend without her boyfriend. Lord, I pray that Kim heard the Easter message that You died for her!

Let's Pray Together

Dear Lord, our family structure could collapse under the pressure of this crisis with our daughter. Help us to maintain a firm foundation built on You and Your principles so our family will be strong and healthy. You knew before time began that we would have this struggle. It's no surprise to You. Give our family the sense of security and normalcy that comes from knowing we are being led and protected by You, the Great Shepherd. Amen.

Family and Support Group Discussion

1. What steps have you taken to maintain "normalcy" in your family life?

2. How are your other children reacting to having a prodigal sister?

3. What reassessments have you made of your parenting guidelines, and how did you explain any changes to your children?

4. If you have had to let go and let God bring your daughter back into the fold, share what helped you make this decision and how you are dealing with it.

Your Prayer Journal

How are you holding up? Can you look at the big picture, as God sees it, and let Him shepherd your sheep when you can't? What does it feel like when normal isn't normal anymore?

MAKING IT ALL ABOUT HER

Pride leads to disgrace, but with humility comes wisdom.
PROVERBS 11:2 NLT

Since we were doing all the "right things,"
parents who had "wayward" children must
be doing the "wrong things."
I was sure my children would never be prodigals.
I've learned the important lesson that pride is a terrible sin,
and I was so prideful when Sarah was the "perfect child."
I've also learned empathy for others going through the same pain.
BETTY

MAKING IT
ALL ABOUT HER

❖

*When we judge ourselves by our children's behavior, we tend to
see all of their mistakes and few of their successes. We miss
developing a relationship with the people they are because we are
so focused on the people they aren't.*[1]
CARLA BARNHILL

♡ A Praying Mother Shares
(Continued from chapter 12)

We had to grapple with our own pride. Both my husband and I worked
at a Bible college. What would happen when people found out our
daughter, Jennifer, was living with someone? How would it affect our
ministries? We even questioned whether we should continue in our jobs
and volunteer ministries. While she was growing up, Jennifer and her
dad had been very close. Now he was hurt and angry, refusing to talk to
her or her live-in boyfriend for almost three months. Finally he realized
that his behavior was not a reflection of a heavenly Father longing for
His child to come home.

Our minister was a great resource during this time and helped us realize our daughter was an individual making her own decisions. It's
amazing how many families in the church have stories similar to ours.

I wish I had a happy ending. But I don't. Only God knows what the
future holds. However, we continue having a relationship with our
daughter and her boyfriend and pray they come back to a Father who
loves them very much.

—*Leslie*

My Daughter Kim Shares

Mom, I always felt like you were proud of me. You introduced me to all your friends at church and in the Woman to Woman Mentoring Ministry and never brought up in front of them how you felt about what I was doing that you didn't approve of. They all seemed to accept me and were kind, so I knew you must have told them good things about me. I always felt cherished and loved . . . as you have always called me "your baby."

Making It All about Her

When crisis hits, it's a natural response to make it all about us. As parents of a prodigal daughter, we focus on how she's messing up *our* life, *our* career, *our* reputation, *our* plans, *our* ministry, *our* finances, and *our* family. We worry about how others might be judging *our* parenting skills or how we handle *our* problem child. We wonder how quickly this situation will pass and if we can even survive it.

These worries lead to stress, depression, and maybe even assuming a victim or martyr mentality. "Poor us," we wail. Why did God let this happen? Why *our* family? Why *our* daughter? It's embarrassing . . . humiliating . . . frightening. We want it fixed right away so we can get *our* lives back on track. Then we wonder why that's not happening.

Pride is subtle and sly—slipping into our behavior without our even realizing it. Pride focuses on self. You might be saying, "But this is happening to *us*. It affects the whole family; didn't we talk about that in the last chapter?" Yes, but we also talked about not letting the enemy win. If we make this all about us, he surely will. Our emotions, our health, our relationships, our jobs, our ministry, our parenting will all crumble under the stress—and that's not going to bring our prodigal daughter back to us and to God.

We think, *If only we can let her know how badly she's hurting us, she'll go back to being the loving daughter she was before.* But that's wishful thinking. Right now she's not thinking about us, no matter how much we might be suffering, or she wouldn't have wandered in the first place. Any self-centered actions on our part will only drive her further away.

As the opening Bible verse reveals, humility, the opposite of pride, is the first step to obtaining wisdom and, thus, making better choices. For example, when we are pridefully focused on ourselves, we often steer conversations to what's going on in our lives—in our case the trials and tribulations of having a prodigal daughter. However, if we can humbly recognize that we're talking constantly about our troubles, wisdom will help us realize that we're talking so much because we long for empathy, not sympathy. We want someone to understand our pain, and there are better ways to achieve that—maybe by joining a support group, which we'll talk about later, or talking to a biblical counselor.

Or admitting that we live in fear of someone finding out about our prodigal daughter can help us make a wiser choice of simply disclosing that we have a problem daughter and asking for prayers. We get the benefit of others' prayers while we release the hold our "dark secret" had on us as we weighed every word and maybe even began to isolate ourselves from others.

Life isn't fair, and the Bible never promises that it will be. Though we strive to lead a good life, there's no guarantee that things will always go our way. But what the Bible does say is that instead of grumbling about our circumstances, we should embrace them as an opportunity for growth. James 1:2–3 puts it this way: "Dear brothers and sisters, when troubles come your way, consider it an opportunity for great joy. For you know that when your faith is tested, your endurance has a chance to grow" (NLT).

This is a difficult verse to accept. I understand—it hits me right between the eyes too. I don't want to rejoice in my troubles, I want to wallow in them. I wish my faith didn't have to endure hardships—like dealing with a prodigal daughter. But if we focus on God's plan and purpose instead of how our prodigal-daughter situation impacts us, our prayers will be more effective as we align ourselves with His plan for our daughter and for us. I know this might seem harsh, but sometimes we need a reminder that, hey—this isn't about us. Our daughter is making choices we can't control. That's humbling. Up to this point, she has been in our "protective custody." It strikes a blow to our egos that now she thinks she can make her own decisions, and we are powerless to stop her from making bad ones.

It hurts to admit that we can no longer protect our daughter from harm. It's what we've done her entire life, and now she's trying to take that role away from us. Peace comes when we finally realize that we'll do what we can, but we have to let God be God. He's omnipotent, we're not. Only God can protect her right now and help her make the right decisions. This isn't admitting defeat—it's admitting we cannot do this alone. We need God. Our daughter needs prayer.

Abandoning the dreams and plans we had for our daughter may be the hardest point for us parents to reach. A wise person once said, "Never try to make your daughter another you; one is enough!" Growing up, I felt my mother was living her life through me. She hadn't gone to college, so I had to—but she picked the college and the major she would've wanted, and I went along with it. I married a man who met her criteria. She'd never had a career, so it was important to her that I did. She meddled in my life to the point that I didn't know where she ended and I began. It always was all about her. If I tried to deviate from her plan, she used guilt and manipulation to get me to do things her way.

Even though I married the man of *her* dreams, she didn't approve of when and where we married, so she didn't attend the wedding. As usual, she managed to turn the attention toward her absence instead of toward my being a bride.

Even my eventual divorce upset all my mother's plans for the life she thought I should have, and the fallout left us estranged for fifteen years. I know firsthand the devastating effect a self-centered, controlling parent can have on a child, and my backsliding prodigal years were an attempt to find out who I was apart from my mother. Like all rebels, I was the one most hurt by my actions.

So when Kim went to her dad's and my alma mater, I wanted her to experience the same college dorm life and campus activities that I had enjoyed, but I realized that was *my* dream for her. I had to relinquish it to the choices *she* was making for her college life. Even though I cringed every time I had to explain her living conditions and became defensive if any of my friends said anything judgmental, I had to continually ask myself if I was more worried about what they thought of her or what they thought of me.

Remembering how I felt when my mother manipulated and controlled my life and how I rebelled helped me keep Kim's decisions in perspective. While I could not support many of her choices and I feared for the consequences they would bring in her life, I would not use guilt or manipulation to try to turn her around to my way of thinking. I would take my concerns to the Lord in prayer and ask Him to take control of her life.

Some people may feel that having a prodigal child precludes parents from serving in ministry. I was happy to hear that praying mother Leslie and her husband sought counsel from their pastor, a wise step for anyone feeling conflicted about this issue. Jesus didn't come to minister to the healthy, He came to heal the sick; and no one knows better what a sick person needs than someone who also has been sick.

We discussed in chapter 8 that none of us has a perfect family or life. If we eliminated from service everyone who had a problem in his or her family, few would be left to serve in our churches today. As Jesus said, "If any one of you is without sin, let him be the first to throw a stone at her" (John 8:7).

Admitting we have a prodigal daughter will keep us humble and compassionate—the perfect servant's heart. We lose credibility when we try to maintain the illusion that everything is fine. But if we're open and honest, without exploiting our daughter or our situation, it might encourage others to share their pain so we can minister to them.

I started Woman to Woman Mentoring in the midst of my daughter's prodigal years. I didn't tell her story then because I didn't have her permission, but I did tell my own account of being a prodigal daughter.

My heart went out to every woman who came into the ministry sharing the story of her own prodigal years or the heartbreak of having a prodigal child. God often uses our painful times to help others going through a similar experience. Don't let your family problems stop you from serving the Lord and offering your heart and hand to help others. That's the mission of the church.

Parent to Parent

Often we can learn from the mistakes of others. In fact, this book is my sharing with you the things I learned from my own mistakes in dealing with Kim's wayward years. I tried to remember what had made me not want to be around my mom during my prodigal times, and do the opposite with Kim. The tips below are some of the things that helped me keep it all about Kim.

I do believe that if we ask God to give us wisdom in how to help our prodigal daughter and don't just focus on how having a prodigal affects us, He will answer and give us insight into how to help her. And you know what? I did . . . and He did . . . and He will do it for you too.

Tips for Keeping It All about Your Prodigal Daughter

Don't . . .

1. withdraw your love or affection.

2. remind her of all the things you've done for her and how ungrateful she is.

3. tell her how ashamed you are of her.

4. try to make her feel guilty for ruining your life and plans.

5. boycott things she is still a part of.

6. cut off communication.

7. set ultimatums.

8. complain or gossip to others about her.

9. stop praying for her.

Do . . .

1. continually tell her how much you love her.

2. continue doing nice things for her—but be careful not to appear to be trying to buy her back. Just do the things you've always done.

3. be honest that you don't like her choices, but you still love her.

4. talk about what's going on in her life.

5. go if she invites you to something.

6. stay in communication if possible—in person or by phone, e-mail, voice mail, or snail mail.

7. maintain the boundaries and consequences for stepping outside them, but not with an "or else" or threatening attitude.

8. speak lovingly of your daughter. You don't have to like her actions, but be sure others know you still like her.

9. pray for her more than you pray for yourself.

From My Prayer Journal

FEBRUARY 19, 2007

Lord, please help me not to make Kim's move to Idaho all about me and how sad I will be without the grandkids near. It's hard. I want Your best for her . . . but it hurts.

Let's Pray Together

Father, You know how our hearts break, and it's hard not to think about ourselves and what this difficult situation is doing to our life. You tell us to think of others more highly than ourselves. Lord, we need to do that now with our daughter. Yes, we're hurting, but she's hurting more. She needs our best right now, and we need to remember that the first step in healing ourselves is to help others—please remind us that it's not about us! With Your help we can do this. Amen.

Family and Support Group Discussion

1. How successful have you been in not making your daughter's crisis all about you? What did you learn from this chapter that might help you avoid that trap?

2. How does focusing on ourselves affect our prodigal daughters?

3. What steps can you take not to let having a prodigal daughter— or pride—ruin your life?

4. What one thing can/will you do today to share your source of joy and minister to another hurting parent?

Your Prayer Journal

What you are going through is tough. Express how it is affecting your life. Then ask God to help you release the hold pride or fear has on you.

_____

_____

_____

_____

_____

_____

_____

_____

CHAPTER

16

CONFRONTING OUR OWN MISTAKES

If we claim to be without sin, we deceive ourselves and the truth is not in us. If we confess our sins, he is faithful and just and will forgive us our sins and purify us from all unrighteousness. If we claim we have not sinned, we make him out to be a liar and his word has no place in our lives.

1 JOHN 1:8–10

I prayed, "Lord, You take care of them [her prodigals]. I need to settle some things in my own life with You."[1]

RUTH BELL GRAHAM

CONFRONTING OUR
OWN MISTAKES

❖

The real injury [is] you tried to heal your daughter
when the hurt was in you. . . . You thought,
"I'll just forget about me and I'll redo it. I'll do better in her."[2]
DR. ROBIN SMITH

♥ Two Praying Mothers Share

When my daughter disappeared, she left without saying good-bye, as if I no longer mattered to her anymore. On some level, that was probably true. I've learned that God never wastes an opportunity to get our attention, and I now see He wanted me to look inward and understand my error, too, that contributed to her leaving.

Abandonment played a big role in my childhood, and I grew up without a sense of family. When I finally had my own family, I experienced the thrill of loving and receiving love in return. I placed too much value on my relationship with my only daughter. I loved our times together. I was so consumed by my personal joy in our relationship that I guess I never stopped to consider whether she was getting anything from it. That's a lot of weight to put on one relationship. Maybe my love became a burden to her heart—I never thought to do a barometer check. When I lost her, my knees buckled and my heart felt like it cracked into a million ragged pieces.

—*Sharron*

(*Continued from chapter 2*)

My daughter, Liz, has chosen to cut off her relationship with me. I made many wrong choices that hurt her. I'm so sorry and have apologized many times, but Liz refuses to forgive me. I'm saddened by the wall she's built to protect herself from being hurt emotionally again.

My guilt over Liz plagued me. I felt captive by her refusal to forgive me. I've beaten myself up for not being the perfect mother and not saying or doing the right things. The truth is, I make mistakes all the time. I hurt people—not intentionally—but it happens when I'm thinking of myself and not of how my words and actions affect others. With God's help, I'm working on changing that part of my character. In the meantime I continue praying that God will soften Liz's heart so she'll be able to forgive me and any other person who has hurt her.

—*Alice*

My Daughter Kim Shares

Mom, when you asked me to forgive you for your past mistakes in raising me, I felt really uncomfortable that you would come to *me* and ask for forgiveness. Parents admitting they're wrong was a foreign concept. I didn't understand or appreciate what you did then. But now that I truly understand God's forgiveness and what you were trying to do—I see it the way you meant it. At the time it was just too strange; but now I know it was an act of humility and not weakness.

Confronting Our Own Mistakes

I appreciate praying mothers Sharron's and Alice's vulnerability and willingness to share and confess openly their mistakes. Before we can truly come before the throne of Christ and petition Him on behalf of our daughters, we must be sure our own hearts are clean. Do we have unconfessed sin or harmful behavior in our lives that we haven't dealt with openly? When we became Christians, we confessed all our sins and asked God's forgiveness, which He graciously granted. However, in our humanness, we continue sinning. You do, I do, we all do. We live in a fallen world where sin reigns.

There's a cute joke about a man praying to the Lord and proudly announcing that he hadn't sinned at all that day. "And now, Lord," he continued, "I'm getting out of bed." Actually, I can sin in my mind before I even get out of bed! So we need to confess our sins daily. We need to ask God to forgive us and provide the courage and fortitude not to repeat the same sin again. Here's an easy way to confront and confess:

+ Admit there's a problem

+ Ask for forgiveness

+ Repent

+ Learn what we can from it

+ Pray for wisdom to avoid repeating it

Even when we believe God forgives our sins, some of us are haunted by the memories of past transgressions. If this describes you, I have a great suggestion. Prayerfully write them all down. Present the list to God in prayer, asking Him not only to forgive you but also to remove the guilt, shame, and memory. Then tear the list into shreds or light a match to it and symbolically rid your mind and heart of the things holding you back from being the man or woman you want to be today. How freeing to know that we can be cleansed from the guilt of the past. As Hebrews 10:22 says, "Let us draw near to God with a sincere heart in full assurance of faith, having our hearts sprinkled to cleanse us from a guilty conscience and having our bodies washed with pure water."

Now comes the harder, but just as freeing, part. We all are living with consequences of poor choices we've made in the past, some of which have affected our children. It's easy to look at our prodigal daughter and point the finger at the sin in her life, when maybe we should be pointing first at ourselves. If we look back at what prompted us to do some of those things we now regret, it might provide insight into our daughter's current behavior. Maybe it'll open a door that allows us to reach out to her and meet her where she is—offering her understanding instead of condemnation. Sharing with our children what could have prevented us from making similar mistakes is far more effective than simply dismissing or criticizing their choices.

Tricia Goyer uses her past mistakes to mentor others and her own children:

> It's taken me years to deal with some of the issues from my past. . . . For me, healing from my past involves helping others who face the same struggles. My heart is renewed when I help others find hope.
>
> The additional benefit is that my children now have a mother who has wholeness in Christ. They've heard about my mistakes, and they've seen me reaching out. They've also gained conviction in these areas, following what I say . . . and what I do.[3]

She also encourages parents:

> Just like us, our kids will mess up. Sometime, somehow. But what a great example we can model for them to mimic—transforming our past mistakes into future causes for Christ. . . . Think of the model you can be for God's restoration process—not only as you give it to God, but also as you struggle, turning to Christ and try again.[4]

We don't need to tell our children every foolish thing we ever did. That would serve no purpose. But if we're self-righteous and legalistic, our children will see right through us. They know we were kids and did wrong things. When we display an attitude of "I'm perfect and you're not," they see it as hypocrisy and want nothing to do with our lifestyle or, worse, our God.

When Kim moved to college with her boyfriend, I had to take ownership of having modeled that behavior for her. The majority of her growing-up years, I was materialistic and lived a sinful life—we even had lived with one of my boyfriends. By the world's standards, I was a good mother. Kim had everything she wanted, and I provided a great material life for her—but not a good example. She didn't know that though. She loved me and put me on a pedestal, wanting to be just like me—the me I was then. When I changed direction by rededicating my life to the Lord, marrying a godly man, and going into full-time ministry, I pulled the rug out from under her and expected her to want to be the *new* me.

When that didn't happen, I searched my heart and realized the choices she was making were a reflection of the poor choices I had made while she was growing up. I had asked God for forgiveness, but I hadn't asked Kim to forgive me. I knew what I must do.

I went to visit her at college and planned a day with just the two of us at the beach. I told her what a wonderful daughter she was and how proud, grateful, and honored I was to be her mother. Then I listed my past transgressions and asked her forgiveness for the way I had lived my life while she was growing up.

And here's the best part. She said, "I forgive you, Mom." Even though she didn't understand at the time, she extended grace. Kim never has used those past transgressions manipulatively or brought them up to condemn or hurt me. Just as God forgave me, so did my daughter. I often listen to moms and dads who regret the years of parenting before having Jesus in their life, and I ask if they've asked their children to forgive them for those times. I usually receive a shocked look and something to the effect of, "Are you kidding!? I could never do that!" I try to reassure them that they don't have to list all their mistakes and sins. Just say, "I'm sorry I was not a godly parent, and I hope you can forgive me. I want to do better now, with God and the Bible as my parenting guide."

Still I get resistance. Alice, from the opening story, is one of the few parents I know who actually did this. It goes back to what we talked about in the last chapter—pride. God hates pride because it stops us from doing the right thing, but as Proverbs 3:34 says, He "gives grace to the humble." We have to stop and ask ourselves, are we the prideful, "I'm always right" kind of parent? Or are we the humble, "I've made mistakes too, but with God's grace I'll do better" kind of parent?

Unfortunately, not every daughter will forgive her parents. But we'll learn in the next chapter and in chapter 24 that our purpose in asking for forgiveness isn't to achieve a change in the other person; it's to change us—to free us from the bitterness of an unforgiving heart.

I'm not insinuating that our past mistakes are the cause of our prodigal daughter's current problems. Maybe they are and maybe they aren't. We'll take a closer look at that in chapter 19. What I am suggesting is that we take a moment to look at our own lives honestly—past and present—and determine how they're affecting our relationship with our prodigal today.

Sometimes we see a reflection of our past self in our prodigal daughter, and it either hurts so badly that we don't want to go there with her or we can't see it clearly. An *Oprah Winfrey Show* featured girls concerned about their appearance at very young ages. One woman lamented that her four-year-old was worried about looking fat in her clothes. The cute little girl was actually quite thin. The mother could not understand her daughter's behavior. As the interview continued, the mother admitted she had struggled with anorexia in her youth but quickly recounted, "I've worked through this. It doesn't affect my life now. This has nothing to do with my daughter's behavior."

Dr. Robin Smith helped her see that she was in denial and it had everything to do with her daughter's behavior. Unknowingly, the mom was passing down to her daughter some of the same issues she'd struggled with as a child—or maybe, subconsciously, still deals with as an adult, even though it doesn't surface in the form of anorexia. Often we think we've worked through our problems, when maybe, as we talked about in chapter 8, they're resurfacing in the next generation. Dr. Smith advised, "I want you to start thinking about what was hurting in [you] a long time ago. . . . [Those wounds are] showing up in our little babies."[5]

I know the things that irritate me most in others are the very things that irritate me about myself. It's much easier to identify these failings in other people than to acknowledge that I might be thinking or acting in the same way they do. Could we be projecting this tendency on our daughter too? We see things in her that we detest in ourselves, so we reject it in her—maybe rejecting her at the same time. We may not be aware we're doing this, but she is.

Unless we face our own issues, acknowledge that they affect our children or our reactions to our children, and take steps to change our behavior, we can find ourselves in the same situation as the formerly anorexic mother—in denial about our part in the problem.

☕ Parent to Parent

The purpose of this chapter is not to fix blame on parents for a prodigal's behavior. Most of us are good at doing that for ourselves. What I do hope you are starting honestly to address are the questions: How have my past and current behaviors and actions influenced my prodigal daughter? And even though she's making my life miserable right now, do I need to ask God and her to forgive me? I know that seems contrary to our natural instinct—shouldn't she be asking us to forgive her? That's the world's way. In the Lord's prayer, God tells us that asking for forgiveness is just as important as forgiving those who have hurt us: "Forgive us our sins, as we have forgiven those who sin against us" (NLT).

Why not try it? What you've been doing so far isn't working. What do you have to lose? Perhaps it could be the first step in winning back your daughter. What a role model for her you could be, taking the initiative in asking for forgiveness.

📝 From My Prayer Journal

MAY 17, 1994

Thank You, Lord, that Kim forgave me! Please give her understanding of the mom I am today. Help her want to follow me as she has in the past.

Let's Pray Together

Lord, we admit that we've made mistakes and need forgiveness. We know You've seen it all, and we aren't fooling You any more than we're fooling our daughter. Humble us to ask our daughter to forgive us. Forgive us of our sins and help us to be quick to forgive others. Amen.

Family and Support Group Discussion

1. What parts of your past have you identified that might be influencing your actions today and might be reflected in your daughter's current behavior?

2. Have you been able to confess them to the Lord and receive relief? What did that feel like?

3. Have you asked your prodigal and her siblings to forgive you for not being a godly role model at times? If you have, describe that experience. If you haven't, how can you find the courage to do so?

4. Are you free from guilt and remorse? Can you move forward with the Lord guiding your parenting path? What will be your first steps?

Your Prayer Journal

Write down any past mistakes that still have power over you, and ask God to release the hold they have on your life. Then journal what it feels like to receive God's restoring forgiveness.

_____

_____

_____

_____

RESOLVING CONFLICT

"In your anger do not sin";
Do not let the sun go down while you are still angry,
and do not give the devil a foothold.
Do not let any unwholesome talk come out of your mouths,
but only what is helpful for building others up
according to their needs,
that it may benefit those who listen.
EPHESIANS 4:26–27, 29

It's easy to become very angry at the repeated betrayal of a
prodigal. Without help that anger can become dangerous, both to
the parent and to the child. Anger is normal and only through
God's strength can we be angry and not sin (Ephesians 4:26).[1]
CHRIS ADAMS

RESOLVING CONFLICT

❖

*In any close relationship, whether it is between relatives,
spouses, friends, or parents and children, there are
bound to be conflicts, arguments, and frustrations that
leave one or both people angry. It is perfectly normal
to feel angry at your child from time to time.*[2]
LAURENCE STEINBERG, PhD

♥ A Praying Mother Shares

We are an adoptive family, with two boys and one girl. After adopting our older son from Ukraine when he was four, we wanted more children, so we decided to try an easier route by becoming foster parents. We received a call to pick up a little girl whose foster mom wanted her out of the home that night. Being "good Christians," we went. Driving there, I wondered, *Why the urgency over a five-year-old? Could it be that bad?* When we arrived, out walked the most beautiful little girl with green eyes and long, curly pigtails. She looked so sweet and perfect. But in a few days the testing and deviancy started. We later discovered she had been bounced around to twelve foster homes because of her behavior. My husband and I vowed this would be her final stop. I had no idea how much that decision would test my faith.

She was a prodigal from the beginning, trying to push us away. I endured most of her tantrums and raging outbursts: they lasted for hours. Often I just held her through it to keep her safe. I'd sing hymns, mostly trying to calm myself so I wouldn't say words I'd regret as she yelled horrible things. But somehow worshipping God aloud also quieted her soul, and she would relax and calm down. I sang the song "Change My Heart Oh God"—some days for her, other days for myself.

For three years we saw no progress. Many days I cried out to God in anger, "Why do You think I'm the right mother for this child?" She brought out ugliness in me. Often I wanted to send her away. The day before we finalized her adoption, I told my husband, "We don't have to do this." Walking over to the window, he looked out and said, "I don't see anyone waiting for her."

We became her forever family. Even though the raging has stopped, it's a daily struggle trying to connect with her. It's been six years, and I can't say I'm "in love" with my child. I love her, and God's grace and mercy continue to push me into a deeper relationship with her, but we have such a long way to go.

I feel I became the prodigal. I know God brought us together, and without her, I wouldn't be the person I am today. It may have looked like God was saving my daughter, but I'm the one He saved. I'm now closer than ever to the Lord, and I love how He brings people into my life to draw me closer to my daughter. Whenever I want to give up, He renews my strength.

—Gail

My Daughter Kim Shares

Mom, you know how I hate conflict and confrontation. I'd rather just go along with things than take a stand. Not wanting to disappoint people, I often say yes to everyone, and then they're angry when I can't fulfill my promises. Growing up, I especially had trouble saying no to you or telling you the truth if it was something I knew you didn't want to hear. That led me to lie rather than face a confrontation.

Today I consider you my best friend, and I tell you everything. I don't always like to hear what you're going to say, but now I don't feel I can keep secrets from you—and I don't want to. A good example is recently when my Pampered Chef business was going slowly, and I came across an opportunity to be a wine consultant and put on wine-tasting parties. I was excited about it. Nobody in my area had done it before, so I would "own" the market. It would be a great opportunity to make a nice part-time income.

Everything was great, except in the pit of my stomach I knew you wouldn't be pleased. Not wanting a confrontation, I even debated whether I should tell you. Toby said we respected the counsel of you and Dave and always ran major decisions by you first. If I was so resistant to telling you, then I must know in my heart what you were going to say.

I did tell you, and you reacted pretty much the way I expected, but I was determined to do it anyway. I talked with Christian friends, and they didn't think it was such a bad thing, but the *one* person I wanted to give me the okay—you—didn't.

I decided not to go through with it because it just didn't feel right doing something you were so adamantly against. You said you wouldn't pray for my new venture to be successful because you didn't agree with it, but you would pray for my Pampered Chef business to thrive, and this past month has been my most successful yet!

Resolving Conflict

The presence of a prodigal daughter creates conflict, confrontation, and unrest—not only with her but also among parents, family members, and even those outside the family. If any unresolved issues are simmering under the surface, having a prodigal daughter blows them out of proportion. Stress, worry, fear, anger, and uncertainty are just a few of the ingredients for conflict, as well as differing opinions about how to deal with a prodigal daughter.

I imagine, like all couples, you've had a few disagreements about how much freedom to give, what tactics to use to bring her back, when to use tough love, and when to let go—just for starters. Times of crisis bring out our differences in personality and temperament and can lead to conflict.

The tension in the home has probably increased the bickering among the other siblings as well. They're likely just as resentful as we are that their sister, our daughter, has inflicted this pain on the family. Our fear and pain may lead us to lash out at anyone who is near and to come down harder on the children and each other than we otherwise would. Naturally, that just makes everyone even angrier.

Siblings of prodigals often have feelings they don't know how to express, so they communicate them negatively at school, at play, toward each other, and at us. Choosing and controlling how we respond could be the biggest character-building lesson of this crisis. Healthy conflict actually clears the air and helps everyone deal with negative feelings. It's important for parents to learn to stay cool when things get heated.

As a child I learned to suppress my real feelings and stay passively compliant because my mom was emotionally fragile after my dad's death. Whenever I tried to disagree with her or do something she didn't approve of, she acted as though I didn't love her, and consequently, she couldn't love me. But eventually compliancy reaches its limit. Often such "perfect" children turn into prodigals, and the parents don't know what hit them. That's exactly what I did. Not having had healthy experiences in dealing with conflict and saying no, I succumbed and said yes to the world. In turn, I passed this pattern on to my daughter. She told me what I wanted to hear but subversively did as she pleased.

Kim's wine-business story shows how our relationship has matured. Her first inclination was the old pattern of avoidance when she knew I wouldn't approve: don't tell Mom. After reconsidering, she confronted me with the plan even though she knew I wouldn't approve. That was a huge step.

Dave and I had a choice too. We could have avoided stating our opinion, but then there would've been unspoken tension among all of us. Instead we prayerfully made the decision to confront her. We lovingly explained why we wouldn't support the wine business but that we would continue praying for her Pampered Chef business to flourish. And as Dave and I diligently prayed, Kim soon had more Pampered Chef business than she could handle. She recognized this increase in business as an answer to her parents' prayers. This easily could have gone the other way, and we would've had to practice what we talked about before—not condemning her while not condoning her actions.

In discovering that she can disagree with people who are important to her and not lose their love, a child's fears of abandonment dissolve, and she learns to stand up against peer pressure. Kim has said that because she grew up a child of divorce, she did fear abandonment and therefore was fearful of voicing her opposing opinions. For example, if I asked if she was okay with my going out in the evening, she would say yes instead of expressing her true feelings: "No, please don't go. I'm afraid when you aren't here. I hear noises."

Our inclination as parents is to silence a child who disagrees or argues, but that's a mistake. A child's words, even those that are hard to hear, are one of the best tools to help us figure out how to understand and appropriately respond, because her words let us know what she's thinking and what we're dealing with. A compliant, passive child can be a time bomb waiting to go off. When my toddler grandchildren are making lots of noise and chatter—even if it's crying or screaming—I know where they are and what they're doing. I panic when the house gets quiet because they're either off-limits, scheming, or already in trouble. Likewise, when our prodigal daughter is quiet, we should become concerned. It could mean she's given up on us or doesn't care anymore what we think and is headed for even deeper trouble. Our children have to be engaged in a relationship with us to fight back. Even arguing is still communication.

Cloud and Townsend explain it this way:

> When children have permission to ask for something that goes against the grain—even though they might not receive it—they develop a sense of what they need.
>
> Below are some ways you can help your children:
>
> + Allow them to talk about their anger.
> + Allow them to express grief, loss, or sadness without trying to cheer them up and talk them out of their feelings.
> + Encourage them to ask questions and not assume your words are the equivalent of Scripture (this takes a secure parent!).
> + Ask them what they are feeling when they seem isolated

or distressed; help them put words to their negative feelings. Do not try to keep things light for a false sense of cooperation and family closeness.[3]

The home of a prodigal is a volatile environment; the relationship with a prodigal is an argument waiting to happen. Acknowledging the potential for conflict allows us to be proactive. Since we know the importance of presenting a united front to our daughter and other children, how can we work through differences? The answer is to work through conflict in the biblical way. We set an example as role models for any watching eyes.

I'd like to share with you some steps to resolving conflict that I have found very helpful in almost any situation. You might look at them and think: *You have to be kidding. That would never work in our family.* Admittedly, it may be a new way of resolving conflict for you, but it works—with husbands and wives, parents and children, employers and employees, friends, ministry workers—in any relationship. You might modify the steps when dealing with young children, but once they understand how it works, you'll have given them a wonderful tool for peacefully working through conflict for the rest of their lives.

Until everyone gets used to communicating this way, make a copy of these steps for each person to keep as a reference. Keep your Bibles handy to look up the Scripture references, and pray together before you go through these steps.

Seven Steps to Resolving Conflict

1. *Take the initiative to resolve the conflict* (Matthew 5:23–24; 18:15–17). The moment you sense a problem in your relationship, take the first step toward righting it—even if you think the other person was wrong and you've done nothing to provoke him or her. Approach the person face to face; conflict seldom is completely resolvable via e-mail, letters, or phone calls because we can't read each other's face, eyes, or body language.

2. *Focus on goals bigger than your personal differences* (Ephesians 4:3). Before starting a discussion, establish that the relationship is more important than any disagreement.

3. *Listen attentively as the other person tells how he or she sees the situation* (James 1:19–20). Let the other person speak first while you "listen" with your heart, eyes, and ears without becoming defensive or angry. Try to hear the hurt in the person's voice and empathize. Don't interrupt. Let the person complete his or her story.

4. *Validate the person's feelings without minimizing his or her concerns* (Proverbs 18:13). Acknowledge his or her points, and don't argue. Then ask if the person will listen to you.

5. *Tell your story* (Proverbs 18:17). Indicate that you understand how the person may have perceived the situation in a different way than you meant it. Avoid assigning blame, although it's okay to let the person know how the situation hurt your feelings.

6. *Apologize and ask forgiveness for your part in the disagreement* (1 John 1:9). Don't expect the person to say he or she is sorry or to ask for forgiveness. Forgive with no hidden agenda or expectations (Colossians 3:13). For a more in-depth discussion of forgiveness, go to chapter 24.

7. *Talk briefly about how to avoid future conflict* (Proverbs 17:14). Set ground rules for the relationship going forward. Close with prayer.[4]

Learning how to resolve conflict the biblical way allows us to keep our cool and humbly communicate in a peaceful, loving manner—Christ's way. Unresolved conflict causes unrest, disunity, anger, revenge, yelling, and screaming—Satan's way. When we resist Satan by adopting Christ-like behavior, the enemy retreats—at least for the moment. He'll be back with a new strategy, but don't allow him to get a foothold.

Following are some tips for how and when to confront. Discuss them with everyone in the family, and keep each other accountable for honoring them—even in conversations with your prodigal.

Ten Helpful Tips for Confronting Conflict

1. *Pick your battles.* Not every issue is worthy of a heated discussion. Sometimes we really have to let some things go. And don't tuck it away as ammunition for another time.

2. *Stay in the moment.* Stick with the issue on the table. Don't bring up past disagreements or something the person did last year, last week, or even yesterday.

3. *Don't use attack words.* Some words make things personal and raise the other person's defenses: words like *you, always, never, all, every time, stupid, worthless, dumb, good for nothing,* and *lazy.* Never resort to curse words, name-calling, or taking the Lord's name in vain.

4. *Don't verbally abuse the other person.*

5. *Don't raise your voice.*

6. *Don't walk out of the room in the middle of a discussion.*

7. *Don't disagree in front of others—especially the kids.*

8. *Don't discuss multiple grievances.* Stick to one topic per discussion.

9. *Don't assume the other person is guilty.* Think the best before thinking the worst.

10. *Don't procrastinate.* Deal with issues as they occur, but don't start a discussion while the other person is driving or in the middle of a project, like preparing dinner.

If the anger and conflict are too thick and you feel as though you've run up against a brick wall, you may need to seek professional counseling. Be sure to find a biblical counselor who bases his or her methods and advice on God's Word.

Parent to Parent

If we're in communication with our prodigal, we can modify the above steps specifically for confrontations with her. Perhaps we've been talking to everyone else instead of telling her face to face what we're thinking. Our discussions probably have been heated and have resulted in yelling matches that resolve absolutely nothing. That may allow us all to vent, but in the end we're still angry and she's still a prodigal.

When backed into a corner, prodigals often come out swinging—sometimes literally. Here are some tips for having a civil conversation with a prodigal daughter.

Ten Tips for Confronting Your Prodigal Daughter

1. Take the initiative. Ask if you can meet with her and talk.

2. Meet face to face in a neutral place over a Coke or cup of coffee.

3. Pray together, asking God to mediate and direct the conversation.

4. Assure your daughter of your love for her and your desire to resolve the issue.

5. Ask her to tell her side of the story. At this point, just listen without interrupting.

6. If you sense that she's lying, ask if what she said is true. Be firm but not accusing. If you still think she's lying or have evidence that she is, tell her you can't continue this conversation until she's honest. If she becomes defensive or continues lying, pray, give her a hug, express love, and explain that when she's ready to tell the truth, you'll listen without reacting.

7. If she won't talk, ask genuine questions. Avoid sarcasm. For example, "Are you enjoying living on your own?" can sound either sincere or cynical. Be sure you ask sincerely.

8. Listen to her answers without reacting, responding, or lecturing.

9. When she's finished, ask if she'll listen to your side. Don't preach or lecture. Simply state how you perceive the situation. Keep the conversation about your own feelings.

10. Try to keep the conversation two-way. If you've managed to stay civil and get to this point, chances are there's been a breakthrough in your relationship.

Even if it didn't work this time, don't give up. Try again.

Before any tips for conflict resolution can work with our prodigal daughter, we have to be convinced of the value of confronting rather than letting things slide or burying them. Our tendency is to think we're the parents and what we say goes. "Why should we have to go through all of this?" we protest. Well, something isn't working, or we wouldn't be in this conflict, so why not try a different approach? Everyone will be helped by learning a new way to work through disagreements and reach solutions. We might not reach the resolutions any of us expected or wanted, but at least we're talking.

From My Prayer Journal

APRIL 5, 1999

Lord, Kim's comment that the way I say things makes her defensive was like a knife to my heart. Thank You for helping me learn to ask questions and listen when confronting her.

Let's Pray Together

Lord, learning how to handle conflict Your way is new. Help us to listen and not always be ready to justify our own position. Give us courage to face issues rather than avoid them. Humble us so we can admit when we're wrong. Keep us alert to our daughter's lies and manipulation. We don't want to see that, and even more, we don't know how to confront it in a good way. But You do, and we ask Your wise counsel. Amen.

Family and Support Group Discussion

1. Where have you encountered conflict in your family besides with your prodigal daughter?

2. Are you willing to try the ideas presented in this chapter, and if so, how will you use them in your family?

3. Role-play through the "Seven Steps for Resolving Conflict" to see how it feels. How do the scriptures apply to each step?

4. Role-play the "Ten Tips for Confronting Your Prodigal Daughter" so you're comfortable when you need to use them.

Your Prayer Journal

How do you deal with conflict? Ask God to help you learn to confront biblically.

SUPPORTING EACH OTHER

All praise to the God and Father of our Master, Jesus the Messiah! Father of all mercy! God of all healing counsel! He comes alongside us when we go through hard times, and before you know it, he brings us alongside someone else who is going through hard times so that we can be there for that person just as God was there for us. We have plenty of hard times that come from following the Messiah, but no more so than the good times of his healing comfort— we get a full measure of that, too.

2 CORINTHIANS 1:3–5 MSG

Parents need support for sure. It's so important to "survival."
CHRIS ADAMS

SUPPORTING
EACH OTHER

♡ A Praying Mother Shares
(Continued from chapter 13)

The one thing that helped me more than any other thing (other than God's presence, of course) was a friend who had a very similar situation [with a prodigal daughter] and was transparent with me while my children were still preschoolers. I saw her walk in faith and peace even though she was hurting deeply. She trusted her daughter to God and never wavered in her faith. She was Jesus "with skin on" for me. When our situation became evident, she was the first person I called because I knew she would understand. If she'd never shared her situation with me years before, I would not have known her openness to help me. I could call and ask her how she got through each day and she would give me words of encouragement and empathy. I desperately needed a mom who had been there. Now I am that mom who shares with other prodigal's [*sic*] parents in pain. I understand the comraderie [*sic*] in common pain and desire to use my experience to help others walk in faith.[2]

—*Chris Adams*

♡ A Prodigal Daughter Shares

At thirty-six I was homeless, jobless, had no bank account, and—I thought—no future. My downward spiral started at age twelve, when I began experimenting with drugs, which led to a life of addiction. In my late teens I entered an abusive dating relationship followed by numerous dysfunctional relationships. I tried to escape through even more drugs.

I was jailed twice in four months for using methamphetamines. The police booked me a third time for failing to appear in court—I couldn't get out of bed. I was trying to turn things around, but I was trying to do it on my own—I was destined to fail. Even the love and support of my family wasn't enough.

The court ordered me to spend ninety days in a residential treatment center. Several years earlier I'd tried a thirty-day program and learned the twelve-step system that included letting God work in my life. But I couldn't fake believing in a power greater than myself. I had a sense of hopelessness. I battled lack of self-worth, fear of failure, even fear of success.

After completing the drug treatment program, I dared to believe that my life has value, and I moved into WISEPlace (formerly the South Orange County YWCA), a nonprofit agency serving women in crisis. I learned to set goals and work toward them, one small step at a time. Somehow, in my struggling years, I'd missed that lesson. WISEPlace is a community of women reminding and supporting each other that "Today, I can become the woman I want to be." I graduated with new ideals, new friends, and an appreciation for accountability. My message of hope is that if it can happen for me, anyone can make the same massive turnaround.

—*Jenny*

Supporting Each Other

God doesn't want us being "Lone Ranger" Christians. He made us to enjoy community and fellowship with each other. His plan was for us to help carry each other's burdens—to grieve with those who are grieving and laugh with those who are laughing. Unfortunately, having a prodigal daughter may lead us to distance ourselves from people and activities right when we most need to stay connected.

I've noticed a recurring phenomenon in small-group Bible-study settings: suddenly someone stops showing up when he or she is going through a crisis. I've never understood this response to life's problems, because one of the major purposes of small groups is to create a community of people who will support each other during the good and bad times. We pull away, though, for many reasons, as Rebekah Montgomery, a mother of a prodigal, articulated: "Some parents don't want to admit their child is prodigal because the admission opens them up to criticism and condemnation. Some parents of prodigals have lived with the grief so long they don't want to pray for their child anymore. And some parents are so brokenhearted they cannot pray. But a band of prayer warriors is crucial to winning the war against Satan."

I love the translation of Ecclesiastes 4:12 in *The Message*: "By yourself you're unprotected. With a friend you can face the worst. Can you round up a third? A three-stranded rope isn't easily snapped." Or, as my pastor Rick Warren says, "We're always better together."

We find comfort in surrounding ourselves with people with whom we can share our hurts and hang-ups, knowing they'll love us anyway. Ideally, we find this solace in our families; but sometimes they're too close to the situation and we're wise to seek godly counsel from someone who isn't so intimately involved.

An e-mail prayer loop I've joined was discussing the topic of prodigals. It was as if a bottle of shaken seltzer water was uncorked and allowed to spew in a safe environment. The loop was flooded with e-mail posts of mothers' heartaches and burdens for their prodigals, while others shared stories of their own prodigal background. They poured out their pain, successes, and prayer requests to people—many of whom they had never even met.

I read about the sorrow of a mother who said it seemed she was only hearing about returning prodigals while, sadly, hers was still lost. Though group interaction can bring such feelings and frustrations, being around people who can support us and understand what we're going through is incredibly comforting. However, we must be careful not to let support groups become places for negative, "poor me" gripe sessions but instead to keep them focused on prayer and encourage-ment. Joining or starting a "Parents of Prodigal Daughters Support Group" or a small-group Bible study can help us survive life with our prodigal. God assures us He will join any group where He is welcome: "When two of you get together on anything at all on earth and make a prayer of it, my Father in heaven goes into action. And when two or three of you are together because of me, you can be sure that I'll be there" (Matthew 18:20 MSG).

Our charge is to "help each other in troubles and problems. This is the kind of law Christ asks us to obey" (Galatians 6:2 NLV). The kind-est, most empathetic help often comes from someone who has had simi-lar experiences. God doesn't let us go through character-building experiences just for our own benefit. He's going to put someone in our path who is experiencing something similar so we can share that been-there-done-that understanding and let others know that "with God's help, I made it through and you can too." That's the heart of mentoring. And the bonus is that using the wisdom gleaned from our experiences to help others heals us.

My local newspaper featured a "Moms of Military" support group meeting at a local church, and the article was accompanied by a picture of the moms praying together. In describing their group, one mom said, "We are here for each other, and we all share our feelings, our concerns and our worries and our fears. We have the same heart, and we know what it's like when you wake up in the middle of the night—it's daytime over there [in Iraq]—and you just pray."[3] Parents of prodigals also un-derstand waking up in the middle of the night and wondering if our daughter is in danger . . . or even alive. The value of a group is the reas-surance that we're not alone—other parents understand exactly what we're going through and know how to pray for us as we pray for them.

Whether it's a small group, support group, or another family we share and pray with doesn't matter; what does matter is that we receive and give loving support. One dad with two prodigal daughters said that he and his wife couldn't have made it without another wise couple that came alongside them and mentored them through their prodigal experience. Now they're helping the mentoring couple with a crisis in their lives.

Sometimes professional, biblical, Christian counselors can provide the help we desperately seek.

A prodigal daughter needs support too, especially after she returns. We can help her make right choices by finding a support group, rehab center, camp, or facility where she can acknowledge the difficulties she's facing and receive encouragement from others going through similar struggles. It's important, though, that those extending a helping hand have worked through their own struggles and are coming from a biblical perspective.

Our daughters can benefit from being in a community of repenting, returning prodigals led by someone who has successfully recovered from a wayward lifestyle. However, since most recovering prodigals are taking it one minute at a time, it's wise to have a co-leader in an advisory and overseeing role who is not recovering from a troubled past. A pastor or youth leader might be ideal. He or she could inject biblical perspective as well as discern when someone in the group backslides, possibly with the risk of taking others with them.

Saddleback Church, where Dave and I worship, has a twelve-step biblical recovery program (now in many churches) called Celebrate Recovery. It offers groups with trained leaders for people recovering from "hurts, hang-ups, and habits" as well as for family members. Life Hurts—God Heals is a biblically based, eight-step program developed by the founder of Celebrate Recovery specifically to help teens acquire lifelong healing tools. If these programs aren't available at your church, your pastor can help you locate other biblically based programs in your area. The Internet is also a great resource. Remember to check to see whether the program is Christian and how long it's been in operation, and obtain references.

Megan Hutchinson, who is in youth ministry at Saddleback Church, wrote a book titled *I Want to Talk with My Teen about Addictions*. In it, she advised: "Teen treatment centers are available in abundance. At first, you may feel nervous at the thought of getting help or 'treatment,' but think of it this way: *What if you don't?* Or better yet, think of what *could* happen if you took this giant leap of faith. There are trained counselors and programs ready to help you and your family heal."[4]

Your prodigal daughter may not want to join a group, so attendance might be part of the conditions you establish for her returning home or staying home. Such a condition is sure to benefit her as well as you. If appropriate and if your daughter agrees, you might attend one of these programs with her. A family that recovers together rejoices together!

Parent to Parent

Saddleback Church has a support group for almost every topic imaginable, but it doesn't have a "Hope for Parents of Prodigal Daughters Support Group." Maybe it's time for my husband and me to start one. Pray to see if God is leading you in that direction at your church too. If He is, here are some helpful guidelines to get you going.

Support Group Guidelines

1. Let each participant tell his or her story once.

2. Listen to each other. Wait your turn to speak.

3. Empathize with each other's pain; don't focus only on your own.

4. Don't try to fix another person's problems. Share what worked in a similar situation, but don't try persuading others to follow the same course. Conversely, be discerning when hearing others' advice.

5. Ask questions and listen to the answers.

6. As a group, practice praying God's will versus "our will."

7. Read a book or work on a Bible study together. I designed *Praying for Your Prodigal Daughter* for this very purpose, with discussion questions at the end of each chapter. This will help participants focus on working through the difficult time rather than staying stuck in it.

8. A major step in healing is helping, so assist each other and look for ways to help in the community or at your church.

9. Open and close each session in prayer. If you commit to praying for each other between meetings, then do it.

10. Set aside time each meeting to pray God's Word back to Him. You can use the "Forty Days of Praying Scripture for Your Daughter" in the appendix of this book.

11. Confidentiality is crucial. Make sure that what's said in the group stays in the group and isn't passed around as gossip. The exception to that would be if someone reveals something of a criminal or unsafe nature or talks about doing harm to themselves or others. Then you need to be responsible and report the information to the appropriate authorities, as well as to your pastor if your group is associated with a church. The group members all need to know and agree that this will be the procedure.

12. Be careful not to let meetings turn into gripe sessions or pity parties. If you're not part of the solution, you're part of the problem.

From My Prayer Journal

JULY 10, 1996

Please, Lord, surround Kim with Christians who encourage her to go to church or to the church singles group. Bring her into contact with people who will be a good influence on her.

Let's Pray Together

Lord, You tell us not to go through troubles alone. You're always with us, but sometimes we need a human hug, words of encouragement, or a shoulder to lean or cry on. Please guide our daughter and us to a group that's just the right fit. If our daughter is to go into rehab or we're to see a therapist or counselor, please help us find a biblical one. And, Lord, if You're asking us to start a support group, please speak to our hearts and give us ears to hear and a willingness to obey. Amen.

Family and Support Group Discussion

1. If you've been using this book in a family or support group, how has it helped you?

2. If you and/or your daughter are not yet in a support group, discuss what might be the benefits of joining one. What's holding you back?

3. What are your thoughts about the possibility of starting a support group in your church or area?

4. What steps are you ready to take to reach out and give or receive support?

Your Prayer Journal

How have others helped you in this crisis, and how might God want you to help others?

_____

_____

_____

_____

_____

_____

_____

Questioning Your Role with Your Prodigal Daughter

Answer me when I call to you, O my righteous God.
Give me relief from my distress; be merciful to me and hear my
prayer. . . . Know that the LORD has set apart the godly for
himself; the LORD will hear when I call to him.

PSALM 4:1, 3

Why do you look so dejected?
You will be accepted if you do what is right.
But if you refuse to do what is right, then watch out!
Sin is crouching at the door, eager to control you.
But you must subdue it and be its master.

GENESIS 4:6–7 NLT

CHAPTER

19

WHAT DID WE DO TO CAUSE THIS?

Children, obey your parents because you belong to the Lord, for this is the right thing to do. "Honor your father and mother." This is the first commandment with a promise: If you honor your father and mother, "things will go well for you, and you will have a long life on the earth." Fathers, do not provoke your children to anger by the way you treat them. Rather, bring them up with the discipline and instruction that comes from the Lord.

EPHESIANS 6:1–4 NLT

My daughters Heather and Jessica couldn't have been further from God or me in their late teens and early twenties. But now I realize how far from God I was in those years, even as I tried to live by religious rules. I'd love to have been the mother I am now with my daughters in their youth, but I'm experiencing God's redemptive work in our relationships.

ROBIN

WHAT DID WE DO
TO CAUSE THIS?

❖

*I think it's common for parents with prodigal children
to wonder what they have done wrong.
I have second-guessed myself at every step.
"What if" became a big question in my mind.*
LESLIE

♡ A Praying Mother Shares

(Continued from chapter 18)

As a parent of a prodigal, the range of emotions experienced is very wide. Guilt is the first major issue. We tend to blame ourselves for what we did or did not do that might have changed the situation. My husband and I had to come to terms with the fact that we were not perfect parents, but we did all we knew to do at the time to help our daughter be a confident young woman and to turn her life around when she began to stray. It was another part of letting go that we had to deal with to keep our sanity.[1]

At times we had to forgive ourselves for failures but then go on.

—*Chris Adams*

♡ My Daughter Kim Shares

Mom, at first I liked it when we went shopping together after church— but then you started dressing more like me, and that bugged me. I had a black mini skort (shorts in back, skirt in front), and you bought one just like it! It wasn't something a mom should wear.

You dated a guy who got you listening to my radio station—alternative/punk rock. You even put one of the station's calendars on the fridge.

You went riding on the back of his motorcycle, but you wouldn't let me ride on the back of my boyfriend's motorcycle. Another time you dated someone closer to my age than yours.

My friends and I sneaked into concerts, and you wanted me to sneak you in too. I remember thinking something just wasn't right about that. I didn't want to be responsible for you. Where were your friends? Why did you want to hang out with my friends and me?

Another major factor in the decisions I made as a young woman had to do with the fact that I didn't have my dad in my life. I was looking for a man to fill that hole. Divorce isn't healthy for kids; it breaks us down. We make wrong decisions based on our need to be accepted and the fear of losing anyone else.

What Did We Do to Cause This?

The decisions we make as parents have consequences that will affect our children for good or for bad. We need to take ownership of that. Many stories in this book are from parents who admit their mistakes and are on their knees praying for God to have mercy on their children. They are changing what they can change and striving to be parents pleasing to God.

The truth is that we've all failed at something with our children, but guilt isn't a healthy response. It's paralyzing rather than energizing. And although God wants us to be remorseful because it leads us to repentance, feelings of guilt are not from Him. It's imperative that we move on. We can't change the past, but we can change the present, which will impact the future. It starts when we admit that we're not perfect parents and when we come to realize that we can't parent effectively without God's guidance. Next we must evaluate our parenting style honestly and realistically. Here are three common laments of parents with the best intentions:

"I did the best I could."

Often I hear a parent say, "I did the best I could"—and that could be the problem. Why? Because the central figure is *I*. When we think we're capable alone of figuring out what's best for our children, ourselves, and our families, we have forgotten to call on the Great "I AM" (Exodus 3:14). Our best is never as good as God's best. We can't do it on our own, but God assures us: "If parents who are called by My name put away their pride and pray, and look for My face, and turn from their sinful ways, then I will hear from heaven. I will forgive their sin, and will heal their daughter" (personalization of 2 Chronicles 7:14 NLV). If we stay close to God, He will equip us to raise godly children in an ungodly world. Isn't that good news!

"I raised all my children exactly the same way, so why did one stray?"

Honestly, it's impossible to treat all our children, born to us in different seasons of our lives, the same. That wouldn't even be healthy, because each child is a one-of-a-kind creation of God. Just like fingerprints, no two people are identical. Learning how to celebrate the unique imprint God has put on each of our children allows each one to become his or her own person. We live in the same house, but we treat each of our children differently. This is a good thing, as long as we don't play favorites. We have to search our hearts to know if we do this.

Remember the story of Jacob and his twelve sons? "Jacob loved Joseph more than any of his other children" (Genesis 37:3 NLT). That blatant favoritism caused jealousy among the brothers and turned them into prodigals who hated Joseph and tried to kill him. I was the first-born in my home, and I remember being the "favorite" of my Granny Hazel, but my baby sister was the favorite of my grandpa's new wife because she wanted a baby of her own. Often these dynamics are overt in a family, and they always lead to dissension.

"She was raised in the church."

We've read stories in this book of daughters raised in Christian homes, or "raised in the church," who became rebels and prodigals. Perhaps this is your experience as well. Maybe you, like other Christian parents of prodigals, have echoed Gideon's question in Judges 6:13: "If the LORD is with us, why has all this happened to us?" Be careful not to confuse the tendency to do "Christian things"—such as hosting or leading small groups, serving in ministry, and taking our children to church every Sunday—with leading our daughters to a personal, life-changing relationship with Christ. They won't pick up Christianity by osmosis. Just because we love the Lord doesn't mean they will. Or, like my daughter, they may mistakenly believe they can get into heaven on our faith.

Research confirms that most Christian parents rely on the church to train their children to become spiritually mature. But it's our job as parents to be absolutely sure our children have accepted Jesus and personally nurture that relationship. As the opening scripture advises parents, "Teach them in their growing years with Christian teaching" (Ephesians 6:4 NLT). What will determine whether our children walk away from sin or succumb to temptation is whether they really *know* Jesus or just know *about* Jesus. We can't just hope or guess about something this crucial; we must be certain.

I sent Kim to church youth camp but never even knew she had accepted Christ there. Even if I had known, I'm not sure I would have understood that she needed discipling. I probably would have expected God and the church to teach and train her.

I learned my lesson. When Kim went to Marriage Builders with Toby, I asked every week what they talked about in the class. The night she casually said, Pastor Pete said the "sinner's prayer," my heart raced as I inquired what she and Toby did during the prayer. She openly said they asked each other that same question on the drive home, and discovered both had made a renewed commitment to the Lord. They'd both accepted Christ at youth camps years earlier, but neither had lived a Christian life. I knew exactly what to do this time—Dave and I needed to mentor and disciple them and stay involved in their lives. They might be adults physically, but they were babies in the Lord.

The Lord answered Gideon, "Go in the strength you have. . . . I will be with you" (Judges 6:14, 16). God is our strength in raising our children. He will help us defeat the enemy that targets and attacks our precious daughters. We won't always be with them when they're tempted, but Jesus will. "Because he himself suffered when he was tempted, he is able to help those who are being tempted" (Hebrews 2:18). We need to be sure our daughters know that.

One way to determine if our daughter is walking with Jesus is to look for the fruit of the Spirit in her life—love, joy, peace, patience, kindness, goodness, and faithfulness (Galatians 5:22). If we don't see the fruit, there's a good chance she hasn't made a firm commitment to Christ, and we still have a lot of praying and parenting to do.

We also need to ask ourselves, Are we the real deal? Do our children see the fruit of the Spirit in our lives? Do they look at us and see God at work, or have we made other things—our work or our possessions or our children—our gods? How much of the world invades our Christian homes? To what influences do we expose our children? Do they see two parents living their Christian walk? We each have to answer for ourselves and make the appropriate changes.

It's difficult to think we might have done something to cause our daughter's troubles. However, it's important to take an honest inventory of our parenting, especially for the sake of any other children. Is this situation the result of our own behavior, decisions, or parenting, or does it have some divine purpose? We can ask God to help us discern the difference.

Kim mentioned the devastating effect divorce can have on a child. If you're divorced, you can't change that, but acknowledge how it affects your children. Think seriously about it, especially if you're contemplating divorce. We fool ourselves if we don't think divorce will damage our children. I regret that Kim didn't have a two-parent family. I divorced her father without a passing thought as to how it would affect her. I mistakenly believed what so many of us say and think: "Oh, she'll be better off if I'm happy." But unless there are safety issues, a single-parent home is seldom better than the most flawed dual-parent families.

How sad and naive of us to think that the decisions of the "big people" won't affect the "little people." Yet that's what many people think while they're getting divorces or making life-changing decisions for the entire family. Conversely, those of us who have prodigal daughters know that the "big people" also have to live with the decisions made by the "little people."

Certainly, not every divorced or single parent is in that situation by his or her own choice. My mom raised her two young daughters as a widow. Many of us find ourselves alone, even though it's not how we wanted or planned to raise our children. Just because a child comes from a divorced or single-parent home doesn't mean she'll become a prodigal, but it stacks the odds against her. Parenting alone is harder, but doable. God will help us if we let Him. If I'd been consulting God, I wouldn't have made many of the choices I did as a single parent, and there's a good chance Kim wouldn't have made her same choices either.

Please, if you're considering divorce, think first about the impact it'll have on your children, and explore all options before making that decision. Meet with pastors and seek wise, trusted Christian counsel—remember, your children may need counseling too.

There is no universal composite of a "perfect parent"—only God has that distinction. It's difficult to say what makes some kids prodigals and others not. Carla Barnhill, in her article "Help! I'm Wrecking My Kids!" articulated the paradox: "People who were raised by lovely, godly people still find ways to mess up their lives. And many wonderful, faith-filled adults grew up in homes where God's name was only uttered in vain. There is no formula. There are no guarantees. . . . Trying to live up to the myth of the perfect family leaves us stressed and anxious, and it's no picnic for our kids either."[2]

As Carla concluded in her article, there's no magic formula to raising children.

☕ Parent to Parent

Some Things Mothers Should Prayerfully Consider

1. *Dress our age.* What's more important: looking trendy in the latest fad or hip clothes, or looking like we're proud to be our daughter's mother? For years, to Kim's dismay, I looked and

dressed younger than I was. Most daughters want their mothers to wear what is becoming and appropriate for their age.

2. *Don't compete.* As daughters develop, it's time to let them shine. She needs to increase as we decrease. It's her rite of passage.

3. *Project a healthy physical, mental, and spiritual attitude.* Mothers transfer how they feel about themselves to their daughters. One beautiful teenager was cutting herself, thinking she was ugly. Her attractive mom constantly dieted and fretted that she was unattractive. The daughter came to see this self-berating as "womanly" and imitated it, taking it to the level of self-mutilation. Anorexia or obesity can have similar root causes.

In her book *Girls Will Be Girls: Raising Confident and Courageous Daughters,* JoAnn Deak, PhD, reported that "by age thirteen, 53 percent of girls are unhappy with their bodies; by age eighteen, 78 percent are dissatisfied with their bodies. Eighty percent of ten-year-old girls are on a diet, and the number one wish of *teenage girls* and *adult women* is to lose weight. Eight million American women suffer from eating disorders, and 90 percent of them are adolescents"[3] (emphasis added).

4. *Model the woman we want our daughter to become.* Mothers are their daughters' closest feminine role model. That's a huge responsibility, but God will guide us if we stay close to Him through reading His Word and prayerfully asking His direction.

5. *Surround ourself with godly women.* We can accomplish this by joining a women's group at church and studying how to be a woman after God's own heart. Also by seeking out a wise and trusted female mentor—and as we grow older and more mature in Christ, we can in turn mentor a younger mother (Titus 2:3–5).

Some Things Fathers Should Prayerfully Consider

1. *Don't leave raising the kids to Mom.* Your children need the strengths, gifts, and prayers of both parents poured into their lives.

2. *Don't wait until your daughter gets older to spend time with her.* Be creative in finding ways to interact with her. She needs time with you just as much as sons do. It's never too early for a night out with Dad.

3. *Treat your wife with respect and honor.* Show your daughter how a man displays healthy, lay-down-my-life-for-you love for his wife.

4. *Surround yourself with godly men.* Join a men's group at church. Study how to be a man after God's own heart. Find a wise and trusted male mentor, and as you grow older and more mature in Christ, be a mentor to a young father (Titus 2:1–2).

Some Things Both Parents Should Prayerfully Consider

1. *Be a parent instead of a friend.* Don't try to talk our daughter's jargon or listen to her music. I prided myself on being a "cool mom." Kim needed a godly mom. Today Kim calls me her best friend, and what an honor that is; but I wish I'd been the parent I am today in her teen years.

2. *Maintain integrity.* When our children are young, we think they're so little that they won't notice we're smoking, drinking, lying, overeating or undereating, depressed, gossiping, or _____ (fill in the blank). Kim cringed when I bought her "child" ski-lift or movie tickets even though she was past the age limit. She wanted to be her age; I wanted to save a few bucks. I modeled that lying is okay when it serves your purpose. So why should I have been surprised, years later, that she lied to me when it served her purpose? Do our daughters see us . . .

+ reading our Bible or tabloids and racy novels?

+ watching appropriate movies and family TV programs or R-rated films and trashy TV?

+ bringing Jesus into our home daily or just going to church on Sunday?

+ giving or being selfish?

+ praying with and for her or just saying we're praying for her?

+ feeding our family's minds, bodies, and souls with healthy and nutritious food or junk food?

+ speaking sweet and gentle words or being argumentative and critical?

+ allowing the husband to be the spiritual leader of the home, or mom does all the leading?

+ showing our spouse respect and love or berating him or her?

+ admitting when we're wrong or always having to be right?

+ living out what we preach or being hypocritical?

+ loving others more than ourselves or always putting ourselves first?

+ taking care of our bodies or abusing them?

+ speaking the best of people or gossiping?

3. *Shower our daughter with compliments and encouragement.* Don't base our accolades solely on performance or accomplishments.

4. *Be home for dinner, and don't bring work home.* This might mean a job change so we don't have to commute. Those valuable hours on the freeway could be spent with family. There always will be work to do, but we'll only get one shot at raising our daughter.

5. *Attend to both our inner and outer beauty.* It's important to develop a spiritual life and stay physically fit by eating healthy and exercising.

6. *Know what's going on in our daughter's life.* Ask questions, and listen with interest to her answers.

You might be reading these suggestions and thinking, *Well, this all sounds great, but it's too late now.* Or, *Our daughter doesn't want to spend time with us anymore.* But hope comes from knowing it's never too late. God isn't on a limited time schedule. Remember, you're praying for your daughter to repent or come home, and when she does, it'll be to the new you. That might be what this is all about—learning how to break old patterns and ways of relating. Don't wait for her to change. You take the initiative. The change she sees in you could be what draws her back.

We all learn from the prodigal's journey. The Christian life is a process of shedding the old self and putting on the new creation we are in Christ. Renewing our mind every day means we are changing every day—drawing closer and closer to the mind of Christ (Ephesians 4:22–24). Don't go through this trial and stay the same. Pray that your prodigal will someday be the person you are becoming.

📓 From My Prayer Journal

MAY 12, 1994

Forgive me for the times I left Kim alone so that I could work and play—and the many other mistakes I made while raising her. Thank You for protecting her. Please continue watching over her until she makes a decision to follow You . . . and the new me!

🙏 Let's Pray Together

Father, what a sobering thought to think that our actions and lack of parenting skills might have contributed to our daughter's problems. But we know You are the God of many chances, and we're praying for another opportunity to do it right this time. Help us become parents who please You and are a joy to our daughter. Amen.

Family and Support Group Discussion

1. This was a tough chapter. What impacted you the most?

2. In what areas do you need to change?

3. What steps will you take to accomplish that?

4. If you're a couple, how can you have a marriage you want your children to emulate? If you're single, how can you become a godly role model for your daughter?

Your Prayer Journal

Ask God to reveal the areas He wants to refine in your life and in your parenting.

_____

_____

_____

_____

_____

_____

_____

_____

_____

_____

20

WHAT IS UNCONDITIONAL LOVE?

Love is patient and kind. Love is not jealous or boastful or
proud or rude. It does not demand its own way.
It is not irritable, and it keeps no record of being wronged. It
does not rejoice about injustice but rejoices whenever the
truth wins out. Love never gives up, never loses faith, is always
hopeful, and endures through every circumstance. . . .
Three things will last forever—faith, hope, and love—
and the greatest of these is love.
1 CORINTHIANS 13:4–7, 13 (NLT)

I don't have to arm wrestle my daughter back to Jesus.
I love her—and let God handle the rest.[1]
PATRICIA RAYBON

WHAT IS UNCONDITIONAL LOVE?

❖

*I focus on our love for her and not her rebellion to
God through her lesbian lifestyle. Only God,
the Holy Spirit, can convict her of sin.
As much as I love her, God loves her more.*
BETTY

♡ A Praying Mother Shares

(Continued from chapter 8)

My love for my prodigal daughters is beyond my understanding. I choose daily to meet them as Jesus has met me, right where they are. Only now, I meet them with the same extravagant, redeeming love I experience through His Living Word *every day*. I just have such an ache waiting for my prodigal daughters to return from rebellion to share and live in the abundant life with Christ. I find myself lingering much in the presence of our Lord to learn what to say and His timing to say it—and just *love* them to pieces the rest of the time.

—*Robin*

♡ A Prodigal Daughter Shares

When I came to know the loving grace of my heavenly Father, I wanted to believe it was possible to find that same forgiveness from my mother. But my mother could only use the law to point out I was fallen . . . a prodigal. There was no embrace to return home to, only graceless judgment.

I knew I was a prodigal daughter, but I longed for a grace-filled relationship with my mother. But she was not a believer, and she could not find it in her heart to welcome me home. Yet still I wanted to believe that if she could taste the sweet peace and love known through Christ, she could let me into her life a little. I longed to be close enough to feel the beat of her heart so badly hardened by the loss to cancer of the husband of her youth.

I often wondered what it would feel like to spend a speechless moment in close proximity to the woman who brought me into the world. To know acceptance just as I was and feel, for a moment, good enough just because I breathed the same air, blinked with her same mischievous twinkle in my eye and smile, and wrinkled my nose in the same shy-girl fashion along the same laugh lines she did. What joy it would be to sit together with my mother in the holy, peaceful, forgiving presence of God's unconditional love—knowing all is well, and the only thing that matters is that we've both returned to . . . love.

Through my relationship with Christ and His grace, I learned that I could escape the judgment under which I'd been living all these years. Yet still I long for my mother's loving embrace. I pray for her to know the forgiveness I know. I hope someday I can welcome home my prodigal mother into God and my grace-filled arms.

—*Cynthia*

What Is Unconditional Love?

Cynthia's story resonates with mine. My mother too was a widow whose heart was hardened toward the Lord. She saw me through the same judgmental eyes as Cynthia's mother and could not love me unconditionally either. Like Cynthia, I longed for my mother to experience the same love of Jesus that I had found and for us to have a mutually grace-filled, loving relationship. But that was not to be for prodigal daughters Cynthia or me.

I grew up in a family where love was given and taken away at will. When I did what my family approved of, I was loved. When I didn't, love was withheld. Various family members were estranged or disowned through the years. It was a perilous, insecure way to live. I vowed that when I had children, I would love them no matter what they did.

Wanting to keep the lines of communication open while Kim was at college, I called her every Sunday, and we chatted. We both looked forward to those phone calls. I didn't scold or preach. We talked about her classes, friends, and what she was doing in college; and I told her what was happening in my and Dave's lives. I ended every conversation as I always have: "I love you, baby." And she responded, as she still does today: "I love you too, Mom!"

When Kim was going through her prodigal years, I made sure she always knew how much I loved her. I didn't like what she was doing and openly told her so, but I also let her know that it didn't change my love for her. I know Kim never doubted my love. Now almost every birthday or Mother's Day card I receive contains these sentiments: "Thank you for being such a great mom and loving me unconditionally. I love you!"

Unconditional love sounds like a great concept, but it can be difficult to live out when our daughters rebel against us and everything we've taught them and value. Here are three concrete, practical ways to help us unconditionally love our prodigal daughter regardless of her actions or whether she shows love back to us.

Unconditional love demands that we honestly and lovingly tell the truth.

Ephesians 4:15 says, "We will speak the truth in love" (NIrV). We appear critical, legalistic, and judgmental when we forget the "in love" part of that verse. But by the same token, we are cowardly when we avoid "the truth" by overlooking sin or minimizing our daughter's bad behavior. Unconditional love is a delicate balance of loving grace with honest factualness.

Jimmie L. Davis, author of *Girls' Ministry Handbook*, wrote about a prodigal daughter who, looking back as an adult, wishes her parents and others had been more straightforward with her: "I needed adults to be honest with me—really honest. I needed them to tell me that although

God is love, He is also fair and just. I did not comprehend the concept of Him allowing me to face consequences. I needed someone to be real with me and tell me the dangers of believing the world's lies."[2]

Unconditional love is respectful—even in the face of disrespect.

It's important to remain respectful to our daughter and speak respectfully about her even when she is doing things we detest. It's easy when we're upset with her to say things about her or to her that we'll later regret. As disillusioned as we might be with her and her actions, we need to remember that we love her . . . and how do we speak about people we love?

I was reminded of the answer to that question one Christmas when Kim was home from college. We received one of those annual holiday newsletters from a family we knew. It was full of detailed stories about numerous prodigal and wayward activities of their children. Kim was sitting next to me as I went through the mail, and I read the letter to her. I commented that I couldn't imagine sending out such a letter to everyone on the Christmas list. Kim laughed and said, "Yeah, Mom, that's like you sending out a letter saying, 'Kim's living in sin.'"

Her words gave me insight—she knew her lifestyle was sinful. But it also was a reminder that while I didn't respect what Kim was doing, I did need to respect Kim.

Unconditional love is tough—yet vulnerable and at risk of rejection.

Our daughter might use our love to manipulate us. Showing her unconditional love doesn't mean we don't show her the door if she won't live appropriately in our home. That's "tough love," or grace meeting truth. We give her the opportunity to abide by boundaries. If she chooses to ignore them, we love her by staying consistent in our words and actions and letting her experience the consequences. Otherwise, we enable her to continue on her wayward path. But regardless of her choices and lifestyle, we never stop showing her grace—undeserved love. We pray, asking God to watch over her, and then we pray some more. Someday she might thank us for loving her enough to let go and entrust her to God's capable hands.

The story of the prodigal son in Luke 15:11–32 is an example of unconditional, tough love. The selfish, foolish youngest son wanted his inheritance so he could leave home in search of what the world had to offer. The father gave it to him and sent him on his way. Sometimes, letting our daughter go, letting her live on her own, or not bailing her out is the most loving thing we can do. Chris Adams and her husband had to make that difficult decision: "Our prayer in not enabling has been that she would come to the point of having to make some changes for her own survival and well-being without anyone coming to her rescue each time she made wrong choices."[3]

After squandering all his money and living on the streets, the prodigal son returned home. And Dad was lovingly waiting for him, showing him grace with open arms. Later you'll read that Chris also had the joy of embracing her returning prodigal.

The parable of the prodigal son is an illustration of God's love for us. Wanting to do things our own way, we often rebel against our loving Father, who gives us so much. Yet God continues loving us unconditionally. He waits patiently even as we hurt Him by squandering our blessings, breaking His rules, and ignoring His pleas for our return. He never stops loving us. Our behavior will bring consequences, but not the withdrawal of His love. And that, my friends, is how we must love our prodigal daughters.

Offering such love to a prodigal is painful, heartrending, agonizing. Rarely does she seem to appreciate it, but we're called to do it anyway. "Don't just pretend to love your daughter. Really love her. Hate what is wrong. Hold tightly to what is good. Love each other with genuine affection" (personalization of Romans 12:9–10 NLT). Maybe our unconditional, unwavering, genuine love will light the way for our prodigal daughter to find her way home.

Unconditional love is not an emotion but an action.

I'm an emotional person, and I had to learn that love isn't an emotion; it's an action. I figured that out during an *aha!* moment in church one day. We don't fall in and out of love. Love is a choice. Emotions wane, circumstances change, but love remains steady through it all—if we let it. Romans 12:9 reminds us: "Love must be sincere." Putting on a pretense of love when we're seething inside is not sincere love. Acting our way into feeling loving can be a start, but we can't stay in this first stage. Our children will see right through it if we're doing what we're supposed to do as "loving parents," but in our hearts we harbor anger, resentment, bitterness, and maybe even malice toward the child who has hurt us. We must come to the point where our hearts—from which our love or hate flows—match our embraces and the smiles on our faces.

Synchronizing loving actions with a loving heart can be a slow process, and not one we can master on our own. Loving a rebel goes against everything inside us that screams out for fairness and justice. *It isn't right*, our minds protest. *I love her, but she's treating us like dirt. She has no regard for our feelings.* Sound familiar?

The Bible is full of what I call "the great reversals"—passages that ask us to do difficult things like love our enemies, turn the other cheek when we're hit, or willingly give more when someone has already taken too much. Jesus is the ultimate example of doing the exact opposite of what our natural tendencies would lead us to do. He loved us when we were unlovable, and He laid down His life to redeem us while we were still sinners. That's genuine, radical, sincere love that knows no boundaries and isn't reliant on our loving Him back. He loved us into His arms, and we can do the same with our daughters. Only Jesus can give us a heart that loves while it's breaking.

Christian author and speaker Patricia Raybon, in an interview in *Today's Christian Woman* magazine, discussed the sense of responsibility she felt when her two daughters strayed from the Christian faith. When asked, "What would you do differently?" she answered: "Love them! I was a strict, inflexible parent. In hindsight, I'd love them like crazy. Then

I'd make sure they understood why—because finally I know Who love is: His name is Jesus. That's what praying in his name means—to walk in his character. A woman can change her entire household this way."[4]

The interviewer later asked, "What's your advice for parents dealing with a prodigal child?" Patricia responded, "I'd say take the problem to the altar and leave it there—then stand back! Because the Lord will first change you. That's the spiritual answer.

"The practical answer is to ask God to show you how to love her . . . I love my beloved daughter [who is now Muslim]. Frankly, we have a closer relationship now than when she was attending church as a teen. . . . I listen when she talks. I'm not exhausted with sorrow and I don't preach. I'm trusting in God's love for her."[5]

Our daughter is God's gift to us, and God asks us to love her more than we love ourselves. She came with no guarantees as to how her life would turn out. But a child loved unconditionally from the day she's born will have a much better chance of withstanding the pressures awaiting her as she goes out into the world. Most of us are way beyond the day she was born; but we can start today by vowing that our family will learn to love each other with the love of Christ.

☕ Parent to Parent

How do we love like Jesus? How can we show unconditional love when our daughters have broken our hearts or said and done terrible things? It's hard not to say, "I love you *but* . . . or *if* . . . or *when* . . ." Or, "I'm too angry to love you." Or, "You don't deserve our love."

We start by looking at what God says about unconditional love. His Word provides a new perspective of the word so freely used to mean many things and shows us how to love our prodigal daughters in spite of their transgressions. Prayerfully personalize with me 1 Corinthians 13:4–8, 13 (NLT): "The Love Chapter."

I am patient and kind. I don't become annoyed, irritable, or critical. I notice it doesn't add, if she's patient and kind back.

I am not jealous. I don't wish my daughter were more like someone else's or my other children, who would be easier to love. If I feel this way, she'll sense it.

I am not boastful. I don't imply that I or others are better than she is by bragging about my own accomplishments or those of others.

I am not proud. I'm proud of my daughter without turning the focus to myself. For example, "I'm so proud of her" with the hidden agenda, "because it makes me look good."

I am not rude. I make my point without being sarcastic or cutting, even when that's how my daughter is speaking to me.

I do not demand my own way. I'm open to looking at an opinion that might differ from my own. I don't have to agree with it, but I listen.

I am not irritable. I stay calm. Everything in me may want to lash out and unleash my anger and frustration, but I won't.

I keep no record of being wronged. I don't retaliate or bring up all the bad things my daughter did in the past. I stay in the moment and truly forgive with no strings attached.

I do not rejoice about injustice. I don't have a "you deserved that" mentality or a "you got what was coming to you" attitude. I'm sad when she's wrongly treated and even sadder when she wrongs others.

I rejoice whenever the truth wins out. I lovingly let her know the conversation stops when she starts lying, and I'm always truthful with her.

I never give up. I may have to let go, but I'll never stop loving and praying.

I never lose faith. I believe all things are possible for those who trust in the Lord.

I am always hopeful. I believe our God is the God of miracles, and He answers prayers.

I endure through every circumstance. I remain strong, not just in some circumstances or only the tolerable times but in every experience.

I love forever! I never stop loving my daughter or forfeit love—no matter what. Three things will last forever—faith, hope, and love—and the greatest of these is love.

And let's finish with this personalized passage from Philippians 1:6: "I am confident that He who began a good work in my daughter will carry it on to completion until the day of Christ Jesus."

I'd like to put my name in those verses and love like that all the time, wouldn't you? Truth is, I don't. None of us do; but it's what we should strive for.

From My Prayer Journal

AUGUST 8, 1998

Lord, please enable Kim and me to love like You love us! I love her with the purest love I've ever known. Thank You for allowing me to be her mother and to experience unconditional love both from her and for her.

Let's Pray Together

Lord, we marvel at how You love us unconditionally, no matter what we do. Your arms are always open. Make us like You, and never let our love for our daughter die. May it burn so brightly that she longs to be back in our embrace. Help us to remember that love for her isn't based on what she does or doesn't do, and give us wisdom and grace to communicate that to her in both words and actions. We remember how much You loved us when we broke Your heart, and that knowledge will strengthen us to love our daughter now. We love You, Lord. Amen.

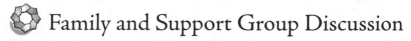 Family and Support Group Discussion

1. In what ways has it been difficult to show your daughter unconditional love?

2. What are some practical ways you can practice not condemning your daughter without condoning her behavior?—What changes can you make to ensure that grace will meet truth in your dealings with your daughter?

3. How can you love her when she is being unlovable?

4. Read the entire chapter of 1 Corinthians 13. Then discuss the characteristics of love and how you can better show love to your family.

Your Prayer Journal

Sit and soak in how much God unconditionally loves you, and write what that feels like.

_____

_____

_____

_____

_____

_____

_____

_____

CHAPTER

21

WHAT WILL OUR FRIENDS THINK?

Friends love through all kinds of weather,
and families stick together in all kinds of trouble.
PROVERBS 17:17 MSG

We even lost friends over how we dealt with our prodigal when
they didn't agree, but they weren't in our shoes.
CHRIS ADAMS

WHAT WILL OUR FRIENDS THINK?

❖

*Even our closest, most caring friends can appear clueless to the
divine dimensions of our dilemma. Yet we need those who know
us best to listen, pray, and encourage. They provide a perspective
that we may have missed in the confusion and consternation.*[1]
JUDI BRADDY

♡ A Praying Mother Shares
(Continued from chapter 14)

We told close friends about Bobbi's disappearance, and they joined us in praying for her. We had faith in our God, but strangely, we also had faith in our daughter. She usually exhibited a good deal of maturity and common sense. The boyfriend she ran away with was another matter.

We felt hurt, sad, disappointed, and even embarrassed by what Bobbi had done, but we loved her very much and desperately wanted her back. Often my husband and I would say to each other, "Any word from Bobbi?"

The answer to our prayers began unfolding with a phone call from Bobbi's boyfriend. He wanted bail money so he could get out of jail! "Yes, she's pregnant," he sighed. "She's working at a card shop and has an apartment in the desert. We're not together anymore. The last time I saw her was a couple months ago."

Immediately we contacted friends who lived in the desert and told them all that had happened. They checked every card shop in the area. It was a happy day when they phoned to say they'd found her, she was healthy, and she wanted us to come see her. We all breathed a sigh of relief. Thank You, thank You, thank You, God!

—*Mary*

My Daughter Kim Shares

Mom, I always was very concerned about what my friends thought. When we first moved to Orange County, it was hard for me to make friends and fit in, so when I did, I wanted to keep them. I probably did crazy things in high school just to fit in and not be different. And when you were gone so much, they were there for me.

Some of my friends actually weren't happy about me moving to college with my boyfriend, but I thought it was because they didn't like him. Most of them didn't go away to college, so it seemed they just didn't understand or were jealous.

Now I'm the one telling girls not to live with someone. It seldom turns out well and isn't a good foundation for a lasting relationship. Most don't listen, just like I didn't.

Taking the Marriage Builders class made Toby and me want to hear more about what the Lord had to offer us, so we decided to start going to church. When we met with Pastor Brett about our upcoming wedding and told him what we'd been learning at Marriage Builders, he suggested we take the next step, baptism. You'd left that up to me because you wanted it to be my decision, but growing up I always wished you would've done it for me as a baby so I didn't have to go through the embarrassment as an adult. I always feared what my friends would think.

I now understand that baptism is a personal decision, and it's our public announcement to the world that we've accepted Christ. Toby's making the decision with me to let Christ into our hearts, and our marriage made it so much easier. I didn't care what anyone else thought anymore when the person I loved the most was right there beside me. (You don't count.)

What Will Our Friends Think?

Friends are important, but when we need them most, sometimes they can disappoint us; or as with Kim, striving for acceptance by friends can pull our daughters down the wrong path. On the other hand, friends like

Mary's can support us, encourage us, pray with us, and maybe even help make it possible for us to reunite with our prodigal. The dilemma comes in deciphering whom we can trust with our secrets, our hearts, and our pain. Who will come through for us, stand with us, and be a positive influence; and who will disappoint us, disappear, or compound our pain?

In my book *Dear God, They Say It's Cancer*, I discussed this quandary of how much do we tell others, to whom do we tell the whole story, and who should do the telling? The same issues apply when we're dealing with a prodigal daughter. We feel torn because we want prayers and need support, but we fear we'll be judged and condemned instead. Even though our daughter is causing us pain, we don't want anyone to think badly of her—or of us for the way we're handling the situation. As Chris said, others aren't in our shoes and probably won't understand. That might lead us to conclude that we're better off trying to handle the crisis on our own or within our immediate family. But friends like Mary's will pray for our daughter and for us. If we don't tell them what's going on, we'll miss out on those valuable prayers.

If our prodigal's ordeal stretches on for a lengthy time, people will find out anyway. Remember, it'll be difficult for younger children to keep news about their prodigal sister to themselves. We don't want to put them in a position of disappointing us with the inevitable—they're going to tell one of their friends, who will tell a parent or someone else. Siblings of a prodigal are under a lot of stress and pressure as it is, so try not to make news about your prodigal another load for them to carry as "a secret."

Besides, most of us would rather deliver embarrassing news ourselves than let the gossip machine put its spin on it. So how do you go about breaking the news of your prodigal daughter's latest indiscretion? Here are some suggestions:

1. Pray together as a family, asking God for guidance in what to share with whom, as well as when and how to share.

2. Make a list of your friends—and the children's—whom you feel should be told.

3. Compose a family statement to which everyone can agree. It could go something like this: "Our daughter (my sister) has left home (or is having problems), and we/she could really use your prayers."

4. Discuss polite and practical ways to change the subject when people pry or ask for more details. For example, "I'm not comfortable talking about it right now, but if you really want to help, please pray for her. God knows the details."

We know the people who support us or who drag us down. We need support right now; we're feeling down enough. Hopefully, you have a few close friends to whom you can pour out your heart without fearing judgment or fueling gossip. In a crisis we discover who our trustworthy and steadfast friends are. We'll also likely discover new friends who have experienced and can understand our pain, even as we lose some who are clueless or insensitive. People don't usually mean to say the wrong thing, but often they do, and it's hurtful. From embarrassment and/or ignorance, some feel compelled to minimize our pain, give unwanted advice, tell stories of other parents' trials, or evaluate our actions—none of which is helpful.

When Kim was in college, a friend of ours mentioned the godly son of a mutual friend. I commented that I wished Kim would meet someone like this young man. My "friend" responded piously, "Oh, he wouldn't be interested in someone like Kim." Ouch! I learned that she wasn't a "safe" person to confide in about Kim. I needed people to pray for my daughter, not judge her or us. And so do you! As Jesus said in response to those who had condemned a sinful woman and wanted Him to do the same: "If any of you is without sin, let him be the first to throw a stone at her" (John 8:7). Sadly, my friend now has a prodigal daughter herself.

When we have friends who understand without judging and who support us, comfort us, and believe in us, it's much easier to let what other people think roll harmlessly off our backs. Such friends share the load and make our burden lighter. It's comforting to know we're not alone in our struggle. When I tell people about the book I'm writing, many raise their eyebrows, recognition flickers in their eyes, and they pour out their own story. I wonder if I'm the first "friend" they've told.

Hurting parents are everywhere. When I was having my contacts adjusted, I explained to the contact lens specialist that I needed to see the computer so I could write. He asked what I was writing, and when I told him *Praying for Your Prodigal Daughter*, he asked if I had personal experience. When I said yes, he told me about his own prodigal daughter who wanted nothing to do with God and how painful this was for their family. I doubt he ventured onto this topic with many patients, but when I was open about my story, I no longer was just a patient; I was a safe friend.

Friends are valuable at any age, but we would all agree that they're *essential* to young people. Much of what drives a prodigal daughter's actions is consideration for what her friends think. Peer pressure and acceptance by others is of paramount importance and can be a force for good or for evil. In high school Kim's best friend went to our church, so it was "cool" going to church and being involved in youth groups with her friend. But when that friend moved away, Kim's other friends didn't go to church—and as you read in her opening story, she was very concerned about their opinions. She worried that if they saw her as a "church girl," she might not fit in. Later, her boyfriend's family "wasn't religious," so she wasn't going to be either.

After Kim stopped being involved at church, the youth group leaders continued calling and inviting her to church and events, but she wouldn't return their calls. She no longer had a friend to go with, and she wasn't going alone. I encouraged her to stay involved, but I didn't take an active enough role. I lost my window of opportunity. Friends had started to influence her more than God and I did. I'm sure you've experienced something similar. I hope you can take comfort to know that with time and lots of prayer, today Kim calls me her best friend. I know that might seem a long shot for you at the moment, but it's hope to hold on to.

Even when our friends and daughters let us down, our eternal Best Friend, Jesus Christ, will never leave or forsake us. Jesus tells us in John 15:14–15, "You are my friends when you do the things I command you.

I'm no longer calling you servants because servants don't understand what their master is thinking and planning. No, I've named you friends because I've let you in on everything I've heard from the Father" (MSG). Those are words of a Forever Friend!

☕ Parent to Parent

It's wise to be discerning in our sharing, but when we know we have an ally, the sharing can be a common bond that allows us to help each other. Remember, this is our life, and no one can live it for us. Not everyone will agree with our decisions regarding our prodigal daughter. But God is the only friend we need to please anyway, so don't waste time and emotional energy seeking approval from those who offer drive-by opinions.

Consider the source of every piece of advice and remarks about your prodigal daughter. Look at the life of that person. Is he or she someone you should be listening to? If the answer is yes, then pay attention. If no, then let the advice roll off like water on a greased surface: it doesn't penetrate but just slides down into a puddle and evaporates.

📝 From My Prayer Journal

JUNE 9, 1994

Thank You for all our friends who are praying with us for Kim's salvation. Please Lord, bring Christian friends into Kim's life. I know they'll have to come from You, because she isn't putting herself in the right places to meet believers.

✌ Let's Pray Together

Lord, give us wisdom to recognize friends who will stick by us. May we not burden them with our problems but seek their prayers and encouragement. For those who have said hurtful things, help us to forgive them and move on. In most cases, they don't realize what they're doing. Thank

You for the friends who love us unconditionally and for the new friends we'll make on this journey. Thank You for calling us Your friends and for laying down Your life for us. Amen.

Family and Support Group Discussion

1. As a family, compile a list of friends with whom you feel comfortable sharing about your prodigal situation.

2. What are you going to tell them? What might you choose not to share?

3. How do you feel about forgiving those who have said hurtful things or discontinued their friendship with you?

4. How can you use the experience of telling others about your struggles to be a witness to God's faithfulness?

Your Prayer Journal

Tell your Best Friend, Jesus, how you feel about having a prodigal daughter and how well-meaning friends have hurt you.

_____

_____

_____

_____

_____

_____

_____

_____

WHAT IF SHE NEVER REPENTS?

A parent's endurance is inspired by hope in
our Lord Jesus Christ.
PERSONALIZATION OF 1 THESSALONIANS 1:3

*Waiting for our prodigal daughter, or daughters in my case,
to come home is never easy.*
ROBIN

WHAT IF SHE
NEVER REPENTS?

❖

*I had to totally trust my daughter in God's hands
and give her up to Him often throughout the day.*
CHRIS ADAMS

♡ A Praying Mother Shares
(Continued from chapter 20)

Waiting on the Lord has proven to be one of the best things I could do for my two prodigal daughters, my marriage, and my life. Daily I'm learning to practice surrendering by being a godly example of a wife and mother. My life is now rooted in the truth of His Word, and I live on His promises daily. I believe all things are possible through Christ because I'm living proof that He is who He says He is—my Redeemer, Savior, and Lord of my life—and one day He will be that for my prodigal daughters too, when they choose to turn to Him. He'll be waiting—just before they return to me with their whole hearts. What a glorious thought!

I always wanted to trust that my daughters would return one day to the Love of their lives and fall in love with Him all over again, as they did in their youth, and we would live happily ever after. I now stand on the words of Jeremiah 31:15–17: "This is what the LORD says: 'A voice is heard in Ramah, mourning and great weeping, Rachel weeping for her children and refusing to be comforted, because her children are no more.' This is what the LORD says: 'Restrain your voice from weeping and your eyes from tears,' declares the LORD. 'They will return from the land of the enemy. So there is hope for your future,' declares the LORD. 'Your children will return to their own Land.'"

I'd like it done now, please! I rest in God's assurance that it'll happen in His perfect time. After all, He promises to finish the good work He starts in each of us (Philippians 1:6). I believe God, and "happily ever after" doesn't seem like a fairy tale anymore but a destination I long to reach.

—*Robin*

A Prodigal Daughter Shares
(*Continued from chapter 11*)

I often initiated debates over Christianity, even with my mother. I drove her into a corner with my intellect. It was my education, I justified, that led me to doubt and question the areas where she blindly followed the herd on faith. She never answered my questions—or, rather, objections—but always said, "You just have to have faith. Without it, there's no hope" and concluded each time with, "I just hope someday you'll come back to Christianity."

She always had to have the last word. Deep down, I knew I was the one driven into a corner by that thought: "Without faith, there is no hope." I had gotten to the point where I really had no hope. I too wanted to come back, but I was so lost and far away, I couldn't. I wanted to believe the Bible was true, but I had embraced a delusion that wouldn't let me. My flesh loved the darkness, and the light switch was moving farther and farther from my reach.

My mom worried about me and the distance I had created between us; but she had no idea how destructive my worldview really was. Ours wasn't a model Christian family, but I certainly grew up knowing and fearing the Lord. My mom despaired that her daughter might never "come back."

—*Loren*

🌅 What If She Never Repents?

My friend Kathy, whose daughter came home with the surprise "Believer" tattoo back in chapter 12, had to pack up her prodigal son's belongings and ask him to leave their house, but she set a place for him at dinner every night. She never lost hope that he would return: he never lost his place at the table. It was a reminder that he was part of the family, and they were praying for him. When his friends continued coming over for dinner, they saw the place set for him and word got back to her son that his family was faithfully awaiting his return.

For some of you, it's been many years since your daughter walked away from God and from you, and you're still awaiting her return. Maybe she has even come back to you but not to God, and you're devastated knowing that she's not living according to God's best plan for her. The time comes when, for our own sanity, we have to let go of our dreams and plans for our prodigal daughters; but we must *never* let go of God's plan of salvation for her. As Lamentations 3:26 reminds us, "It is good to wait quietly for the salvation of the LORD" (Lamentations 3:26). Hope of that day is what keeps us praying and interceding for her year after year.

Those of us who always want to be in control have a hard time with hope because there's no time frame and we don't know the outcome. But when we put our hope in what God can do, we demonstrate our faith. That's the essence of faith: "Faith is being sure of what we hope for our daughters and certain of what we do not see" (personalization of Hebrews 11:1). Discouragement comes from Satan, who wants us to believe it's not possible. When we put our trust in God, we believe that all things are possible!

Some of you may be saying, "I had hope, but I'm at the end of myself. I've run out of words to plead with God. I'm just so tired." Be comforted, because the Holy Spirit will intervene for you:

> We parents were given this hope when we were saved. (If we
> already have something, we don't need to hope for it. But if

we look forward to something we don't yet have, *we must wait patiently and confidently.*) And the Holy Spirit helps us in our weakness. For example, we don't know what God wants us to pray for our daughter. But the Holy Spirit prays for us with groanings that cannot be expressed in words. And the Father who knows all hearts knows what the Spirit is saying, for the Spirit pleads for us believing parents in harmony with God's own will. And we know that God causes everything to work together for the good of those who love God and are called according to his purpose for them (personalization of Romans 8:24–28 NLT, emphasis added).

Chris Adams shared:

> One thing I had to learn was to let go. This is the hardest lesson a parent probably ever has to learn. A minister on the staff I was serving with had some difficult issues with all three of his children during their teen years. I asked him one day how he dealt with it and continued to minister to others. He lifted his open hand, palm up, and told me he had to release them to his heavenly Father. I began doing the same thing, sometimes several times a day, trusting God to take care of my daughter and love her more than her father and I did. I continued doing it until I felt the peace of letting go. The alternative would be to go crazy with pain and fear. It didn't eliminate the pain, but it gave me peace in the midst of it.[1]

You may have heard the phrase "Let go and let God." In fact, that's what some may have counseled you to do, and you wondered, Let God do what? The phrase simply means to fully and completely put our hope and trust in the Lord and His plan for us—and our daughter—as we continue reading and praying His Word and His promises. Even though our daughter may be out of our sight, she's never out of God's sight. He's omnipresent—something we could never be. Like us, He's shedding tears for her, but He's also battling Satan for her life. Our part in that battle is to pray. When Kim was far from God, I continually prayed that He would surround her with Christians everywhere she turned.

It can be painful completely giving up our illusion of control and entrusting our daughter to God's will. Maybe, as with the prodigal son in the Bible, God's plan is to let our prodigal daughter sink to the depths of consuming what's fit only for pigs before she can understand the good life she left behind. But in some cases, a prodigal daughter will stay in that pigpen and wallow in the filth for the rest of her life while our hearts break. Some prodigals repent on their deathbeds. My father was a highway patrolman who was killed in the line of duty. My grandmother's biggest heartbreak came from not knowing if my father was a believer. I remember her torment, and now, being a parent, I can empathize with her, as can you.

If we don't see our daughter return, we wonder, *Wasn't God listening? Did He turn a deaf ear to our prayers? Why didn't He bring her back?* These are all legitimate questions—and hard ones not to have answered. Many things in life will be beyond our understanding until we get to heaven. Maybe our daughter accepted Jesus but walked away and has led a terrible, miserable life on earth. God still welcomes believers home: "God so loved our daughter that he gave his one and only Son, so that if she believes in him she will not perish but have eternal life" (personalization of John 3:16). The enemy can steal her earthly joy and peace, but he can't steal her salvation, because "the one who is in her is greater than the one who is in the world" (personalization of 1 John 4:4). This is the hope and faith that gives us peace.

It's hard to be comforted when the baby girl we cuddled, nurtured, loved, and rejoiced over is destroying herself. But we must not let it destroy us too. As much as we're hurting, our family—or others—need us. What's more, some people we're not even aware of are inevitably watching to see how Christians handle such a trying situation. Is our God truly a God of comfort and solace? Do we seek the Lord's strength when we want to crawl under the covers and wake up to the life and daughter of our dreams?

I know parents who had dreamed of helping their daughter plan a lavish wedding only to hurriedly throw together a simple ceremony because she was pregnant. Or they'd dreamed of being by their daughter's side when she delivered her first baby but learn that she gave away a child, or maybe had an abortion. The list goes on. Each of us has our own story of heartache and loss.

Don't give up. Don't stop praying. *Do* allow yourself to grieve and mourn for the loss of your daughter or the vision you had for her. Then trust God and wait for Him to work.

It's hard to wait. It's especially difficult when the stakes are high and we realize there's little or nothing we can do to change or hurry things. Yet, as Philip Yancy wrote, there's purpose even in the waiting: "The very tedium, the act of waiting itself, works to nourish in us qualities of patience, persistence, trust, gentleness, compassion—or it may do so, if we place ourselves in the stream of God's movement on earth. It may take more faith to trust God when we do not get what we ask for than when we do. Is that not the point of Hebrews 11?"[2]

Faithful waiting means entrusting our daughters to God and faithfully praying with the expectation of the goodness of God's sovereign plan in His perfect timing. And so we pray for God's will, and we wait for His answer.

Parent to Parent

In *Dear God, They Say It's Cancer,* I discussed the stages of grief that follow a diagnosis of breast cancer. These also apply to grappling with the pain of having a prodigal daughter. I adapted them for those of you whose little lost lamb has not returned to the fold and who grieve for the daughter you once knew.

The Steps of Grief

- *Shock* is our first reaction. The punch or sinking sensation in the pit of our stomach—dizzying, nauseating, room-spinning, unbelievable!

+ *Denial* is a survival reaction until we get our bearings. "This can't be happening to us." We hold on to the possibility it's all a mistake and try ignoring it.

+ *Acknowledgment* replaces denial. Now we must face it head-on, and it hurts so bad and makes us so mad!

+ *Anger* is intense at our daughter, those who influenced her, ourselves, and maybe even God.

+ *Acceptance* follows anger because we can't be angry at something we haven't accepted.

+ *Sadness* seeps in as the dust settles on anger and acceptance, and the emotional pain engulfs us.

+ *Depression* is the deepest form of sadness and can become debilitating and dangerous if we don't take steps to move through it.

+ *Joy* can be the aftermath of healthy grieving. With prayer, support, and counsel, God says, "You will grieve, but your grief will suddenly turn to wonderful joy" (John 16:20 NLT).[3]

That's the hope to which we cling: that somewhere—somehow—our daughter makes her peace with God. And on that glorious day, when we're ushered into His throne room, we'll have a reunion with our precious daughter, washed clean as snow of her sins, just as we have been. As Robin said at the beginning of this chapter, for those of us who believe in God, this isn't a fairy tale: it's the long-awaited happy ending.

Until then: "Rejoice in our confident hope. Be patient in trouble, and keep on praying" (Romans 12:12 NLT). Your daughter needs your prayers now more than ever. Flood the heavens with them.

From My Prayer Journal

NOVEMBER 23, 1997

Dear Lord, I pray for Kim's deliverance. May she know You, Lord, and not be persuaded by a cult or stay lost in the world. Surround her with Christians who will show her Your love. Show me what You want me to do to persuade her, Lord. She's so skeptical of Christianity.

Let's Pray Together

Father, we pray for lost daughters who haven't yet returned to You or to their families. What heartbreak is ours as long as we don't know where she is or what she's doing. Bring her back, Lord. Bring godly people into her life whom she'll listen to. Protect her. Save her. We release our daughter to You fully, completely, trustingly. We give You full control over her life, knowing we never really had it anyway. We love You, Lord. In Jesus's name we pray, amen.

Family and Support Group Discussion

1. What are your feelings regarding your daughter's lack of repentance?

2. Where are you in the stages of grief, and how can your group pray for you?

3. How successful have you been in surrendering your daughter completely to God? What do you do when the inevitable times come when you doubt God?

4. What gives you hope?

Your Prayer Journal

Express your feelings regarding your daughter's lack of repentance.

Welcoming Home Your Prodigal Daughter

Pray like this:
Our Father in heaven, may your name be kept holy.
May your Kingdom come soon. May your will be done on earth,
as it is in heaven. Give us today the food we need, and forgive
us our sins, as we have forgiven those who sin against us.
And don't let us yield to temptation,
but rescue us from the evil one.
If you forgive those who sin against you,
your heavenly Father will forgive you.
MATTHEW 6:9–14 NLT

CELEBRATING
HER RETURN

There is more joy in heaven over one lost sinner who repents
and returns to God than over ninety-nine others who are
righteous and haven't strayed away!

LUKE 15:7 NLT

One day, sooner or later, hopefully sooner,
I'll run to meet my daughters on the road home, because I'm
watching and praying for their return, and we'll celebrate like
we've never celebrated before!

ROBIN

CELEBRATING HER RETURN

❖

*My mom and Aunt Kim are beginning to trust me. . . . My entire
family is happy that I am whole again and part of them. I pushed
them away for so long, and now they have welcomed me back. I
am touched, sometimes floored, by their love and acceptance.*[1]
ASHLEY SMITH

♡ A Praying Mother Shares
(*Continued from chapter 21*)

Our hearts were pounding with anticipation as we knocked on Bobbi's
door. There she stood—the daughter we hadn't seen in many months.
She looked great! We hugged, we kissed. We talked about her reasons
for running away, her plans for the birth of her child, her life as a single
mom of seventeen. Oh, it was good to see her again and to know she
was alive and well. We had all missed her so much. God, thank You for
keeping her safe and bringing us to this wonderful moment!

Bobbi decided she wanted to stay in the desert for the birth of her
baby but asked if she could come home to complete her high school education. It was the plan we had prayed she would want. Anticipating
Bobbi and our new grandchild coming home was just what we needed
to melt the pain of the long months we'd endured. It was time to forgive
and forget and look to the future.

Bobbi never left our hearts, only our house. We welcomed her back
with open arms. She ran away a teenager—scared, embarrassed, and
pregnant. Because of God's grace, she returned home a young woman—
a mother ready and eager to handle the challenges ahead of her. We
would help her, but we knew she could do it.

—*Mary*

🐦 A Prodigal Daughter Shares

(Continued from chapter 22)

When I entered college, I had sunk so deep into sin, I adopted a new worldview that justified my lifestyle and lifted the guilt. Whatever Christian roots I had were gradually deteriorating, and ultimately, I found myself disillusioned and resentful at the way I was brought up and didn't consider the Bible to be in tune with the "real world."

Shortly after 9/11, there were rumors of an impending terrorist attack in Los Angeles. My roommate and I decided, "If this is the last night of our lives, we might as well live it up and party all night!" So we shared a bottle of tequila. I recall lying in complete blackness with my head spinning, thinking that if this were going to be the night our world ended, I should probably call my family to tell them I loved them. I called my sister. She thought it was a suicide message. I told her I loved her and said, "Tell Mom and Dad I love them too." I didn't want them to know how intoxicated I was. It didn't matter if I missed talking to my parents, since I would see them in heaven. Then it hit me—if I'm too ashamed to face my parents and couldn't even tell them I loved them, how could I stand before the almighty God of the universe? There's no way I would deserve to go to heaven . . . that's *not* where I would go!

That realization, along with the fact that I valued the pleasure of sin more than my relationship with my family, was profoundly shocking. At that moment all my intellectual reasoning, debating, and rationalizing meant nothing. I became very aware of the eternity that was always written on my heart. I was haunted by the relentless thought, *What if I'm wrong?* That "someday" I kept vaguely thinking about was supposed to be *now*. This epiphany led me on a search for absolute truth and to change my lifestyle. What suddenly mattered more than anything was living the way God intended. I asked God to reveal the truth so I could believe it.

The conversion didn't happen overnight. At one point I didn't want to live anymore; yet I didn't want to die either. I was desperate. I found myself in church on the premise of observing. The Lord led me to a series of apologetics seminars, where my mind finally met the place where God was guiding my heart. I actually ran out of excuses and repented of the rebellion. I was baptized again, this time to symbolize my eternal commitment.

—*Loren*

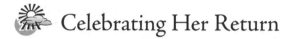 Celebrating Her Return

Not every homecoming is as joyful as Bobbi's. Some parents erroneously expect everyone's troubles to be over when their daughter returns home. A recovering meth addict's mother lamented, "I thought she would come home from drug rehab 'fixed,' and never want another fix. Like you put the car in the shop when it needs work, and it comes out repaired." But as Loren said, it doesn't happen overnight. We seldom pick up where we left off before our prodigal went astray—and we shouldn't. The dynamics of the family have changed. Our daughter has to prove she's trustworthy, and that takes time. For our part, we can encourage her by looking for things she's doing right and welcoming her home.

Her prodigal days will probably have consequences—maybe a child . . . jail time . . . money to pay back . . . relationships to break or restore. We can't settle everything in the first week or month. Everyone needs time to adjust and work through the process of the prodigal's restoration to her family and, hopefully, to God. When we come to God, He doesn't list our previous sins or meet us with a stern, disapproving, "I know you're going to mess up again" attitude. He greets us with open arms, tells us He's been praying and waiting for this day, and if we let Him, He'll help us not to stumble again. This is how we greet our prodigal too.

Addicts talk in terms of how many years, months, days, and sometimes minutes they've been clean or sober. Doing the next right thing *every* time they have a choice is the most difficult hurdle. Many prodigals go through rehab programs but fall back into their addiction when they let their guard down. Sometimes it takes several attempts.

Others return home just long enough to get a good meal, sleep in their old bed, steal money and things to sell, and hit the prodigal road again, often in the middle of the night. I also know parents who've spent thousands of dollars on attorney's fees and bailing their child out of jail only to have her turn around and land in jail again. We want to believe our daughter is sincere when she rushes back into our life and arms, but we should be cautious until we see whether her heart has truly changed.

Sharron wrote: "After we found her, I just wanted my precious daughter safely back home. She did come home for a while, but she didn't stay—circumstances were against us. She had grown up and become a woman; but we were estranged. Even though it wasn't her desire, her leaving a second time broke my heart all over again."

We should be excited about our daughter's return, but we can't let our emotions overtake our better judgment. So first, stop and pray, thanking God for this miracle! Then ask Him for wisdom and discernment as to how sincere your daughter is and how you should proceed. Next, take an assessment of the things we talked about in chapter 19 and address any changes you might need to make. Maybe as parents you were enablers in the past, but now you'll be accountability partners. It's a two-way relationship—everyone readjusts and reassesses.

If she's returning to your home, review chapter 12, bring out your Family Survival Plan, and go over each point, asking your daughter to agree to abide by it. Right from the beginning, set up consequences, outlining what will happen if she doesn't. Then stick to your guns. Sometimes true repentance takes a few tries.

If we really want to help our returning daughter, we can't be too lenient, overly strict, expect perfection, or bring up all the things she's done wrong in the past. She's painfully aware of those, and rehashing them will probably push her away. However, we do need to be honest. We tell her we want to believe her. We won't be looking for her to do things wrong, but we won't be turning our backs either.

Our prodigal daughter won't shed dysfunction like changing her dirty clothes. She may have a great deal of baggage from the life she's been leading, so her first step in returning is admitting she needs help.

And for parents, it's admitting we don't have all the answers. Our returning prodigal might need to agree to counseling or going to a day or live-in rehab center or camp. If drugs are an issue, random drug tests are appropriate. No addiction is easy to break, and we definitely need professionals helping guide our daughter and us.

Youth minister and author Megan Hutchinson advised: "There are things you can do to nudge your struggling teen toward a heart of change, leading him [or her] (hopefully) to choose healthier behaviors. To help a teenager heal, he [she] must be surrounded by caring adults who will support him [her] through the healing process. It's important to remember that addictions don't happen overnight, and neither does healing. . . . With every story of recovery or healing, deliberate and practical steps toward change were taken."[2]

Not every prodigal is a teenager or an addict, but the process of healing and "coming home" is similar. As one mom put it, "They don't come home one day smelling like a pigpen and get up the next morning smelling like a rose—doing everything the way you'd like."[3]

It's important to determine whether our daughter truly is repentant. That means saying she's sorry, asking for forgiveness, being willing to make restitution, and agreeing to change. We'll talk more about forgiveness in chapter 24, but if she calls on the phone or shows up on our doorstep saying, "Okay, I'm ready to come home now," we make a big mistake if we don't stop and try to discern whether she's broken in spirit and truly ready to repent of her sins. How can we know that?

Vickie Arruda counseled, "Only when parents have learned to let go and turn over their children to God will they be in a position to recognize true brokenness." Vickie also pointed out that although the father of the prodigal son threw his arms around his son and kissed him upon his return, "the father did not call for the robe, ring, or shoes until after hearing his son's brokenness."[4] "Father, I have sinned against heaven and against you. I am no longer worthy to be called your son" (Luke 15:21).

If our daughter is prideful, defiant, belligerent, angry, or manipulative, she's not broken in all the right places. She may be broke, but not broken. There's a difference, and we set ourselves up for more heartache if we try to lean on our own understanding and don't ask God for wisdom. Chances are you've been down that road before.

A prodigal may quit her addictions and bad behavior but not give her heart to Jesus. Or she may say she believes in God but isn't ready to go to church or change her lifestyle. Let me warn you: This isn't a truly repentant prodigal, and it's almost impossible for her to stay clean of her sinful behavior without God at the center of her life. Forcing her isn't the answer, but keeping the discussion open is.

I've found with Kim that asking questions is far more effective than lecturing. Often she works her way through to the resolution I was hoping for. So ask, "Why don't you want to go to church?" Point out that saying she loves God but doesn't want to go to church is like saying she loves you, but she never wants to come to your house. Find out the reason. Then you'll know better how to pray that this barrier comes down.

You might learn that she is embarrassed to go to church . . . feels she won't fit in . . . feels guilty . . . is afraid people will ask embarrassing questions . . . doesn't feel worthy or accepted. Those are legitimate feelings and concerns, and it doesn't help to tell her she shouldn't feel that way, because she does. But now you know how to pray for her. *Show* her church. Invite godly people into your home. Pray at meals and include her in family devotions. Love her back into the church by showing her the love of Christ.

It might be time to check out a new church, where she'll feel more comfortable and where no one knows her story. Maybe a biblically based recovery program will be her "church" for now. Assist her in finding a place where she feels she fits in with others who've been through a similar journey. With your daughter home, you'll have a better chance to influence her healing. Don't stop praying daily, but don't be discouraged if she doesn't have an immediate spiritual heart change or reawakening.

When Kim called after college graduation and asked if she could come home, I was ecstatic. I thought, *Here's my chance to win her for the Lord.* It was during this time that I found out she had "gone forward" at a church youth camp. I was so excited that I brought home pamphlets on baptism and was sure she'd want to start going to church with us.

But she wasn't ready for either. We had made headway, but it wasn't going to happen all at once. I needed to stay on my knees in prayer, and God still had work to do in her heart. My part was not to be disappointed but to stay diligent. I continuously prayed, thanking God for the small victories, and kept my eye on the big one: her complete and total surrender to God. What I didn't know then was that surrender was still a couple of years away.

When the glorious day did come that we baptized Kim and her fiancé Toby two weeks before their wedding, I knew they were babies in the Lord. They were going to need mentoring in how to live a godly life. Kim was living with a roommate, Toby had moved into the apartment they would live in after they were married, and Kim was starting to move her things over to that apartment. I knew how tempting it would be for her to move in completely.

I prayed for the right words and simply had an open and honest conversation suggesting she live at our house the remaining weeks before their wedding. She moved back home that night. I cared enough to confront. I knew she was treading water as a new Christian and might need a lifeguard.

Help your daughter be successful, no matter what her age. If she shows a desire to change her ways, guide her to the right way. Don't set your expectations so high, though, that you can't celebrate small milestones. This is what we've been praying for. This is the long-awaited miracle. We want to be like the prodigal's father in the Bible, standing at the gate with open arms, covering our prodigal with embraces, putting her at the head of the table to signify her return to her rightful place in the family, and then throwing a party!

☕ Parent to Parent

What to Do When She Repents and Returns

- ❖ Thank God for giving her and you this opportunity.
- ❖ Celebrate! Cook or go out for her favorite meal.

+ Surround her with love—and with accountability.

+ Review the boundaries of living at home and/or your relationship.

+ Commit to helping her be successful.

+ Keep your eyes open for backsliding or lack of true repentance, and confront it.

+ Stay on your knees before the Lord, praying for success in restoring your family.

+ Give God the glory for your reunion.

From My Prayer Journal

OCTOBER 28, 1998

Lord, please give Kim the strength to withstand the evil darts that may come at her as a new Christian. Give us wisdom to disciple her and Toby.

Let's Pray Together

Lord, we praise You that our daughter is back. Please guide her to a good and fruitful life, and guide us in how to help her. Give us eyes to see and words to share the truth—thank You for Your truth that sets our daughter free. Help her to be successful. Keep us supportive and patient. Amen.

Family and Support Group Discussion

1. How do you feel about your daughter's repenting of her ways?

2. In what ways are you prepared to help her be successful?

3. What obstacles will you both have to overcome?

4. How can you celebrate her return?

 Your Prayer Journal

Your daughter is home! Scream, yell, praise the Lord, sing songs of praise, fill the pages with your joy. You've waited a long time for this.

_____

_____

_____

_____

_____

_____

_____

_____

_____

_____

_____

_____

_____

_____

_____

_____

_____

_____

EXTENDING UNCONDITIONAL FORGIVENESS

Lord, if you keep in mind our sins
then who can ever get an answer to his prayers?
But you forgive! What an awesome thing this is!
PSALM 130:3–4 TLB

We must forgive them even if they never repent.
It will destroy us if we don't.
CHRIS ADAMS

EXTENDING UNCONDITIONAL FORGIVENESS

❖

*The concept of forgiveness is as slippery as a greased watermelon
in a swimming pool. The harder you squeeze it,
the more slippery it becomes.*[1]
EVERETT L. WORTHINGTON JR.

♡ A Praying Mother Shares

After my daughter walked out the door, the stillness in my apartment
sent a chill down my spine. The walls closed in, and I felt suffocating
panic. What just happened? I wasn't unreasonable. I loved my daughter
and wanted what was best for her. I shivered. Where would she go?
How will she survive? I shouldn't have yelled.

As night fell, I couldn't move even to turn on the light. *Oh God, what
am I going to do? Linda is only eighteen. Have I failed as a mother because
I didn't let her take advantage of me? Please, please keep her safe. Bring her
home soon.*

She'd come home with a boyfriend asking if he could move in. I said
no. Without saying a word, Linda went to her room, reappeared with a
backpack, and defiantly said, "Then I'm leaving!" My heart and mind
struggled to unravel why Linda had become a prodigal. She'd been hurt
and angry after her dad left us, and her present actions probably were
another way of acting out that anger.

Hours passed with no word. After making several phone calls, I
learned that none of her friends had seen her. The next day I prayed repeatedly, "Please, Lord, keep her safe, and bring Linda home." Two days
later I prayed, "Lord, I don't know where she is. I need to know." The call
finally came: "Mom, we're living with one of Greg's friends in Newport

Beach." I went to see her and pleaded, "Linda, how are you going to manage? Come home and finish school." "No, Mom. My life is none of your business."

Wow! What had I done to deserve this? I drove home in tears. That night I prayed, "Lord, I give my daughter to You. You love her enough to die for her, so I know You have a plan for her life."

Six weeks later, Linda called: "Mom, we're living in Palm Springs. I love you, and I'm sorry. Now I understand how hard it is to be responsible and pay rent and bills. I appreciate how you took care of us." I said, "I love you, too, Linda. And the door is always open."

I continued praying. When she invited me to visit, they were living in an unfurnished vacation home and sleeping in sleeping bags. Even under those circumstances, a new, loving relationship developed between us. I knew I had to show her unconditional forgiveness for her actions and the way she had hurt me. If I rejected her, the cycle of anger would continue. I trusted God to show me how to love her without condoning her choices. God led me to Proverbs 10:12, which says, "Hatred stirs up dissension, but love covers over all wrongs."

Three years passed before the day I'd been waiting for—Linda came home. I helped her get a job, and joy returned. At twenty-three, she married a wonderful young man. I'd never stopped praying for Linda to come back to the Lord. That day arrived too. I realized I had not been alone in wanting the best for my daughter—God wanted it too.

Karen

My Daughter Kim Shares

Mom, when you and Dad first divorced, I saw my dad frequently. Over the years, I saw less and less of him. I missed him and the relationship we once had, and I know I've made many wrong choices trying to fill that void in my life.

I became angry and resentful of the consequences of the divorce. I plotted how one day I would get revenge. That was until Toby and I both accepted Christ, and I felt my heart starting to change.

I remember telling you through tears and sobs about my new, strange feelings of suddenly not wanting revenge but wanting to forgive instead. I asked you, "Is this what it means to be a Christian—to forgive those who had hurt me?" You said yes.

I find forgiveness is a daily process. However, I know what it feels like to operate out of revenge and anger, and I never want to go back to letting bitterness control my feelings.

Extending Unconditional Forgiveness

When Kim asked me those questions about forgiveness, I was full of joy because I knew for sure that this time she really had accepted Jesus as her Savior. I could see the evidence of His softening her heart and renewing her mind right before my eyes. She had accepted Christ's forgiveness, and one of the first things she wanted to do as a new Christian was to forgive others. I remember praying, "Thank You, Lord! She really is a believer. This time it took!"

Acceptance is something our daughters crave—from their peers and from us. If they don't get it, they search for it in all the wrong places. Now is our chance to give our daughters the acceptance they so long for by unconditionally forgiving them as Christ forgave us: "If your daughter sins, rebuke her, and if she repents, forgive her" (personalization of Luke 17:3).

If our hearts hold even a speck of malice or anger toward her, she'll sense it, and we won't be able to wholly restore our relationship. Instead, it will teeter precariously as we just wait for her to do something wrong again. Then the feelings we've been harboring inside will flood out, confirming that we haven't completely forgiven her: "For out of the overflow of the heart the mouth speaks" (Matthew 12:34).

Praying mother Sharron knows about pent-up anger:

At first I was incredibly hurt by my daughter's behavior. The friendship I thought we had now felt like betrayal. I believe God wanted me to let go of any rights I felt I had—or deserved: the right to a good, loving relationship with my daughter . . . the right to mutual respect between us. It's surprising how we feel entitled to such a long list of "rights."

I became surprisingly aware of anger stored in my heart toward my own mother, and it forced me to evaluate other areas where I harbored anger. Thank God, I reached a place of sorrow where I couldn't harbor anything that wasn't right before Him. I recognized how much forgiveness I needed from God. In my brokenness, my heart overflowed with the warmth of His love—I could not help but feel a deep forgiveness for my precious daughter.

The primary reason we forgive is because Christ forgave us. Ephesians 4:31–32 instructs us, "Get rid of all bitterness, rage and anger, brawling and slander, along with every form of malice. Be kind and compassionate to one another, forgiving each other, just as in Christ God forgave you." Think back to your actions before knowing Christ. Harrowing isn't it? Now visualize them listed on a white board and Jesus taking an eraser and wiping the board clean. Then He says, "Go and sin no more" (John 8:11 NLT). The Lord doesn't bring our transgressions back to our minds, but Satan does. He loves making us feel guilty and unworthy, and he tempts and torments us to go ahead and sin again. Sometimes we give in, but when we confess and ask for forgiveness, Jesus is ready with the eraser. Can we not do the same for our daughters? I believe Jesus would say to us, "If you forgive your daughter who sinned against you, your heavenly Father will forgive you" (personalization of Matthew 6:14 NLT).

However, God doesn't wipe away the consequences of sin. Our daughter—and we—must live with those consequences. Often we need to ask for forgiveness from others we've harmed as we've gone along our sinful way—and so will our daughter. That's a key point. When we forgive our daughter, we forgive her for how her actions affected us. We cannot forgive her for what she inflicted on others or on herself. Only they and she can do that. For example, let's say she drunkenly hit someone with our car. We can forgive her for damaging our car, but only the person she hit can forgive her for the damage she did to him or her. And that person may choose not to forgive. Only our daughter can forgive herself, as will God if she asks Him, for harming someone else through her actions. Or if she has had an abortion, we can forgive her for depriving us of our grandchild, but again, only she can forgive herself, and God will too, when she asks, for causing the death of her own child.

Unconditional forgiveness means we give up the right to visit an incident ever again. We address new offenses with new acts of forgiveness. *Webster's Encyclopedic Unabridged Dictionary of the English Language* defines *forgiveness* as a "disposition or willingness to forgive."[2] It isn't something we can be shamed or talked into—our hearts have to be ready. Unconditional forgiveness isn't dependent on what the other person does or on whether she returns or repents. It's extended freely, regardless of whether it's accepted or reciprocated. And we don't have to confront the person to do it. Even if we haven't seen our daughter in years, we can choose to forgive her. Forgiveness isn't dependent on her presence, just our predisposition.

Many times I tried reconciling with my mother; but she wouldn't agree to meet unless we attached blame to every offense. Of course, she never "felt up to that," so for fifteen years we lived estranged. One day I was sitting in church when Pastor Rick Warren said that if you harbor unresolved anger or unforgiveness, you'll never experience genuine love. The Holy Spirit tugged on my heart. I'd been single for almost seventeen years, and I knew that until I made peace with my mother, I'd never have true love.

My mother was in a nursing home, so I sent a letter saying that Kim and I were coming to visit, and we went. I asked Mom for forgiveness, but as I expected, she never asked for my forgiveness. That wasn't the point of the meeting. I just needed to let her know that I was sorry for my part and that I forgave her. I didn't let the conversation go back to old wounds. Even when she slung verbal arrows, they bounced off instead of penetrating as they had in the past. Miraculously, it wasn't long before I couldn't remember the bad things my mother had done. Instead, I found myself, just as when I was a young girl newly saved, trying to share Jesus with my mother and praying for her heart to soften. That same year, I met and married my husband, Dave, and the next year my mother died.

Why should we forgive the seemingly unforgivable? Because it frees us from bitterness and having a hardened heart and all the repercussions those bring about in our own lives—including leading us to sin. When my father was murdered, my mother blamed God. She lived with the bitter root of unforgiveness strangling her heart, and she experienced physical, spiritual, and emotional illness. Unforgiveness holds us back from the best God wants for us. The replayed anger, hurt, bitterness, hatred, hostility, and fear are destructive emotions Satan uses to get a foothold in our relationships and our lives.

Author Frederick Buechner graphically described the ravages of anger and unforgiveness: "To lick your wounds, to smack your lips over grievances long past, to roll over your tongue the prospect of bitter confrontations still to come, to savor to the last toothsome morsel both the pain you are given and the pain you are giving back—in many ways it is a feast fit for a king. The chief drawback is that what you are wolfing down is yourself."[3]

Unconditional forgiveness means forgiving even when the person has not repented or asked us to forgive her. Even when she doesn't say she's sorry. Even when she continues to sin. Only through daily prayer and conversations with God is such forgiveness possible. In our humanness, we cannot do it; but with the Holy Spirit indwelling us, we can. The Holy Spirit prompts us to obey the teachings in Romans 12:14–19 to turn over every unforgiving thought to God: "Bless those who persecute you; bless and do not curse" (verse 14). "Live in harmony with one another" (verse 16). "If it is possible, as far as it depends on you, live at peace with everyone. Do not take revenge, my friends, but leave room for God's wrath, for it is written: 'It is mine to avenge; I will repay,' says the Lord" (verses 18–19).

God will take care of things while we keep our minds focused on "whatever is true, whatever is noble, whatever is right, whatever is pure, whatever is lovely, whatever is admirable" (Philippians 4:8). When we keep our minds focused on positive things, we're told: "The God of peace will be with you" (Philippians 4:9). Ah . . . living peacefully—doesn't that sound wonderful?

I hope you see that when we don't forgive a prodigal daughter, we allow her to control our lives and emotions. It makes us victims, and we take on a victim mentality. Our prodigal daughter may try pulling this one on us: "You did or didn't do something, and that's why I'm the way I am today." It may be true, but it doesn't excuse her behavior. As godly parents, we must not match her poor behavior. Forgiving will be a big step in our own recovery from this crisis and will set a great example for her to follow.

On our own, this isn't easy. We know in our heads to forgive; however, it can't be solely an act of the mind and will. It must be an inclination of the heart. Forgiveness takes time and much prayer, but it's an essential step to healing both our relationships and ourselves.

☕ Parent to Parent

Here are some common myths that might hinder us from forgiving our daughter.

Ten Forgiveness Myths

Forgiveness . . .

1. makes what our daughter did okay—it condones her behavior.

2. wipes away her offenses and actions as if they'd never happened.

3. lets her off the hook. She won't have to suffer consequences.

4. frees her to go and do it again. We turn our backs to what she did or still has potential to do.

5. can be extended to those who didn't personally offend or hurt us.

6. is forgetting what happened.

7. requires reconciliation even if she could potentially harm us.

8. expects her to make up for all the hurt she caused.

9. means she has to change.

10. obligates her to say she's sorry and/or ask for our forgiveness.

None of these statements is valid. They reflect the world's idea of forgiveness—not God's. Let's take a closer look at how and why we forgive. Let me reemphasize that it's truly impossible to forgive completely without the help and promptings of the Holy Spirit, who dwells in a Christian's heart. Forgiveness isn't something we can work at; we just need to look inward and upward. We pray for the Holy Spirit to give us strength to do what we cannot do alone. Now let's look at the truth about forgiveness.

Ten Forgiveness Truths

Forgiveness . . .

1. does not make what our daughter did okay—it doesn't condone. Her behavior still is wrong or sinful. Forgiveness means choosing to forgive in spite of what she did.

2. does not wipe away her offenses and actions as if they'd never happened. They're real, and we must address them.

3. does not let her off the hook; it lets us off the hook. She will live with the punishment and/or consequences of her sin, but we won't live with the consequences of an unforgiving heart.

4. does not free her to go and do it again. We're not ignoring her transgressions; we're facing them: "We don't like what you did, and you'll face punishment or consequences, but we're not holding it against you for the rest of your life."

5. does not extend universally. We only can offer forgiveness when we're the recipient of the harmful behavior or action. We can't forgive someone for the harm he or she did to others.

6. does not mean forgetting it ever happened. Only Jesus could

truly do that; however, we may find that the angry "tapes" that played repeatedly in our heads are now blank.

7. does not require reconciliation if that means potential harm to us. Often forgiveness does result in reconciliation, but forgiveness is vertical—between God and us. Reconciliation is horizontal—between our daughter and us. We forgive her to set our captive hearts free, but it might not result in reconciliation.

8. does not expect her to make up for all the hurt she has caused. We would be manipulating and sending the message that forgiveness is the reward for good works or behavior. Unconditional forgiveness has no strings that either side can pull.

9. does not mean she has to change. Then it would be conditional.

10. does not obligate her to say she's sorry and/or ask for our forgiveness.

Steps to Forgiving Our Daughter

Focus calmly on just the facts.

Objectively review her offenses.

Recall a time when someone forgave us for offending him or her.

Give mercy. Replace anger with empathy, compassion, and sympathy.

Intercede in prayer for her.

Verbally ask for her forgiveness, and forgive her.

Embrace her if she's near. Nothing melts away pain like a hug.

If we asked Jesus how many times we should forgive our daughter, I'm sure He would answer, "I tell you, not seven times, but seventy-seven times" (Matthew 18:22). Jesus was talking about unlimited, unconditional forgiveness. In other words, if we're counting, it doesn't count.

📝 From My Prayer Journal

DECEMBER 17, 1993

Dear Lord, Kim will need Your forgiveness, and I just pray she'll realize that only You can cleanse her from her sins; and more importantly that she'll realize she has sinned. Please forgive me for the sins I've committed, and give Kim the desire to be forgiven by You.

🙏 Let's Pray Together

Father, thank You for unconditionally forgiving us when we were so undeserving. Help us to extend that same forgiveness to our daughter, and open her heart to forgive us. We long for the freedom that comes from releasing our pain and sadness into Your capable hands. You tell us our burdens should be light and that You're ready to shoulder them, so we surrender any feelings of unforgiveness hiding in our hearts. Release us from their hold, and help our daughter to do the same. In Your precious, holy name we pray, amen.

🌸 Family and Support Group Discussion

1. If you're in contact with your daughter, have you extended to her unconditional forgiveness? Describe how that went and the freeing you experienced. If you don't have contact, prayerfully forgive her before God and your group.

2. Have you been able to ask for forgiveness from your daughter? How did that feel?

3. What, if any, signs of victim mentality do you see in your family or in yourself? How can forgiveness free you from that?

4. Discuss the ten myths and truths about forgiveness.

 Your Prayer Journal

Reflect, reveal, and release anything holding you back from unconditionally forgiving your daughter.

_____

_____

_____

_____

_____

_____

_____

_____

_____

_____

_____

_____

_____

_____

_____

_____

_____

_____

NURTURING THE MOTHER-DAUGHTER RELATIONSHIP

Do not forsake your mother's teaching.
PROVERBS 1:8

*Perhaps no family dynamic is more complex than the one between
a mother and daughter—an emotional cocktail that mixes love
with equal parts defiance and devotion, respect and regret.*[1]
LADIES' HOME JOURNAL

NURTURING THE MOTHER-DAUGHTER RELATIONSHIP

❖

*In that first year, I would often stand over her crib and watch
her while she slept. I would talk to God and plead with Him
to spare her from some of the painful mistakes I had made during
my growing-up years. Would she love me? Would she even
like me? Would we become lifelong friends? Would she come
to love the God I serve? . . . It would be my responsibility
to model to Paige what it means to be a godly woman.
Could I do it? Was I up for the task?*[2]

VICKI COURTNEY

♡ A Praying Mother Shares

(Continued from chapter 22)

I think of how I tried telling my daughters what they needed to do.
Later, I realized that telling them—instead of meeting them where they
were and showing them a good role model—only pushed them further
from me and where I felt they should be. As I've grown in my understanding of how a godly mother relates to her daughters, much like
Jesus relates to us, I've found that listening and setting the example have
drawn them closer to home.

—*Robin*

♡ A Prodigal Daughter Shares

My mom had a hard life. Orphaned at eighteen months and raised by
an elderly aunt in extreme poverty in South America, she later married into an abusive and explosive relationship that ended in divorce.

Relocating my brothers and me to New York, she became a highly respected businesswoman in Long Island, where she lived for forty-five years.

Mom didn't negotiate. She did whatever was necessary, always with honor, love, and dignity. Growing up, we had a rocky relationship. I interpreted her strict and restrictive ways as lacking tenderness, and I became resentful and resistant. I kept things to myself and was insecure, easily intimidated, and afraid of my every decision.

When I married, my husband and I moved to California. I visited Mom, but we couldn't connect. My children were our buffer. I remained guarded and on edge around her, feeling inadequate as a woman and a daughter.

Mom's deteriorating health eventually required moving her to a skilled nursing facility in California just before her eightieth birthday. I was terrified of having her so close, but it was "the daughter's job." The sad truth is, I was so involved in protecting myself that I failed to offer compassion or tenderness. I was so blinded by my fear of being suffocated by Mom's strength that I didn't see her fear and loss.

However, having her near turned out to be the beginning of my healing and the rebuilding of our relationship. This fiercely independent woman was completely dependent upon her daughter for the first time in our lives.

I now see these years as a gift—an opportunity to know Mom differently and to reframe my childhood. Mom was a product of her upbringing. What I felt was criticism, I now know it is how she had learned to love, care, and give. I have a new awareness and understanding of her. I want Mom to know how much I admire her tenacity, survival skills, and strength—she's my hero. What I interpreted as controlling was her way of sharing wisdom acquired through her own hardships and struggles and trying to shield me from those same experiences.

I cheated us; I know that now. My mom has forgiven and accepted me and knows I love her. She's my shining example of how our heavenly Father loves and accepts us even when we act like foolish children and run from His guidance. Mom has given my brothers and me a legacy of strength, steadfastness, goodness, survival, and forgiveness. I'm forever grateful and proud to be her daughter.

—*Brenda*

Nurturing the Mother-Daughter Relationship

Several years ago Kim came to hear me speak at a mother-daughter tea. I read to the audience Kim's own words written to me on a birthday card: "I don't have the words to tell you how much I love you. I can only tell you how fortunate I feel because I have so much more than a mother—I have a friend, someone I know will never let me down."

Then I shared with them the front of the card: "A mother is your first friend, your best friend, your forever friend." I held up a pillow I had given Kim with the inscription, "A daughter is just a little girl who grows up to be a friend." I was speaking on "Forever Friends" and encouraging mothers that even though the teen years are usually tough, they shouldn't lose hope but should keep praying. We wouldn't want to miss the wonderful season when our daughter blossoms into an adult and we can have a beautiful friendship with her.

After the tea, a mother tearfully told Kim she wished she and her daughter had the relationship Kim and I had. Kim humbly assured her that ours wasn't always like that. We'd had our tough times, but we'd made it through, and our relationship on the other side of those rebellious years couldn't be sweeter. A healthy mother-daughter relationship is one of the most rewarding gifts from God and probably one of the most fragile.

All mothers of daughters have unique stories. For mothers of prodigals, the narrative may at times seem like a horror story or a mystery. Parenting can be a painful disillusionment—not what we expected or hoped.

Being a Mom Is about Sacrifice

From the day our precious baby girls are born, we do unbelievably sacrificial things for them. However, we can't pull out the trump card—"After all I've done for you . . ."—in a manipulative or guilt-inducing way when she acts up. I know it's tempting when she ungratefully repays us with bad behavior. But being a child isn't about payback: it's about receiving a mother's unconditional love without a reminder of what the child owes his or her mother in return. Parents are supposed to provide for their children—that's our job. Parenting is a way of fulfilling the biblical mandate to love our neighbor as ourselves. Nothing in the Scriptures tells us to remind our neighbor of what she owes us for our love. I've never seen a child repent based on guilt and manipulation. It usually just drives her further away.

Being a Mom Takes Diligence

It's hard work being a mom, and when we send our kids off to school, it's tempting to let the school raise them. Maybe we go back to work, start a hobby, or pick up the life we set aside when they were born. I'm not saying there's anything wrong with pursuing our dreams, but we can never take our eyes off our children. I made that mistake.

I didn't pay enough attention to the negative influences Kim encountered at school and in the media. I foolishly remembered my own school years and assumed times hadn't changed much. I was wrong. They've changed dramatically, with removing all mention of God and Christianity from the curricula. When schools eliminated modest dress codes and started espousing extremely liberal thinking, our daughters were brought face-to-face with many worldly temptations and pressures. The luring pressure to succumb to the world's ways is intensified with television, movies, and magazines trying to outdo each other in touting the "glamour" of sin.

Vicki Courtney warned Christian mothers in her book *Your Girl*, "We must awaken from our slumber, equip ourselves for battle, and refuse to allow the world to take our girls by the hand and lead them through life. If we don't take action, be assured, our daughters will be indoctrinated into the popular thinking of the day."[3]

Kim came home from high school announcing that she believed in Creationism *and* Darwinism—one learned at church and one at school. Not knowing which authority to believe, she accepted both. I now see that this was the beginning of my declining influence on her thinking. I should have taken more time to help her discern truth from the faulty information she was getting at school, from the media, and from her friends.

Being a Mom Means Letting Go

Watching Kim turn from a teenager into a young woman meant I no longer was a "young woman." If she was maturing, I had to also. Or did I? I fought it, and that sabotaged her sense of security and grounding.

Allowing our daughter to grow into adulthood and become our friend and an extension of us requires a shifting of roles. She has her own dreams for her future, and we can't regain or relive our lost youth and dreams through her or beside her. We had a chance, and she needs hers. It's time for her to step forward and us to step back, into her shadow. Many of us don't accept the natural seasons of a woman's life. I know I didn't until I felt secure in my relationship with God.

Our motherly job is to celebrate the gifts and talents God gave our daughter and help her become a godly woman. The good news is, if we failed at this in the past, it's never too late to start. Kim and I are living proof. Our main goal as mothers should be for our daughter to imitate our faith, even if she doesn't imitate our choices of clothing or career. That's okay. Major on God and minor on what that looks like to her.

If your daughter is in the midst of her prodigal life, she may not want to talk to you or be your friend. She's rebellious, and everything you say probably makes her angry. You want to be the mom she needs, but she shuts the door in your face. As Robin said in the opening story, meet her where she is. Continue being a godly role model, and pray that another godly woman comes into her life to mentor her. I know it's difficult entrusting our mothering to someone else. It might help to read the first chapter of Luke in the Bible, which tells the story of Jesus's mother, Mary, who miraculously became an unwed, pregnant teenager. The angel Michael specifically told Mary to go visit her older relative Elizabeth, who was having her own miracle pregnancy. The Bible doesn't say why Mary didn't stay at home with her mother, but perhaps her mother was embarrassed or unsure of what to do about Mary's situation.

Young girls and their mothers often are too embarrassed to talk to each other about things like sex and boys, but they will talk to someone who's neutral. I live in Orange County, California, where a mother-daughter program is offered through Project Youth. It pairs girls ages twelve to seventeen with adult mentors. In addition, moms and daughters attend workshops separately and together, where they learn about HIV, STDs, and the names of drugs on the street and what they look like. Check to see if there's a program like this in your area.

Even if we're not emotionally distant from our daughter, we might be geographically distant. Again, a mentor can fill the gap. Christian comedian Kerri Pomarolli was away from home as a young adult and starting to stray: "I was a borderline prodigal. . . . I found a mentor who lovingly challenged me to strive for purity in my dating relationships. I learned the concept of accountability for the first time in my life."[4]

Being a Mom Means Being a Spiritual Leader

Sometimes it's frustrating trying to compete with the outside influences to which our daughters are exposed. So we cave in to pressure: "Everybody's doing it." "It's too hard to fight the system." "She needs to fit in." That breaks my heart, because essentially, it's saying we're throwing in the towel. We surrender to the world's ways. We buy into the excuse that "times are different now."

Times may be different, but the Bible is timeless. The laws of morality and truth that were God-breathed centuries ago still apply and are "useful for teaching, rebuking, correcting and training in righteousness" (2 Timothy 3:16). We mothers need to embrace biblical mandates and, with God's help, raise the bar of the standards in our homes. Are our daughters going to rebel? Probably. Will we allow ourselves to be daunted by that? Absolutely not. We have God on our side and prayer as a weapon to fight this spiritual battle. Our heavenly Father will guide and direct us in how we should guide and direct our daughters. All we have to do is ask God for direction and be willing to do the tough work of obeying Him.

Vicki Courtney also challenged mothers: "If you are to take seriously your role as the spiritual leader for your daughter, you must make sure you are providing a Christlike model for her to follow. I'm not asking you to be perfect; I'm asking you to evaluate your life honestly to see how you might need to grow in each of these areas [conformity, self-esteem, modesty, purity, boys, and girl politics] yourself."[5]

Are you ready for Vicki's challenge to be the "spiritual leader for your daughter"? I hope so. I know I am. Even if you've made mistakes in the past, as I admitted to you that I did, it's not too late. Your daughter still may be lost, but you'll pray with renewed fortitude when you accept this leadership role. Fortunately, I came to my senses, and my mission became to exemplify a godly life and retrain Kim.

Pray this verse with me: "I, _____, will instruct my daughter _____ and teach her in the way she should go; I will counsel her and watch over her" (personalization of Psalm 32:8).

With God's help and lots of prayer, Kim and I have reached the point of agreeing "in the way we should go." Hallelujah! I want the same for you and your daughter. I know you do too.

Those of you with adult daughters know the delicate balance of teaching and counseling them while not encroaching on their independence. When Kim and Toby first adopted baby Brandon, I wanted to rush up to their house. I always dreamed of helping with her first child. However, Kim feared that since Brandon had been in a foster home for two weeks, he wouldn't bond with them with someone else around—so she wanted me to wait a week. She asked if my feelings were hurt. I admitted it was disappointing, but I understood. This was more about her being a new mother than my being a new grandmother. I prayed for the right heart to give this little family the time they needed. Of course, after a week of sleepless nights and searching on the Internet to learn what to do with a new baby, Kim greeted me with open arms when I arrived.

Nine months later, when Katelyn was born, at Kim's request I canceled all my speaking engagements and spent more than a month with her, helping her care for her two babies. This time, she wanted me there *before* Katelyn was born. Had I made a fuss about waiting to see Brandon, I might not have been as welcome.

While I wasn't always there for Kim when she needed me as a child, the Lord has fulfilled His promise: "I will repay you for the years the locusts have eaten" (Joel 2:25). I now have my priorities straight. Kim is a wonderful mother, balancing two babies only nine months apart, and I'm her biggest cheerleader. I need to treat her as the adult and mother that she is and be her encourager, friend, and—hopefully—source of wise counsel.

If your daughter is newly repentant, your goal is to help her be successful. Be Christ-like with her regardless of what she has done. Jesus is the one we want her to see in us. Jesus is the one we want to see in her, so we have to show her what that looks like.

Like Brenda in the opening story, we often look back as adults with a much better understanding of our mothers and why they did the things they did. Sometimes we find we've become just like them, as much as we've tried not to. But other times we've successfully corrected the areas in which she was weak and used that knowledge to become better moms ourselves.

My mom didn't have Jesus in her life—I see that now. Instead of becoming an estranged, rebellious daughter, I should have helped her find the Lord. I realized that a year before she died. I don't know if I was too late. What if I'd been praying for her all those years instead of running from her? Mothers need their daughter's prayers too.

☕ Parent to Parent

Remember that daughters never outgrow their need for our prayers. Initially, after Kim's baptism, I thought my work of daily prayer was over, and I put away my prayer journal for her. But it wasn't out of sight for long, because soon she and her new husband were facing many decisions. I knew my best chance to be a positive influence was to continue praying God's will for her life. If God wanted me to intervene, I trusted He would tell me; and if He wanted me to ask her questions, He'd tell me that too. To this day, I still pray daily for my daughter.

Ask your daughter for prayer requests. Rather than just stating, "I'm praying for you," ask, "How can I pray for you today?" Those probably will be the times she opens up the most, and you can discover what's happening in her life. She will come to appreciate and welcome your prayers . . . and to expect them.

Recently, when Kim was leaving after a visit, I sadly put the babies in their car seats and kissed and hugged them good-bye. I again found myself standing in the driveway where, thirteen years earlier, I had sobbed on my knees when Kim drove down the same street in her little blue car packed for college. Now I was crying as I watched her drive a big blue car packed with two babies and all her family's gear, headed to their home four hours away. Suddenly I realized I had forgotten to pray with her for their safe trip. I immediately prayed, then called Kim's cell phone to tell her. She said, "Yeah, Mom, I was wondering why you didn't pray for us."

What a difference years and God can make. And so, we mothers pray for our daughters and pray that we are the women we want our daughters to become.

✔ From My Prayer Journal

JUNE 8, 1995

Lord, let Kim's inheritance be from You. May I leave her a legacy of a Christian mom that she wants to pattern her life after.

Let's Pray Together

Lord, it's hard, and yet so rewarding, being a mother to our daughters. It's a big responsibility, and we make mistakes. Help us to be mothers who gracefully mature and don't live our lives vicariously through our daughters. Instead, guide us in teaching them to live dependently on You and independently of us. Please raise them up to be godly women. For those daughters still in Satan's grip, please loosen the hold. Free them and put them on the path that leads to You. Amen.

Family and Support Group Discussion

1. What's it like being the mother of a daughter?

2. What type of a relationship do you have with your daughter? Are you happy with it?

3. How can you become the spiritual leader of your daughter? If you already are fulfilling that role in her life, share with the rest of the group how you do it.

4. What was your relationship like with your mother, and how does that influence you today?

Your Prayer Journal

Share with God the joys and sorrows of being the mom of a daughter.

_____

_____

_____

_____

_____

26

NEEDING
A FATHER

O Lord, you are our Father.
We are the clay, and you are the potter.
We all are formed by your hand.
ISAIAH 64:8 NLT

*When my father and I were in the car together, we never listened
to the radio; instead we would talk. Sometimes he even told me
about his problems, which was very flattering. I have few
memories of what we talked about. I only remember that he
always listened, always had the right response, always made me
feel not simply loved but treasured.*[1]
LANITA

NEEDING A FATHER

❖

*My dad was unaware of my spiritual turmoil, and while I don't
blame him, there's something sad about spiritual and emotional
distance in a father-daughter relationship.*

LOREN

♡ A Praying Father (My Husband) Shares

I wanted to be the best dad I could be, but I discovered that if you don't
know your heavenly Father, you don't know how to be a good dad. In
my early years of fatherhood, I focused on having a successful career and
providing for my family, as I thought dads and husbands were supposed
to do. But over the years my family relationships suffered. My three children didn't have a dad around to be involved in their lives, and my first
marriage crumbled. It was during my separation and eventual divorce
that I sought to restore my relationship with the Lord and learned what
success really looks like—being a godly man. I wanted my children to
experience Jesus in their lives too, and one by one they all became Christians.

As a single dad I remained a part of my children's lives. My oldest
daughter chose to live with me, and we learned to share life together, including playing on the church softball team. I participated with my children in Young Life, a Christian organization for kids, and often we went
to church together.

When I married Janet, we were determined to make our marriage a
good model for our children. I had become a godly man and understood
the role of being a spiritual leader of our home, and today I mentor my
son and sons-in-law to do the same.

Janet and I have prayed our prodigals home, and I have the opportunity to share what I learned with all our children and their spouses

about how to prioritize their lives by putting God first in each of their families, and families before careers. I pray for my daughters and my daughter-in-law to support and encourage their husbands to be spiritual leaders in their homes.

—Dave Thompson

A Prodigal Daughter Shares

My parents divorced when I was seven. I started out living with my mom and then tried three months with my dad, but I longed for a "family." When given a choice of where to live permanently, I chose my brother and his wife. I accepted Christ as a little girl, but by twelve, I was hanging out with the wrong crowd and experimenting with alcohol and sex. My mother had moved into a trailer with her boyfriend, and my dad had a girlfriend who wasn't interested in his kids.

At seventeen I was sleeping regularly with my boyfriend. When my brother's wife found out, we argued. I went to my dad and complained. His only advice was follow the rules or move out. So I moved into my own apartment, got two jobs, and completed high school. My boyfriend and I continued our wild party life: he was heavily into drugs. It wasn't long before I was too. Then he cheated on me, and we broke up.

I moved in with another brother, who was a Christian, and he tried to help me straighten out my life. Nothing *he* did worked. So knowing only *God* could help me change, my brother prayed. I stopped using drugs and started dating my boyfriend again: he, too, had given up the drug scene. We moved in together, but in my heart I knew it was wrong and prayed God would make things right. That night my boyfriend proposed. We started going to church, and he accepted Christ as his Savior. Today we're trying to raise our daughter in a godly home.

When my mother died, I found a letter from Dad in my baby book telling me how much he loved me and how sorry he was for hurting me when he left our family. I realized I wanted a relationship with my dad. I knew that my anxiousness every time my husband was late stemmed from feeling abandoned by Dad.

I've had to do the reaching out. We started out having breakfast and playing golf together, and today we're working at restoring our relationship. In fact, I'm looking forward to Dad's moving in with us. We have a lot of catching up to do.

—*Valerie*

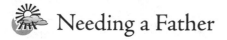 ## Needing a Father

(Note: This chapter is specifically for dads, but moms—especially single moms—will be helped by reading it too.)

I remember waking up and hearing voices. Opening my bedroom door, I noticed that my parents' bed across the hall was empty. Something was wrong. My daddy was a highway patrolman working the night shift, so he always slept late in the morning. Venturing out, I saw a room full of family and friends hovering around my mom, who was crying. Instinctively I knew what had happened. We'd always lived with this threat—now my daddy was dead. Suddenly there was a hole so big in my heart, it seemed nothing and no one could fill it.

The following summer I went to a church camp. Two camp counselors sat on my cot and asked, "We know you've lost your earthly father, but would you like a heavenly Father who never will leave or forsake you?" I said yes and accepted Jesus into my heart at the age of eleven. I excitedly told my mom of my decision to follow Jesus, but she wasn't impressed. Mom was angry with God for taking my father and replied skeptically, "That's nice for you."

My mom never remarried, and growing up I didn't have a godly male role model. I was unsure of men and didn't have my first date until college. I dated on and off throughout college; then, the day after graduation, I married the boy I dated my senior year. I didn't seek wise counsel as to whether we were marrying for the right reasons. I was caught up in the rush and glamour of getting married.

However, I had a ten-year-old's memory of my dad as my vision of what a husband was. My husband couldn't compete with that. After six years, we separated and later divorced. You've read that I became a single prodigal mom of sweet Kim. In my single years I sought approval from men, but never the right men. I always broke off the relationship just as it was getting serious—I was afraid to let anyone get too close. Kim remembers it as a time of lots of boyfriends for Mom. I was repeating the pattern of my daughter not having a godly male role model.

It wasn't until I rededicated my life to the Lord and was willing to turn my dating life over to God that I met Dave, who is now my godly husband. All those years, I was running from what I so badly wanted—a man to love me as my daddy had. No one could do that for me. I had to come to the realization that God was the only Father I needed, and I should look for a man who had His characteristics!

Kim has told me many times: "Mom, I think the father-daughter relationship is priceless. Many of the bad decisions I made growing up stemmed from needing to feel accepted by people. I had low self-esteem because I thought that if even my dad didn't want a relationship with me, I would have to try really hard to get people to love me. So I intend never to get divorced."

Dads must be aware that just as there's a special mother-daughter bond, every daughter wants to be her daddy's princess. She wants to please him and revel in his attention and love and make him proud. A mother called into Dr. Laura Schlesinger's radio program saying her daughter told a "positive lie," claiming she'd won first place in a spelling bee, but she hadn't. Dr. Laura asked the mother, "Who's the most difficult parent?" The mom quickly responded, "My husband is hard to please." Dr. Laura said their daughter lied to win Dad's approval, and if he didn't change and show her how much he loved her regardless of her performance, she'd escalate into exceedingly worse behavior . . . pregnancy, drugs, etc.

It's also from her father that a daughter learns how men should treat women. That's why it's so important for husbands to treat their wives and daughters lovingly. If Dad's abusive, the daughter will most likely continue on the destructive path of expecting physical or emotional abuse. Until we feel accepted by Jesus, we all continually seek approval that never quite fills the emptiness in our hearts.

When my daughter Kim was around ten years old and the relationship with her father was waning, I suddenly realized she needed a godly male influence. The church we attended was conducting a big brother/big sister program, so I signed up for Kim to have a big brother. I wanted her to be assigned to an older, godly man as a big brother. The leaders of the program said that wasn't possible, but I insisted. Eventually they gave in and matched her with a godly grandfather. But it wasn't the same as having a dad. He was more like a family friend or uncle. I jokingly called him our "rent-a-Dad," but Kim didn't see him as a father figure. Her dad was still her dad, and she made it clear that she didn't want anyone filling his shoes. She and my husband, Dave, have a wonderful relationship now—she refers to us as "her parents," and he is "Grandpa Dave" to her kids—but he's not her dad.

Having an absent dad doesn't necessarily lead to becoming a prodigal, but studies consistently show that daughters benefit mentally and emotionally in direct proportion to quality time spent with their fathers. I would add to that, time spent with their heavenly Father—the role model for a godly man. Some Christian men don't live out their faith, so daughters need to learn how to discern a "wolf in sheep's clothing." If Dad's in her life, he can help her learn to make that distinction. If he's not, then it's important for Mom to step in and help her learn the difference.

Without parents providing guidance and direction and staying involved in our sweet daughter's life, she can become innocent prey to a "bad boy's" evil ways. As we have seen in so many stories in this book, including my daughter's and mine, his intriguing lifestyle ensnares her, and she may renounce everything good she ever knew. Or did she ever really know good from evil? That's why an involved dad or father figure is vital. If Dad has been treating his daughter like Lanita's dad (from the opening quote) treated her, chances are significantly reduced that she'll settle for something less. Mom can also help a daughter with this, but somehow hearing it from Dad (or another godly man), whom she knows understands the male mind, makes a greater impact.

Dads, when your daughter starts dating, stay involved. You may think you've lost the chance to influence her life. You haven't! When she was little, if you saw an unsavory person hovering around her, you stepped in and protected her. Don't stop now just because she's fourteen, sixteen, eighteen, or twenty. She needs to know you care. If she's loved and cherished at home by Dad, it's doubtful she'll date a "bad boy." But if she's not receiving positive male attention, she's more prone to seeking it wherever she can get it.

Often Dad steps out of the picture just when his daughter needs him most. Maybe he feels uncomfortable as she turns into a woman or is preoccupied with his career or his own activities and leaves the child-rearing to Mom. After divorce, Dad might stop visiting or participating in his daughter's life. When Dad physically or emotionally abandons his daughter, at any age, she perceives it as rejection—even if Dad is in the home. No matter how old she is, she has an intense longing for Dad to be the most important man in her life, even if she doesn't act that way. If Dad isn't showing her love, she's probably going to find someone or something that makes her feel accepted and wanted.

Divorced dads especially must be aware that even if they stay close and do all the "right things," there's no guarantee their daughter is going to appreciate it. Be there for her anyway. Kauline wrote: "In my teens, I took out all my frustration on the one person who made the most effort to show his love. I began to blame every issue in my life—from bad grades to fighting with my sister—on the divorce. Every time we were together, I looked for a way to lash out at my father. Through all the fighting and hurtful words, he never stopped trying to spend time with me.

"Today my father and I are closer than we have ever been. It would have been easy for him to give up on me, but he did not do that. Instead he continued to love me, and he showed me by giving his time."[2]

God has called godly men to be His earthly representation as husbands and fathers. God is the *heavenly* head, and Dad is the *earthly* head, of the home. That was God's plan—the ideal. In a Christian home, it's important for the family to respect Dad as their spiritual leader. Fathers may not feel worthy of this position, but it's the role God called them to. One of the reasons we see so many confused prodigal daughters today is because few homes actually are led by godly men willing to take on this role. Moms often step into the leadership gap, but it's not God's plan for the family.

Valerie, from the opening story, told me that as she and her husband were quarreling one day, she felt convicted when her sweet little girl observed: "You two are fighting over who's in charge." Out of the mouths of babes! Our children are watching to see who's in charge of our home and our lives. Show them an "in charge" dad who answers to God.

If Dad isn't available or safe, then, Mom, pray for God to bring godly male role models into your daughter's life. Maybe it'll be a youth pastor at church, a schoolteacher, the dad of her friend, or the husband of one of your friends. It's difficult encouraging those types of relationships when we read about abuse and immorality in schools, churches, neighborhoods, and so forth. So do be cautious. Your daughter shouldn't spend time alone with these men, but arrange for her to spend time in their presence when you or other trustworthy adults are around. Have your girlfriend and her husband and kids, or the youth pastor and his wife, over for dinner or do recreational things together. Arranging for godly male influence in your daughter's life may take creativity, but it's worth it.

☕ Parent to Parent

Dads, if you're wondering how to enter into your daughter's world right now to help influence her choice of a safe boyfriend or husband, or to reconnect with her, here are some prayer suggestions. And single moms, take note also, because in the absence of Dad or another godly father figure in your daughter's life, you fill some of these roles, so this will be your prayer too.

Pray . . .

+ for God's guidance in helping your daughter make good choices.

+ that God will help you be (or, for moms, provide) a godly male role model.

+ that God will show you how to advise your daughter in a way she'll accept.

+ for protection of her heart, mind, and body.

+ that your daughter will see God as her Father ... Abba ... Daddy ... Dad ... Papa ... and run to His safe embrace regardless of her earthly father's successes or failings in a relationship with her.

+ that you will not lose hope or give up, even if you feel rejected.

+ that God will help you to be the spiritual leader of the home.

+ for an opportunity for your daughter and you to attend a Purity Ball to celebrate your father-daughter bond. At this ball, daughters are given the opportunity to choose abstinence, and dads pledge: "I, (daughter's name)'s father, choose before God to cover my daughter as her authority and protection in the area of purity. I will be pure in my own life as a man, husband and father. I will be a man of integrity and accountability as I lead, guide, and pray over my daughter and my family as the high priest in my home. This covering will be used by God to influence generations to come."[3] Even if you can't attend a Purity Ball, this is a great vow for every dad to take.

From My Prayer Journal

NOVEMBER 26, 1993

Every daughter needs a relationship with You, Father, and with her earthly father. Help restore Kim's relationship with her dad.

Let's Pray Together

Heavenly Father, we ask You to please put Your imprint on the lives of all dads. Humble them to become the men of God You ordained them to be. Help dads to love their daughter by guiding her to make healthy choices for her life. And help each mom to treat her husband with respect and prayerfully support him as the spiritual leader of the home. We love You, Father. Amen.

Family and Support Group Discussion

1. Dads, how has this chapter impacted you?

2. What might you need to do differently concerning your daughter?

3. If you feel that part of your prodigal's problem is that she is seeking a father figure, what could you do to remedy that?

4. How can you help your daughter to see God as her loving, heavenly Father?

Your Prayer Journal

Ask God to fill in the gaps an earthly father may have left in your life, or praise Him for your godly dad and grandfather to your daughter.

CHAPTER

27

SHARING YOUR TESTIMONY

You're here to be light, bringing out the God-colors in the world. God is not a secret to be kept. We're going public with this, as public as a city on a hill. If I make you light-bearers, you don't think I'm going to hide you under a bucket, do you? I'm putting you on a light stand. Now that I've put you there on a hilltop, on a light stand—shine! Keep open house; be generous with your lives. By opening up to others, you'll prompt people to open up with God, this generous Father in heaven.

MATTHEW 5:14–16 MSG

If we never share our story, God can't use it for His good. Others must hear and know they aren't alone in their journey with a prodigal. We don't have to share details, but just enough for others to know we understand and are available if they have a need. I do want my testimony to be an encouragement to other moms for sure.

CHRIS ADAMS

SHARING YOUR
TESTIMONY

❖

*I do not go to meetings right now because of publicity,
but I plan on going and sharing my story of addiction
and recovery as soon as I can.*[1]
ASHLEY SMITH

♡ A Praying Mother Shares
(Continued from chapter 19)

"God is better than He has to be." I've heard that said, and I truly experienced it this past weekend. Let me start the story a couple of months ago.

After not seeing our daughter for over eight years or hearing from her in four, I felt a compulsion to pray that God would let us know if she was alive. Her twin sister, unaware of my prayers, also was searching on the Internet, but every lead was a dead end.

At the close of our annual LifeWay Women's Ministry National Leadership Forum, I went to my office and saw that I had a voice mail. I listened to two messages, both from my missing daughter! We knew she had made contact with my sister, who had been giving her wise counsel about making a move back toward our family. It must have prompted her to call. God *had* to be in this.

I had my husband, my other daughter, and an accountability partner praying as I returned the call. I didn't know what to expect, but I wanted to hear from God and obey Him. My friend prayed according to Matthew 10:16, that I would be wise as a serpent and harmless as a dove. At first the conversation was a little awkward, but it was a sweet time nonetheless. My daughter knew nothing about my prayers or her sister's searching, which is why this had to be the Holy Spirit nudging each of us toward one another. I discovered she was still married, and we had a fifth grandchild. We set up a meeting for Saturday at one P.M. Nana (my mom) would be with us. My daughter wanted to see her and have her meet her seventh great-grandchild.

Her sister decided not to go with us, needing to first process her feelings. (She has since met with her as well.) I struggled Thursday and Friday with my own feelings of hurt, anger, and fear—what would I say? How would I react when I saw her for the first time in eight years?

On Saturday morning, while praying and weeping, I got an answer from the Lord about how to respond. The previous day, at our LifeWay chapel service, Liz Curtis Higgs, author of *Embrace Grace* and a former prodigal daughter herself, taught from Luke 15:11–32, the parable of the prodigal son. I thought of the father's arms open in love and acceptance as well as the other brother's resentment because he was the son who had stayed. A friend told me as I was leaving the office that afternoon, "Just love her."

My Saturday morning devotion was the Scripture passage where Jesus washed the disciples' feet (John 13). It was an act of love, humility, and servanthood. Praying and weeping, I clearly heard what God wanted me to do. "Just love her." I wasn't to think about the past or the pain (which I didn't think I could do) or worry about the future and if we'd get hurt again. It would be worth the risk just to love her.

While my accountability friend was again praying, God orchestrated every detail. My daughter and I both opened our arms to an indescribable hug. Two years ago, I actually dreamed about hugging her. I remember it as the most unbelievable feeling—that's what I felt Saturday. Thank You, Lord. It was exactly what she wanted, and we had prayed it would be a sweet reunion. Our granddaughter is a precious, happy baby, and our daughter's husband is friendly and kind.

The future is in God's hands, and I won't predict what I think will happen. I couldn't help thinking after I got home, *If I never got anything more than what I had today, it was worth it. If it all fell apart tomorrow, I would still praise Jesus for the precious time we had today.*

Each day I see God's love and grace a little more clearly as He repeatedly forgives and teaches me so much. He doesn't dwell on the past but just loves me today. In each situation in my life, I pray I will extend to others the same love and grace He extends to me. He truly is "better than He has to be"!

—Chris Adams

P.S. Prior to our hearing from our daughter, I asked the question: If I never heard from her again this side of heaven, would I still trust that God is good? Would I still believe He was working in the situation and be able to experience peace? I spoke my answer to those questions at a women's retreat the October prior to our reunion. Tearfully my answer was "YES!" But I'm so grateful I didn't have to wait till heaven.

My Daughter Kim Shares

Mom, I want to share my story in your book because you also need my perspective. How can you effectively write about you and me if you don't know what I was feeling? You can't teach others what to do correctly if you don't know what works and doesn't work with kids. I'm so thankful I've come to know the Lord, that my life is so blessed, and that I didn't make too many serious mistakes along the way. If I can help you save one daughter by sharing my story, then that's what I want to do!

Sharing Your Testimony

Another term for "your story" is "your testimony." A testimony focuses on God, not us. It describes our lives before we turned them over—or returned—to God and on how He changed and transformed us. Or, as with Chris Adams, it can be sharing any story in which we tell of God's mighty work in our lives. The entire family, especially the returning prodigal daughter, will have a testimony of the prodigal journey.

As Chris said in the opening quote, we don't have to give details—then the story may become more shocking than restoring. We don't focus on the awful experience but on how God's redeeming us brings restoration and hope. Simply saying something like, "Running away from home and to the dark side of life took me (her) far away from my (her) fuzzy slippers and the quilt grandma made for me (her) that warms the bed at home." That paints a graphic enough picture. Listeners can fill in the blanks. We highlight how God helped our daughter or us escape that dark place and return to the fuzzy slippers and warm quilt at home and how He will help them too. It's a story of hope. At times it may be appropriate to share more details so others truly can relate to us, but be honest—not sensational.

Your story doesn't have to have a "happy ending" for you to share it. We give our testimonies to show God's faithfulness in spite of the circumstances, to let others know they're not alone, and maybe just to stop someone else from making the same mistakes we did. Loren, who shared with you her own prodigal story, attests that "God uses my experiences of spiritual death to encourage others about the urgency of receiving life with Christ."

In God's perfect and miraculous timing, I actually was writing this last chapter when Chris e-mailed her testimony. Parts of her prodigal daughter's story were included throughout this book, before anyone knew how it would end. By God's graciousness, her story has a happy ending, and I was able to share that with you too. As a public speaker, trainer, and author on staff at LifeWay Christian Resources, Chris has told her story to numerous audiences. When she sent out the e-mails about the wonderful surprise reunion, which she titled "Amazing Grace," I counted eighty-six names in the address line, and she said thousands more had been praying for her over the years! I have the privilege of working with Chris at LifeWay, which is also the publisher of my *Woman to Woman Mentoring Resources*. The first time I met Chris, she openly shared her heartache of having a prodigal daughter.

When people tell me their hardships, I often advise them to begin journaling because it's recording the story that will become their testimony. We must be willing to share our hurts and hang-ups and how God helped us through difficult times. It's our witness to His faithfulness. It's the opportunity to give purpose to a crisis. Otherwise, we spend our lives feeling sorry for ourselves. Revealing is the first step to healing.

The Bible tells us that "the wages of sin is death" (Romans 6:23). Hidden sin has us in a death grip that will kill us from the inside out. But exposed sin loses its power. We don't have to worry about others finding out about our past. We can "thank God we've started listening to a new master, one whose commands set us free to live openly in his freedom!" (personalization of Romans 6:18 MSG). One of the steps in most recovery programs is openly telling one's testimony to a group. Public sharing frees us and allows God to minister to someone in the audience who is going through something similar. When I told people I was writing this book and would be including Kim's story, they often asked, "How does she feel about that?" I assured them she wanted her story told to help others.

Before sharing a testimony publicly, it helps to organize your thoughts and write out what you want to say. Then run it by a friend or mentor or share it in a safe small-group setting. Next, read it to an objective and trusted person who will give wise counsel—maybe a pastor or a godly grandparent. It's fine to read it—most people do. Eventually, it'll flow from the heart, but being nervous is normal, and words on a page keep us focused and on track.

Here are some suggestions for a daughter sharing her testimony and, in parentheses, how we parents can adapt the tips to tell our stories.

Ten Steps to Sharing Your Testimony

1. Pray before you start.

2. Introduce yourself and tell what your life was like before becoming (having) a prodigal.

3. What led you (your daughter) down the prodigal path? For example, was it peer pressure, abuse, family dysfunction, curiosity, rebellion, etc.?

4. When did you realize you (she) had a problem?

5. How did you admit your problem (your part in the problem)?

6. What steps, events, programs, or people helped you (you and your daughter) through your hurt and the consequences of your prodigal behavior (of having a prodigal daughter)?

7. How and when did you accept Jesus as your Savior?

8. How has Christ changed your life?

9. What are you doing now to stay on the path (help your daughter stay on the path) leading away from the prodigal road you were (she was) on?

10. Why do you want your story to be told?[2]

You won't always share your testimony in a public setting. God will bring people across your path or your daughter's, and the Holy Spirit will prompt you to share one-on-one. When people ask Kim and me how we made it through, the best answer we can give them is, "We couldn't have done it without God." And that's your best answer too!

☕ Parent to Parent

Many praying parents and prodigal daughters shared their testimonies in this book to give you, the reader, hope and encouragement. Would you be willing to do the same and share your testimony with others? Kept to ourselves, difficult times with a prodigal can be terrible, painful, and destructive. But using our experiences to help others draw closer to God and to their own healing is liberating.

If you feel it's too fresh and painful to share, write your testimony to God. As a writer, I know the freedom that comes from pouring our pain onto paper, and who better to tell it to than our Father. That's why I gave you space to journal.

When I started writing *Dear God, They Say It's Cancer,* suddenly it seemed almost everyone I met either had breast cancer or knew someone who did. In writing this book, again it seemed that everywhere I went, I met people who have a prodigal daughter or son or knows someone who does! I know this is God's spurring me on to share my story—and Kim's, and the other stories throughout these pages. A world of hurting parents are at the end of their emotional rope. Maybe that was you when you picked up this book, and you needed to hear that when you come to the end of yourself, God is waiting with a life-line. I hope you feel grounded and safe today.

Many parents told their stories in this book to encourage you to do likewise. Chris Adams shared and wrote about her story when she had no idea if her prodigal daughter was dead or alive. But just today—this very day, as I conclude this final chapter—there's another chapter in her story of God's amazing grace. She journaled that story only three days after meeting with her prodigal daughter. Chris didn't want to forget a single detail of God's goodness—she wanted to share that testimony of His faithfulness to parents' prayers. If you're wondering how to make your story into a testimony, Chris's account is a perfect example.

And here's the amazing part—her prodigal daughter gave permission for us to share it! In fact, she's pregnant again and asked Chris to accompany her to the first sonogram. Chris says she counts it a privilege. Chris and her husband, Pat, are examples of never giving up on God or their daughter. This isn't the end of their story either, we hope, but notice that Chris said that if it were—if Saturday were the only day they ever had with their returning prodigal daughter—it would be enough. It would be an answer to the parents' prayers just to have a moment with her and to know that she was alive and well, whether or not the future went the way they hoped.

Can you say that? Can you pray that? I hope so.

From My Prayer Journal

JUNE 30, 1996

Dear Lord, I pray You'll give Kim a testimony and a willingness to share it publicly.

Let's Pray Together

Father, it's scary telling our story, because some people may not understand. They may condemn or reject us. It hurts to remember and reveal the pain and sadness. But Lord, if You can use our testimony to help and encourage others, we ask You to give us the boldness and courage to tell it in a way that brings You all the glory for the great and glorious God You are! We praise You, Lord. Let Your words be our words and Your tears of sorrow and joy be our tears also. Thank you for our testimony. Amen.

Family and Support Group Discussion

1. How can you make your story into your testimony and help your daughter to do the same?

2. Write your testimony and share it in the group. Ask them to critique it.

3. Discuss potential opportunities to share your testimony, and ask the group to do the same.

4. How does it feel to share a story when you don't know the ending?

Your Prayer Journal

Think back to where you were emotionally, spiritually, and maybe even physically, when you started reading this book. How has God met you at each step of the prodigal daughter journey as you learned to pray His will for your daughter and your family?

_____

_____

_____

EPILOGUE

From My Prayer Journal

Today I observed a miracle! Last Thursday, I drove Kim and her two babies four hours back home, after their Thanksgiving visit with us. While the babies slept in the backseat and I drove, Kim wrote some of her thoughts and contributions for this book.

When we arrived, Toby said their church had called, asking if he and Kim would give their testimony of the miracle of baby Brandon's adoption and then discovering they were pregnant with miracle baby Katelyn. The pastor's sermon topic was "God's Still in the Miracle Business."

Are You ever, Lord! This Sunday I was the proud parent and Grammie snapping pictures and listening to Kim give God all the glory and praise for her two children. She talked about her own plan for how she and Toby would start a family—after they'd finished school, bought a house, and traveled, they'd be ready to have a baby when she was thirty. But it didn't happen that way. After three years of trying to get pregnant and undergoing infertility treatment, they felt God leading them to adoption. Then Toby told of the numerous people praying for them to become parents—many people they didn't even know, because Kim and Toby's prayer request had been submitted to numerous prayer chains.

There stood my daughter and her husband, with microphones in their hands, exclaiming the power of prayer. The same daughter who had been so embarrassed by her mother's prayers was now giving a public testimony of answered prayers in her life! Isn't that just like You, God, to bring it full circle.

I started journaling and praying Your will for Kim on November 16, 1993. How gracious You've been over the years to allow me to witness the fulfillment of this mother's prayers for her daughter.

❖

Moms and dads, never stop praying for your prodigal
daughter. I hope that someday she too will have a testimony
of God's faithfulness and yours. I'm praying for you.
Hang in there!
Janet

Appendix

And so I tell you, keep on asking, and you will receive what you ask for. Keep on seeking, and you will find. Keep on knocking, and the door will be opened to you. For everyone who asks, receives. Everyone who seeks, finds. And to everyone who knocks, the door will be opened.

You fathers—if your children ask for a fish, do you give them a snake instead? Or if they ask for an egg, do you give them a scorpion? Of course not! So if you sinful people know how to give good gifts to your children, how much more will your heavenly Father give the Holy Spirit to those who ask him.

LUKE 11:9–13 NLT

FORTY DAYS OF PRAYING SCRIPTURE FOR YOUR DAUGHTER

(All scriptures are personalized.)

Blessed are the parents who make the LORD their trust.
PSALM 40:4

I continue to pray specific prayers that speak to where she is, such as, "She will know the truth and it will set her free."
CHRIS ADAMS

You have read how I daily prayed personalized scriptures to use in praying for my prodigal daughter. It kept me praying God's will for her and not my will. I pray that you find comfort and encouragement, as well as hope and help, from doing the same for your daughter. You can journal your will in the Prayer and Praise Journal starting on page 321. The blank line in each scripture is for you to write in your daughter's name.

Feel free to jump around. These are in no specific order. When you finish, you can start back at the beginning, or maybe you'll want to start fresh, with whatever scriptures God brings to light for you to pray from your own Bible. Remember, this is just a guide and place to start.

Photograph of Your Daughter

1. I pray that my daughter _____ would listen to You, Lord, and that You would quickly subdue her enemies and turn Your hand against her foes! (Psalm 81:13–14)

2. Evening and morning and at noon I commit to pray and cry aloud for my daughter _____. And You, Lord, shall hear my voice. (Psalm 55:17 NKJV)

3. Lord, please teach my daughter _____ to live a disciplined and successful life and help her do what is right, just, and fair. (Proverbs 1:3 NLT)

4. Lord, I know You do not change, and I pray my daughter _____ will return to You, so You will return to her. (Malachi 3:6–7)

5. Oh, God, my Lord, step in; work a miracle for me—You can do it! Get my daughter _____ out of her troubles—Your love is so great! She's at the end of her rope, her life in ruins. She's fading away to nothing, passing away, her youth gone, old before her time. She's weak from hunger and can hardly stand up, her body a rack of skin

and bones. ... Help her, oh, help her, God, my God, save her through your wonderful love; then she'll know that Your hand is in this, that You, God, have been at work. (Psalm 109:23–24, 26–27 MSG)

6. Show my daughter _____ the right path, O Lord; point out the road for her to follow. Lead her by Your truth and teach her, for You are the God who saves her. All day long I put my hope in you. Remember, O Lord, your compassion and unfailing love, which You have shown from long ages past. Do not remember the rebellious sins of my daughter's youth. Remember her in the light of Your unfailing love, for You are merciful, O Lord. (Psalm 25:4–7 NLT)

7. Father, purify my daughter _____ from her sins, and make her clean; wash her, and she will be whiter than snow. Oh, Lord, give her joy again; You have broken her—now let her rejoice. Don't keep looking at her sins. Remove the stain of her guilt. Create in her a clean heart, O God. Renew a loyal spirit within her. Do not banish her from Your presence, and don't take Your Holy Spirit from her. (Psalm 51:7–11 NLT)

8. I pray that my daughter _____ will know the truth and that the truth will set her free. (John 8:32 NIV)

9. Lord, I pray that my daughter _____ will change her wicked ways and banish the very thought of doing wrong. Let her turn to You, Lord, and please have mercy on her. I know that if she will turn to You, God, You will forgive her generously. (Isaiah 55:7 NLT)

10. I pray that my daughter _____ will think clearly and exercise self-control. Guide her, Lord, in looking forward to the gracious salvation that will come to her when she accepts Jesus Christ. Help her to live as Your obedient child. Don't let her slip back into her old ways of living to satisfy her own desires. (1 Peter 1:13–14 NLT)

11. God, please help my daughter _____ believe that You loved her so much that You gave Your one and only Son, Jesus Christ, so that she will not perish but have eternal life. (John 3:16)

12. Dear God, I humbly ask You, please help my daughter _____ to resist the devil so he will flee from her. Draw her close to You, and I know You will come close to her. Wash her sinful hands; purify her heart, for her loyalty is divided between You, God, and the world. (James 4:7–8 NLT)

13. Lord, I pray that You will urge my daughter _____ on whenever she wanders to the left or right. Whisper in her ear: "This is the right road. Walk down this road." Then may she scrap her expensive and fashionable god-images, throwing them in the trash as so much garbage, saying, "Good riddance!" (Isaiah 30:21 MSG)

14. Lord, please guide my daughter _____ along the best pathway for her life. Advise her and watch over her. (Psalm 32:8 NLT)

15. God, You alone are my daughter _____'s refuge, her place of safety; I am trusting You to watch over her while I can't. Please rescue her from every trap, and protect her from any deadly disease or fatality. Cover her with Your feathers, and shelter her with Your wings. May Your faithful promises be her armor and protection. (Psalm 91:2–4 NLT)

16. Lord, my daughter _____ has lost her footing and been swept off her feet by lawless and loose-talking, unsavory people. Please grow her in grace and understanding of You, our Master and Savior, Jesus Christ. Yes, help her to give glory to You forever, Lord. (2 Peter 3:18 MSG)

17. Lord, I pray that my daughter _____ would come to know You and put away the old person she used to be and have nothing to do with her old sinful life. She has been fooled into following bad desires. Make her mind and heart new. Help her to become a godly person. Make her right with You, God, and help her to live a truly holy life. Stop her lying. Help her to tell the truth. (Ephesians 4:22–25 NLV)

18. Lord, my daughter _____ was furious. She lost her temper. She yelled at You, God, and at us. She said, "God! I knew it—when I was

back home, I knew this was going to happen! That's why I ran off!" Lord, I know You are sheer grace and mercy, not easily angered, rich in love, and ready at the drop of a hat to turn Your plans of punishment into a program of forgiveness! Please forgive us for our part in her leaving You and her home. (Jonah 4:1–2 MSG)

19. I pray that my daughter _____ will make You her Lord and seek Your refuge and shelter. Please don't let evil conquer her or disease come near her home. Order Your angels to protect her wherever she goes and to hold her up with their hands so she won't be hurt. (Psalm 91:9–12 NLT)

20. Father, my daughter _____ is lost. Your Son, Jesus, came to seek and save those who are lost. Please save her. (Luke 19:10 NLT)

21. Lord, please help my daughter _____ to say with her mouth that Jesus is Lord and believe in her heart that You, God, raised Him from the dead so she can be saved from the punishment of her sin. You promise that when she believes in her heart, You will make her right with You. Let her testify to others of how You saved her from the punishment of sin. (Romans 10:9–10 NLV)

22. My prayer, Lord, is not that You take my daughter _____ out of the world but that You protect her from the evil one. (John 17:15 NIV)

23. Father, as the deer desires rivers of water, please put in my daughter _____'s heart a desire to know You. Make her soul thirsty for You, the living God. (Psalm 42:1–2 NLV)

24. Lord, the sacrifice You desire is a broken spirit. I pray that my daughter _____'s wayward spirit will be broken because I know You will not reject a broken and repentant heart, O God. (Psalm 51:17 NLT)

25. Lord, when my daughter _____ follows the desires of her sinful nature, the results are very clear: sexual immorality, impurity, lustful pleasures, idolatry, sorcery, hostility, quarreling, jealousy, outbursts of anger, selfish ambition, dissension, division, envy, drunkenness,

wild parties, and other sins like these. You tell us that anyone living that sort of life will not inherit the kingdom of God. Lord, please help my daughter _____ to accept the Holy Spirit, who will produce this kind of fruit in her life: love, joy, peace, patience, kindness, goodness, faithfulness, gentleness, and self-control. (Galatians 5:19–23 NLT)

26. I pray, Lord, that my daughter _____ will forget everything that is behind her and look forward only to that which is ahead of her. Keep her eyes on the prize. Give her a desire to win the race and get the prize of Your call from heaven through Christ Jesus. (Philippians 3:13–15 NLV)

27. Lord, I pray that You will guard my daughter _____'s heart above all else, for it determines the course of her life. (Proverbs 4:23 NLT)

28. Father, please help my daughter _____ make every effort to live in peace with everyone. Give her a desire to be holy, because without holiness she will not see You, Lord. Please don't let her miss Your grace, nor let a bitter root grow up in her heart to cause trouble and defile her. Stop her from being sexually immoral or godless. (Hebrews 12:14–16)

29. I pray, Lord, that soon my daughter _____ will say, "But as for me, I trust in You, O Lord. I say, 'You are my God.' My times are in Your hands." Free her, Lord, from the hands of those who hate her, and from those who try to hurt her. (Psalm 31:14–15 NLV)

30. I pray that my daughter _____ will not be afraid but will believe in Jesus Christ. (Mark 5:36 NIV)

31. I pray that my daughter _____ will think clearly and exercise self-control—that she'll look forward to the gracious salvation that will come to her when You reveal yourself to her and to the world. (1 Peter 1:13 NLT)

32. Lord, help my daughter _____ to become a new person in Christ. Please remove her old life and let a new life begin! (2 Corinthians 5:17 NLT)

33. I pray that my daughter _____ will forget her past and look forward to what lies ahead. (Philippians 3:13 NLT)

34. Father, please help my daughter _____ receive training that will help her have the skill to recognize the difference between right and wrong. (Hebrews 5:14 NLT)

35. Lord, I pray that my daughter _____ will be surrounded by such a huge crowd of witnesses to the life of faith that she will strip off every weight that slows her down, especially the sin that so easily trips her up. Strengthen her to run with endurance the race that You, God, have set before her. (Hebrews 12:1 NLT)

36. Dear Lord, I pray that my daughter _____ will trust in You with all her heart and not depend on her own understanding. Guide her in seeking Your will in all she does, and show her which path to take. (Proverbs 3:5–6 NLT)

37. Lord, please don't let my daughter _____ be impressed with her own wisdom. Instead, I pray that she will fear You, Lord, and turn away from evil so that You will heal her body and strengthen her bones. (Proverbs 3:7–8 NLT)

38. Lord, please save my daughter _____'s soul in peace from those who make war against her. For there are many who fight her. God, You sit on Your throne forever. I know You will hear them and bring trouble upon them, because there has been no change in them. They do not fear God. (Psalm 55:18–19 NLV)

39. Lord, I travel East looking for You—I find no one; then West, but not a trace; I go North, but You've hidden Your tracks; then South, but not even a glimpse. But You know where my daughter _____ is and what she's done. Please cross-examine her all You want, and help her pass Your test with honors. May she follow You closely, her feet in Your footprints, not once swerving from Your way. Help her to obey every word You've spoken, and not just obey Your advice—but treasure it. (Job 23:9–11 MSG)

40. God, please help my daughter _____ to take her everyday, ordi-

nary life—her sleeping, eating, going-to-work, and walking-around life—and place it before You, God, as an offering. Embracing what You, God, do for her is the best thing she can do for You and us. Don't let her become so well-adjusted to the culture that she fits into it without even thinking. Instead, fix her attention on You, God. Change her from the inside out. Help her to readily recognize what You want from her and quickly respond to it. Unlike the culture around her, always dragging her down to its level of immaturity, God, please bring the best out of her. Develop well-formed maturity in my daughter _____. (Romans 12:1–2 MSG)

Amen.

PRAYER AND PRAISE JOURNAL

May the LORD grant all your requests.
PSALM 20:5

Prayer Request	Praise

Prayer Request	Praise

Prayer Request	Praise

Prayer Request	Praise

NOTES

Introduction

1. William Booth quoted in *The One Year Walk with God Devotional: Wisdom from the Bible to Renew Your Mind* by Chris Tiegreen (Wheaton, IL: Tyndale House, 2004), June 29.

2. Janet Thompson, *Dear God, They Say It's Cancer: A Companion Guide for Women on the Breast Cancer Journey* (West Monroe, LA: Howard Books, 2006), 8. Adapted.

Chapter 1: Praying Daily

1. Bill Hybels with LaVonne Neff, *Too Busy Not to Pray: Slowing Down to Be with God* (Downers Grove, IL: InterVarsity Press, 1998), 58.

2. Tiegreen, *One Year Walk with God*, June 29.

Chapter 2: Praying Biblically

1. Kay Arthur, *Lord Teach Me to Pray Workbook: Practicing a Powerful Pattern of Prayer* (Nashville: LifeWay Press, 2007), 19.

2. Tiegreen, *One Year Walk with God*, August 5.

3. Evelyn Christenson, *What Happens When God Answers Prayer* (Wheaton, IL: Victor Books, 1994), 51.

4. Ibid., 50.

5. Ibid., 53.

6. Tiegreen, *One Year Walk with God*, March 10.

Chapter 4: Praying Persistently

1. Tiegreen, *One Year Walk with God*, March 26.

2. Patricia Raybon in an interview by Lisa Ann Cockrel, "Mountain Mover," *Today's Christian Woman*, September/October 2006, 38.

3. Charles Spurgeon quoted in *One Year Walk with God* by Tiegreen, March 7.

4. Ruth Bell Graham, *Prodigals and Those Who Love Them* (Grand Rapids: Baker Books, 1999), 29.

5. Richard A. Burr, *Praying Your Prodigal Home: Unleashing God's Power to Set Your Loved Ones Free* (Camp Hill, PA: Christian Publications, Inc., 2003), 1–2.

6. Tiegreen, *One Year Walk with God*, October 7.

7. Amy Carmichael quoted in *One Year Walk with God* by Tiegreen, March 2.

8. Burr, *Praying Your Prodigal Home*, 35.

9. Corrie ten Boom quoted in *One Year Walk with God* by Tiegreen, March 6.

Chapter 5: Praying Sacrificially

1. Bill Bright, "Basic Steps to Successful Fasting and Prayer," www.billbright.com/7steps.

2. Mayo Mathers, "Radical Gratitude: What a Dying Friend Taught Me about Being Thankful 'in All Things,' " *Today's Christian Woman*, November/December 2006, 44.

Chapter 6: Praying Unceasingly

1. Arthur, *Lord Teach Me to Pray*, 17.

Chapter 7: Praying Thankfully

1. Mathers, "Radical Gratitude," 44.

2. Quin Sherrer and Ruthanne Garlock, *Praying Prodigals Home* (Ventura, CA: Regal, 2000), 54.

3. Graham, *Prodigals*, 50.

4. Ibid., 51.

5. Lloyd John Ogilvie, *Conversation with God* (Eugene, OR: Harvest House, 1993), 19–20.

6. Ibid., 26.

7. Ibid., 28.

8. Card designer and author: Kathy Davis; card publisher: Recycled Paper Greetings; © Kathy Davis Designs, Inc., 2007. All Rights Reserved; www.kathydavis.com

Chapter 8: Praying to Break Generational Sin

1. T. Suzanne Eller, *The Mom I Want to Be* (Eugene, OR: Harvest House, 2006), 21.

2. Dr. David Stoop and Dr. James Masteller, *Forgiving Our Parents, Forgiving Ourselves: Healing Adult Children of Dysfunctional Families* (Ann Arbor, MI: Servant Publications, 1991), 99.

3. "Boarding Schools for Teens," www.usnews.com/usnews/news/articles/931108/archive_016059_5.htm.

Chapter 9: Praying as a Couple

1. Carol Sprock, quoted in "What My Parents Did Right," *Discipleship Journal*, September/October 2006, 50.

Chapter 10: Praying as a Family

1. Tricia Goyer, *Generation NeXt Parenting* (Sisters, OR: Multnomah, 2006), 232.
2. Vickie Arruda and Chris Adams, *Women Reaching Women in Crisis: Prodigal Children* (Nashville: LifeWay Press, 2005), 8.
3. Ibid., 11–12.
4. Stoop and Masteller, *Forgiving*, 50.
5. Goyer, *Generation NeXt Parenting*, 238.

Chapter 11: Defining a Prodigal Daughter

1. John Milton quoted in *One Year Walk with God* by Tiegreen, September 7.
2. Ashley Smith with Stacy Mattingly, *Unlikely Angel: The Untold Story of the Atlanta Hostage Hero* (Grand Rapids: Zondervan, 2005), 160.
3. Kathleen Deveny with Raina Kelley, "Girls Gone Bad?" *Newsweek*, February 12, 2007, 41.
4. K. Emily Bond, "Girls Gone Wild?" *Ladies' Home Journal*, March 2007, 68.
5. Deveny with Kelley, "Girls Gone Bad?" 42.
6. *The American College Dictionary* (New York: Random House, 1962), 966.
7. Dotson Rader, "How Could We Not Have Known?" *Parade*, November 26, 2006, 4.
8. Arruda and Adams, *Women Reaching Women in Crisis*, 14.
9. Rader, "How Could We," 4.
10. Ibid., 5

Chapter 12: Setting Boundaries

1. Jimmie L. Davis, *Girls' Ministry Handbook: Starting and Growing a Girls' Ministry in Your Church* (Nashville: LifeWay Press, 2007), 130.
2. Arruda and Adams, *Women Reaching Women in Crisis*, 8.
3. Natalie Nichols Gillespie, "Broken and Beautiful: On the Road with Angela Thomas," *More to Life*, January/February 2007, 25.
4. James Dobson quoted in *One Year Walk with God* by Tiegreen, March 19.
5. David Walsh, PhD, *No: Why Kids—of All Ages—Need to Hear It and Ways Parents Can Say It* (New York: Free Press, 2007), 157.
6. Dr. Henry Cloud and Dr. John Townsend, *Boundaries: When to Say Yes, When to Say No to Take Control of Your Life* (Grand Rapids: Zondervan, 1992), 190.
7. Ibid., 190.

8. Ibid., 170.

9. Ibid., 191.

10. Arruda and Adams, *Women Reaching Women in Crisis*, 8.

11. Cloud and Townsend, *Boundaries*, 126.

12. Mary Mohler, "Kids Behaving Badly," *Family Circle*, February 2006, 52.

Chapter 13: Surviving in Marriage

1. Raybon interview by Cockrel, "Mountain Mover," 38.

2. Arruda and Adams, *Women Reaching Women in Crisis*, 10–11.

3. Ibid., 10.

Chapter 14: Maintaining a "Normal" Family

1. Judi Braddy, *Prodigal in the Parsonage: Encouragement for Ministry Leaders Whose Child Rejects Faith* (Kansas City, MO: Beacon Hill Press of Kansas City, 2004), 140.

2. Gigi Graham Tchividjian, "I Wasn't Prepared for a Prodigal," *Prodigals and Those Who Love Them* by Ruth Bell Graham (Grand Rapids: Baker Books, 1999), 108.

Chapter 15: Making It All about Her

1. Carla Barnhill, "Help! I'm Wrecking My Kids!" *Discipleship Journal*, September/October 2006, 64.

Chapter 16: Confronting Our Own Mistakes

1. Graham, *Prodigals*, 34.

2. Dr. Robin Smith, quoted from the *Oprah Winfrey Show*, "Healing Mothers, Healing Daughters: The Real Injury," www.oprah.com/tows/slide/200604/20060424/slide_20060424_284_104.jhtml.

3. Goyer, *Generation NeXt Parenting*, 47.

4. Ibid., 52.

5. Smith, "Healing Mothers, Healing Daughters: The Real Injury," www.oprah.com/tows/slide/200604/20060424/slide_20060424_284_109.jhtml.

Chapter 17: Resolving Conflict

1. Arruda and Adams, *Women Reaching Women in Crisis*, 10.

2. Laurence Steinberg, PhD, *The Ten Basic Principles of Good Parenting* (New York: Simon & Schuster, 2004), 153–54.

3. Cloud and Townsend, *Boundaries*, 177.

4. Brenda Hunter, PhD, *In the Company of Women* (Sister, Ore.: Multnomah Books, 1994), 150. Adapted.

Chapter 18: Supporting Each Other

1. Raybon interview by Cockrel, "Mountain Mover," 38.

2. Arruda and Adams, *Women Reaching Women in Crisis*, 12.

3. Adam Townsend, "Moms On a Mission," *Orange County Register*, February 5, 2007, 4.

4. Megan Hutchinson, *I Want to Talk With My Teen about Addictions* (Cincinnati: Standard Publishing, 2006), 84.

Chapter 19: What Did We Do to Cause This?

1. Arruda and Adams, *Women Reaching Women in Crisis*, 9.

2. Barnhill, "Wrecking My Kids," 64.

3. JoAnn Deak, PhD, with Teresa Barker, *Girls Will Be Girls: Raising Confident and Courageous Daughters* (New York: Hyperion, 2002), 5.

Chapter 20: What Is Unconditional Love?

1. Raybon interview by Cockrel, "Mountain Mover," 39.

2. Davis, *Girls' Ministry Handbook*, 131.

3. Arruda and Adams, *Women Reaching Women in Crisis*, 8.

4. Raybon interview by Cockrel, "Mountain Mover," 38.

5. Ibid., 39.

Chapter 21: What Will Our Friends Think?

1. Braddy, *Prodigal in the Parsonage*, 36.

Chapter 22: What If She Never Repents?

1. Arruda and Adams, *Women Reaching Women in Crisis*, 7–8.

2. Philip Yancy, *Prayer: Does It Make Any Difference?* (Grand Rapids: Zondervan, 2006), 238.

3. Thompson, *Dear God, They Say It's Cancer*, 217–18. Adapted.

Chapter 23: Celebrating Her Return

1. Smith with Mattingly, *Unlikely Angel*, 261–62.

2. Hutchinson, *About Addictions*, 82.

3. Sherrer and Garlock, *Praying Prodigals Home*, 199.

4. Arruda and Adams, *Women Reaching Women in Crisis*, 7.

Chapter 24: Extending Unconditional Forgiveness

1. Everett L. Worthington Jr., "Forgiveness," *The Soul Care Bible*, Tim Clinton, exec. ed. (Nashville: Thomas Nelson, 2001), 1520.

2. *Webster's Encyclopedic Unabridged Dictionary of the English Language* (New York: Portland House, 1989), 556.

3. Frederick Buechner, quoted in Wisdom Quotes: Quotations to Inspire and Challenge, http://www.wisdomquotes.com/cat_anger.html.

Chapter 25: Nurturing the Mother-Daughter Relationship

1. "Mother & Daughter, Inc.," *Ladies' Home Journal*, May 2007, 120.

2. Vicki Courtney, *Your Girl: A Bible Study for Mothers of Teens* (Nashville: Life-Way Press, 2006), 7–8.

3. Courtney, *Your Girl*, 11.

4. Kerri Pomarolli in interview by Camerin Courtney, "There's Something about Kerri," *Today's Christian Woman*, November/December 2006, 38–39.

5. Courtney, *Your Girl*, 12.

Chapter 26: Needing a Father

1. Lanita Bradley Boyd, quoted in "What My Parents Did Right," *Discipleship Journal*, September/October 2006), 47.

2. Kauline Sidinger, quoted in "What My Parents Did Right," *Discipleship Journal*, September/October 2006), 52.

3. "The Pledge," Generations of Light, www.generationsoflight.com/generationsof light/html/index.html.

Chapter 27: Sharing Your Testimony

1. Smith with Mattingly, *Unlikely Angel*, 262.

2. Hutchinson, *About Addictions*, 89. Adapted from "7 Steps to Sharing Your Story!"

ABOUT THE AUTHOR

Janet became a Christian at age eleven and was on fire for the Lord throughout her teens. She stayed on course during her college years; however, the day after graduating from college, Janet married without consulting the Lord. Sadly, that marriage only lasted six years; but God blessed her with a daughter, Kimberly Michele. The next seventeen years, Janet was a single parent moving up a successful career ladder. They were times of great backsliding away from the Lord and poor role-modeling for Kim.

In 1992 Janet rededicated her life to Christ and met her future, godly husband, Dave. They married and became a blended family with Dave's three children, Michelle, Shannon, Sean; and Janet's daughter, Kim. Dave and Janet quickly accepted each other's children as their own.

The spring of 1995 Janet received a call from the Lord to "Feed My sheep." Soon God revealed that the "sheep" were women, and the "feeding" was mentoring. So she quit a lucrative career to start the Woman to Woman Mentoring Ministry at Saddleback Church, where she and Dave worship. Three months later, Dave was laid off from his job and was out of work for eighteen months. As friends and family asked if Janet was going back to work, Dave repeatedly answered, "She is working." When asked, "At what?" he replied, "She's about the Lord's work"—thus the naming of Janet's writing and speaking ministry, *About His Work* Ministries. *AHW* Ministries has now expanded to *AHW* Publishing and *Two About His Work,* a speaking ministry with Janet's best friend and co-worker for Christ, Jane Crick. You can learn more about *AHW* Ministries at Janet's Web site: www.womantowomanmentoring.com.

In the fall of 2002, Janet received the dreaded diagnosis of breast cancer. Shortly after finishing treatment, she wrote for her breast cancer sisters the book she had longed to have during her struggle: *Dear God, They Say It's Cancer: A Companion Guide for Women on the Breast Cancer Journey.*

Janet and Dave live in Lake Forest, California, and have been members of Saddleback Church since 1987. Dave is on staff as a community leader in Saddleback's Couples' Ministry and a "Helpmate" partner with Janet in *AHW* Ministries. All four of their children are married and have given them nine darling grandchildren—six boys and three girls! Janet and Dave are enjoying the empty-nest season of life Janet refers to as parents' time to rest—although they often comment that they're busier about the Lord's work than at any other time in their lives!

Janet has a master's of arts in Christian leadership (Ministry of the Laity) from Fuller Theological Seminary. She also is a CLASS graduate (Christian Leaders, Authors and Speaker Services) and a member of AWSA (Advanced Writers and Speakers Association).

ABOUT HIS WORK MINISTRIES

About His Work Ministries is Janet Thompson's writing and speaking ministry. Janet has a passion for today's Christians to live significant lives regardless of their circumstances. She is about His work helping men and women realize the importance and value of relationships and God's call in Titus 2:1–5 to teach and train the next generation of Christian men and women through mentoring and loving them. In 1996 Janet founded the Woman to Woman Mentoring Ministry at Saddleback Church in Lake Forest, California. Through her authored resources *Woman to Woman Mentoring: How to Start, Grow, and Maintain a Mentoring Ministry* and a Bible study series, *Mentoring God's Way*, she has helped numerous churches around the world start Woman to Woman Mentoring in their own churches. In *Dear God, They Say It's Cancer: A Companion Guide for Women on the Breast Cancer Journey* (Howard Books), Janet mentors fellow breast cancer sisters from her own journey with breast cancer. And now Janet, and her "former prodigal" daughter Kim, share their story in *Praying for Your Prodigal Daughter* (Howard Books) and speak together to mentor parents of prodigal daughters.

For more information and to contact Janet:

Two about His Work
Janet and her best friend Jane Crick speak together. To contact them about speaking availability:

Tom Crick—*Two About His Work* Ministries
Phone/Fax 949-380-0690
Tom@2ahw.com
Woman to Woman Mentoring
Woman to Woman Mentoring: How to Start, Grow, and Maintain a Mentoring Ministry
www.lifeway.com
Call LifeWay at 800–458–2772
Visit nearest LifeWay bookstore

Mentoring God's Way Bible Study Series
E-mail: ahwpublishing@yahoo.com
Call *AHW* Publishing at 208–345–3338
www.womantowomanmentoring.com

Dear God, They Say It's Cancer: A Companion Guide for Women on the Breast Cancer Journey (Howard Books, a Division of Simon and Schuster) is available at all fine bookstores.
www.deargodtheysayitscancer.com

Contact Janet Thompson and *About His Work* Ministries
Phone/Fax 949–837–0614
ahw@sbcglobal.net
www.womantowomanmentoring.com
www.deargodtheysayitscancer.com
www.prayingforyourprodigaldaughter.com

Every 3 minutes another woman is diagnosed with breast cancer.

A Companion Guide for Women on the Breast Cancer Journey

Dear God, They Say It's Cancer

Janet Thompson

Author of the Woman to Woman Mentoring Series

"This book has helped me mentally as well as spiritually. I only wish I had this book when I was first diagnosed with breast cancer…I am glad you wrote the book, and I know God had a hand also."

—Carmen Dunn
breast cancer survivor

The need for a guide such as this is apparent as we watch the struggles of those we love. *Dear God, They Say It's Cancer* is like a dear and wise friend who walks readers through the difficult breast cancer journey and accompanies them through treatment and recovery. Offering spiritual, emotional, and practical support, this book is a thorough and gentle guide for women who are hurting.

HOWARD BOOKS
A DIVISION OF SIMON & SCHUSTER